FREDDIE MERCURY

FREDDIE MERCURY

THE DEFINITIVE BIOGRAPHY

LESLEY-ANN JONES

HODDER &
STOUGHTON

First published in Great Britain in 2011 by Hodder & Stoughton
An Hachette UK company

1

Copyright © Lesley-Ann Jones 2011

A CIP catalogue record for this title is available from the British Library

Hardback ISBN 978 1 444 73367 9
Trade Paperback ISBN 978 1 444 73368 6
Ebook ISBN 978 1 444 73370 9

Typeset in Plantin Light by Hewer Text UK Ltd, Edinburgh
Printed and bound by CPI Group (UK) Ltd, Croydon, CR0 4YY

Hodder & Stoughton policy is to use papers that are natural, renew-
able and recyclable products and made from wood grown in sustain-
able forests. The logging and manufacturing processes are expected to
conform to the environmental regulations of the country of origin.

Hodder & Stoughton Ltd
338 Euston Road
London NW1 3BH

www.hodder.co.uk

For my mother and father
For Mia, Henry & Bridie

Contents

Introduction

Montreux

We didn't write it at the time. We took notes, as journalists did in those days, by committing quotes to memory, then making our excuses and heading for the bathroom, where we'd scribble into our notebooks before the booze set in. We had tape recorders, sure, but you couldn't use them. They were conversation-killers, especially if you found yourself somewhere compromising. Where it wasn't cool to be up-front about being a hack.

So we – a couple of scribes and a snapper – had broken rank from the media-fest raging up the road at the conference centre, and had slipped out for a quiet pint at the only pub on Montreux's main drag. Intimate little place, the Blanc Gigi, they called it: the White Horse. Freddie happened to be in that night, with a couple of tight-slacked friends who might have been Swiss or French. This typically English pub was a favourite haunt of his, which I think we must have known. Freddie didn't need a bodyguard. He needed cigarettes. The new bloke from the *Express* was an addict, he always carried four packs. Nights were long for young showbiz reporters. We came prepared.

This was not the first time I'd met Freddie. We'd been in each other's company several times before. A rock fan since childhood – I'd met Bowie when I was eleven, and Hendrix died on my birthday in 1970 (had to be a 'sign'; wasn't everything?) – I was introduced to the thrilling, complex music of Queen the summer I left school by sisters Jan and Maureen Day, fans from Aldershot. This was when I found myself travelling alongside them on a wheezing coach bound for Barcelona and the beaches of the Costa Brava. When everyone had a guitar, and a plectrum that had belonged to George Harrison. No amount of finger stretches was going to get the instrument to weep for me.

Never destined to be a Chrissie Hynde or a Joan Jett, from the early 1980s until around 1992 I reported on rock and pop for the *Daily Mail*, the *Mail on Sunday*, its supplement *You* magazine, and *The Sun*. It was as a rookie journalist at Associated Newspapers that I first encountered Queen. I was sent to interview Freddie and Brian at Queen's Notting Hill offices one day in 1984, and a lopsided acquaintanceship was struck: they called, you came. The years that ensued now seem surreal. The business was simpler then. Artists and journalists routinely flew together, limo'd together, stayed in the same hotels, ate at the same tables, painted far-flung cities the colours of hell.

A precious few of those friendships got to last.

Things hardly ever happen that way today. Too many managers, agents, promoters, publicists, label folk and hangers-on, all on points. If they're not, they pretend. It's in their best interests to keep the likes of me behind the barrier. Back then, we cheeked our way in everywhere – with or without the laminate or an Access All Areas pass. We sometimes even hid them, just to keep our hand in. Blagging was part of the fun.

I had watched from the wings as Queen performed at Wembley for Live Aid the previous year – I wouldn't get a look-in today – and was invited along to a string of destinations on the 'Magic' tour in 1986. In Budapest, I would attend a private reception in the band's honour at the British Embassy, and would witness their historic Hungarian show behind the Iron Curtain, which was perhaps their greatest live moment ever. I like to think I blended in: just another skinny twenty-something freckle-face who loved rock 'n' roll.

What always surprised me was how much slighter Freddie was than you remembered him. Perhaps it was the diet of nicotine, vodka, wine, cocaine, little appetite for food, and being hyped up as a performer. He was so larger-than-life up there on stage that you expected him to be imposing in real life. He wasn't. On the contrary, he seemed quite small, and endearingly boyish. You wanted to mother him, all the girls did. He aroused the same instincts as Culture Club's androgynous Boy George, who became the housewives' favourite after 'confessing', if disingenuously, that he preferred a nice cup of tea to sex.

In the White Horse, Freddie was looking around, eyebrows raised, murmuring 'ciggie' in that distinctively clipped and faintly camp voice of his. It struck me that night what a tangle of contradictions he was. That he could be as humble and unassuming away from the stage as he could be arrogant on it. Later on, I heard him mutter 'pi-pi' in a child-like tone, and watched, fascinated, as one of his number toddled him off to the Gents. That was it, I fell for him completely. I wanted to take him home, stick him in a hot bath, get my mum to cook him a roast. Thinking about it now, it couldn't have been that the big-shot rock star was so helpless that he was unable to go to the john alone. Freddie would have been the most vulnerable of targets in a toilet.

Roger Tavener, the *Express* guy, offered him a Marlboro Red. Freddie wavered before accepting – he'd have preferred Silk Cut. He watched us from his pitch with vague interest as we sparred with the barflies. Perhaps because we didn't pay him too much attention, he came back for another fag. Where were we staying, then? The Montreux Palace: right answer. Freddie had lived there; he'd had his own suite. He and Queen owned Mountain Studios, the only recording complex in this dignified Swiss resort. Mountain was reckoned at the time to be the best in Europe. It was his round now. More of whatever it was we'd had before.

After an hour or so: 'You obviously know who I am', he said, a flicker of recognition in his ebony eyes. Well obviously. He was what we were there for. A few vodka tonics earlier, he might have figured our names. Despatched by newspaper editors to attend the annual entertainment TV festival and Golden Rose Awards (the Rose d'Or was at its peak in Montreux in May 1986), we also covered its side-kick, a widely televised rock gala that was a thinly-disguised excuse for the media to misbehave.

We thought he wouldn't want to be bothered, but he was the one who seemed keen to talk. He didn't care for hacks as a rule. Having been ridiculed and misquoted in the past, he trusted few of us. David Wigg – at that time the *Daily Express* showbusiness editor, and also in town – was a good friend of Freddie's. More often than not it was he who got the scoop.

We were getting too close. Throwing away, we knew, the chance of an official interview. Come morning, Freddie would have sussed us. More to the point, his management and the publicists would have too. Having overstepped the mark, as they'd perceive it, we'd probably never get near him again. This was his bar, his territory. Even so, he seemed vulnerable and edgy, far removed from the star we thought we knew.

'That's why I'm here,' he said. 'This is only two hours from London, but I can breathe here, and I can think and write and record, and go for a walk, and I think I'm going to need it these next few years.'

We sympathised. We joined in about the pain of fame: his problem, not ours. We were keeping a lid on it. Trying to be cool. Willing the killer instinct to subside, the one that would have had us flying at the phone to call our news editors with the scoop of the year, that we had rock's most sought-after showman cornered in a foreign boozer; we swallowed a couple more shots and waited. This was a priceless opportunity. Tavener and I were new partners in crime, out to impress each other, and the titles we wrote for were bitter rivals. We should have been circling each other like great whites. We reassured Freddie that we were used to work-ing with celebrities, that we knew about privacy. That it's the first thing they sacrifice, the last thing they realise they want back. This struck a chord with him.

He squinted into his vodka, swishing the glass.

'Do you know, that's exactly the thing that keeps me awake at night,' he mused. 'I've created a monster. The monster is me. I can't blame anyone else. It's what I've worked for since I was a kid. I would have killed for this. Whatever happens to me is all my fault. It's what I wanted. It's what we all strive for. Success, fame, money, sex, drugs – whatever you want. I can have it. But now I'm beginning to see that as much as I created it, I want to escape from it. I'm starting to worry that I can't control it, as much as it controls me.

'I change when I walk out on stage,' he admitted. 'I totally transform into this "ultimate showman". I say that because that's what I must be. I can't be second best, I would rather give up. I know I have to strut. I know I have to hold the mic stand a certain way. And I love it. Like I loved watching Jimi Hendrix milk his audience. He got it, and so did the fans. But he was a pretty shy guy off stage. Maybe he suffered by trying to live up to expectations, of being the wild man he wasn't really, away from the lights. It becomes an out-of-body experience for me up there. It's like I'm looking down on myself and thinking, "Fuck me, that's hot." Then I realise it is me: better go to work.

'Of course it's a drug,' he said, 'a stimulant. But it gets tough when people spot me in the street, and want him up there. The *big* Freddie. I'm not him, I'm quieter than that. You try to separate your private life from the public performer, because it's a schizophrenic existence. I guess that's the price I pay. Don't get me wrong, I'm no poor little rich guy. The music is what gets me up in the morning. I'm truly blessed.'

What could he do about it?

'I'm being a drama queen about nothing, aren't I!' A flash of the big guy. 'Money pouring in, adulation, we're talking about me living in Montreux and in the flashiest part of London. I can buy in New York, Paris, anywhere I want. I'm spoilt. The guy on stage can do that stuff. His public expects it. I do worry about where it ends up,' he confessed, at last. 'What being part of one of the biggest bands in the world can mean. It brings its own problems. It means I can't just wander about and have an afternoon bun in a lovely *tea shoppe* in Kent. I've always got to weigh that up. It's a heck of a journey, and I'm enjoying the ride, I assure you. But there are times . . .'

Through the casino and out the other side, we were nowhere near dawn. Freddie and a couple of pals, bunked down in some villa beneath the jagged Alps, which Freddie said guarded ancient mysteries and lost treasure, some of it stashed by Nazis during the War. The chilled night air was spiked with pine. Moonlit mountains cast shapes across the yawning lake.

What was evident was how much Freddie adored this retreat: a chocolate-box picture on the Vaud Riviera, famed for its annual jazz festival, its vineyards, for Nabokov and Chaplin, for 'Smoke on the Water' – the inimitably-riffed track penned by Deep Purple in December 1971, after a fan misfired a flare at a Frank Zappa gig. The whole casino burned down, the fumes billowing out across Lake Geneva as Roger Glover watched from a hotel window, bass guitar in hand.

'Just throw my remains in the lake when I go,' Freddie jested. He repeated this at least twice.

Talk turned to the importance of enjoying the simple things in life. The elephant in the room, as we call it now, was that rock-star wealth could buy him the kind of fantasy life here that the likes of us could visit only in dreams.

What did we do with this 'exclusive'? We did nothing. Wrote nothing. Only we knew.

Freddie and his crew were good people. It had been a fun night. He'd been honest. He probably didn't trust us as far as he could have thrown us. He knew who we were, must have assumed we'd stitch him up. Perhaps he wanted us to, to prove a point: that reporters are always bad news. Freddie of all rock stars was used to being betrayed, especially by people like us. If we didn't understand it at the time, his behaviour now makes sense. Freddie may have had an inkling that his days were numbered. He was certainly living like there was no tomorrow. Maybe he just fancied lobbing caution to the wind at that point, imprisoned as he was by fame. Because we knew he was expecting the worst from us, Tavener and I agreed to commit a sackable offence. We would not sell Freddie's confidence for a cheap page lead.

Dawn began to shimmer over the snow-mantled mountains. True colours flecked the water as we faded back to our hotel. No one spoke. Nothing left to say. Tavener smoked his last fag.

'Rock music is vastly important,' declares Cosmo Hallstrom, a renowned consultant psychiatrist who has done four decades with the great and good.

'It represents culture as it is now. It's big money, which makes it a desirable pursuit. It's a phenomenon that can't be ignored. It unifies, it creates a common bond.

'Rock 'n' roll has immediacy. It's about raw, unchannelled, early emotions and simple concepts, driven hard. It's so compelling, you cannot ignore it. You cannot fail to be roused by it. You'd have to be deaf – and perhaps not even then. It speaks to a generation. It validates it, in a way that nothing else can.'

'Being an artist is a cry for help', insists Simon Napier-Bell, the industry's most infamous rock and pop manager, who should know: he wrote hits for Dusty Springfield, made household names of Marc Bolan, The Yardbirds and Japan, invented Wham! and transformed George Michael into a solo superstar. Simon never minces his words, especially not on this subject.

'All artists are terribly insecure people. They are desperate to be noticed. They are constantly seeking an audience. They are forced to be commercial, which they hate, but which I think makes their "art" all the better. They all have the same story, too, which is key. Take Eric Clapton: when I first saw him, I thought, "He isn't an artist, he's just a musician." In John Mayall's band, he played with his back to the audience, he was so shy. But as he evolved, I saw that he *was* an artist. He had the missing father, a sister who was really his mother, a grandma he thought was his mum. Artists always have an abusive childhood – at least in terms of emotional deprivation. So they have this desperation to succeed, to get love and attention. All the others just drop out eventually. Because I'm telling you: it's *absolutely horrible* being a star. It's nice to get a good table in a restaurant, but then you have people coming up to you every thirty seconds throughout the meal. It's a nightmare. Yet stars are perfectly happy to put up with that kind of thing. It comes with the territory.

'They are usually utterly charming with new people,' he goes on. 'But there's a dark side. When they've taken everything they possibly can from you, they have no further use for you and they spit you out. I've been spat out, but I couldn't give a toss. I understand these people, I know what makes them tick. It's no use getting upset or angry about being treated unkindly or cruelly by some star. They are what they are. There is a certain psychological damage which runs through every one of them. I guarantee that if you look through their childhoods, you will find it. What else makes you so desperate to win applause and adulation? So desperate that you'll lead a lousy life you can never really call your own? No normal person would ever want to be a star. Not for any money.'

'Freddie Mercury did the most important thing of all,' counters Dr Hallstrom. 'He died young. Instead of becoming a fat, bloated, self-important old queen, he was cut off in his prime and is preserved at that age for eternity. It's not a bad way to go.'

This is his story.

I

Live Aid

By making this concert, we are doing something positive to make people look, listen, and hopefully donate. When people are starving, it should be looked upon as one united problem. Sometimes I do feel helpless. This is one of those times I can do my bit.

Freddie Mercury

It was the perfect stage for Freddie Mercury: the whole world.

Bob Geldof

There was a time when politicians made great orators. The art has dwindled dramatically in this century. Rock 'n' roll, of all unlikely disciplines, is one of the few remaining professions in which an individual or group can hold an audience in the palm of their hand, controlling a throng of thousands with their voice. Film actors can't do it. Television stars don't even get close. Perhaps it makes the rock superstar the last great compelling figure of our times. This occurred to me as I stood in the curtained wings at Wembley Stadium on Live Aid day with Who bassist John Entwistle and his girlfriend Max. We watched Freddie perform in sweltering heat for close to 80,000 people, and for a television audience of . . . who knows? a lot of figures have been bandied about in the ensuing years, but somewhere between '400 million in around 50 countries via satellite' and '1.9 billion worldwide'. With nonchalance, wit, cheek and sex, he gave it the works. We looked on, open-mouthed. The deafening roar of the crowd drowned out any attempt to speak to them. Freddie couldn't have cared. The raw power that held his audience spellbound was so potent, you imagined you could smell it. Backstage, the most legendary names in rock paused to watch their rival stealing the show. Freddie knew what he was doing, all right. For eighteen minutes, this unlikely king and Queen ruled the world.

We make luck in random ways. Bob Geldof, scribbling in his diary in a taxi one day: that was lucky. This was in November 1984. From the depths of his brain, a 'battleground of conflicting thoughts', as he later described it, came rudimentary bits of lyrics that would soon enough rock the world. It happened shortly after watching Michael Buerk's terrible bulletin from famine-wracked Ethiopia on *BBC News*. Horrified by television footage depicting suffering of biblical proportions, Geldof felt at once shocked and helpless, his gut telling him that he had to get involved. He had no idea how. He could do what he did best: sit down and write a hit single, the proceeds of which he could pledge to Oxfam. But his Irish punk band The Boomtown Rats were by then in decline, having not enjoyed a Top Ten hit since 1980. Their zenith, a Number One with 'I Don't Like Mondays', had been and gone in 1979. Music fans, he knew, would flock to buy a charity single provided the artist was big enough – especially at the Christmas-single time of year. It was a question of finding a sympathetic star to record one. How much better if he could persuade a whole galaxy to join in one song.

Bob spoke to Midge Ure, whose band Ultravox were appearing that week on *The Tube* – a Channel 4 rock and pop show presented by Geldof's then girlfriend (soon to be his wife), the late Paula Yates. Midge agreed to set Geldof's lyrics to music, and to orchestrate some arrangements. Bob then went to Sting, Duran Duran singer Simon Le Bon, Gary and Martin Kemp of Spandau Ballet.

His galactic list stretched as time ticked on to include, among many, Boy George, Frankie Goes To Hollywood, The Style Council's Paul Weller, George Michael and Andrew Ridgeley of Wham! and Paul Young. Francis Rossi and Rick Parfitt of Status Quo went in willingly. Phil Collins and Bananarama followed suit. David Bowie and Paul McCartney, who were otherwise committed, made contributions remotely. These were sent to Geldof to be dubbed onto the single later. Sir Peter Blake, world-famous for his iconic artwork on The Beatles' album cover *Sgt Pepper's Lonely Hearts Club Band*, was recruited to design the record sleeve. Band Aid was born, the name a pun on a common brand of sticking plaster. This was to be a 'band' that would 'aid' the world.

'Do They Know It's Christmas?' was recorded free of charge at Trevor Horn's Sarm West Studios in Notting Hill, West London, on 25 November 1984, and was released just four days later.

At Number One that week was knockout Scottish singer Jim Diamond, with his sublime, timeless ballad 'I Should Have Known Better'. Although Jim's group PhD had scored a hit with 'I Won't Let You Down' in 1982, he had never had a solo hit. The music industry was therefore gobsmacked when big-hearted Jim gave an interview about his chart success.

'I'm delighted to be Number One,' he said, 'but next week I don't want people to buy my record. I want them to buy Band Aid instead.'

'I couldn't believe it,' said Geldof. 'As a singer who hadn't had a Number One for five years, I knew what it cost him to say that. He had just thrown away his first hit for others. It was genuinely selfless.'

The next week, 'Do They Know It's Christmas?' went straight to Number One in the UK, outselling everything else on the chart put together and becoming Britain's fastest-selling single since the chart's inception in 1952. A million copies were shifted in the first week alone. The record held the Number One slot for five weeks, selling more than three and a half million copies. It went on to become the UK's biggest-selling single of all time – ending the nine-year reign of Queen's magnum opus, the 'ba-rock' 'Bohemian Rhapsody'. 'Do They Know It's Christmas?' would only be outsold in 1997 by Elton John's double-A-side charity single 'Candle In the Wind/Something About the Way You Look Tonight', re-recorded as a tribute to the late Princess of Wales.

'Queen were definitely disappointed that they hadn't been asked to appear on "Do They Know It's Christmas?",' admits Spike Edney, a session musician who toured with Queen as the band's fifth member, contributing on keyboards, vocals and rhythm guitar, and who had made his name playing for The Boomtown Rats and a string of big-name acts.

'I was out doing a Rats tour with Geldof, and I mentioned this to Bob. It was then he told me that he was hoping to get a show together, and he was definitely going to ask Queen to play. I remember thinking, "Bollocks. He's nuts. It'll never happen".'

The industry's reaction to what Geldof had achieved so far suggested otherwise. Hot on the heels of the British chart effort came America's contribution, in the form of supergroup USA for Africa and their single 'We Are the World'. Written by Michael Jackson and Lionel Richie, produced by Quincy Jones and Michael Omartian, the session brought together some of the world's most legendary musicians. It was recorded at Hollywood's A & M Studios in January 1985, and boasted a stellar cast, Diana Ross, Bruce Springsteen, Smokey Robinson, Cyndi Lauper, Billy Joel, Dionne Warwick, Willie Nelson and Huey Lewis among them. In all, more than forty-five of America's top artists took part. A further fifty had to be turned away. When the chosen ones arrived at the studio, they were confronted with a sign instructing them to 'please check your egos at the door'. They were also met by an impish Stevie Wonder, informing them that if the song wasn't up to scratch nor down in one take, he and fellow blind artist Ray Charles would be driving them all home. The record sold more than twenty million copies, and became America's fastest-selling pop single ever.

It was after Queen's challenging *The Works* outing that Geldof took his aid campaign up a notch, announcing plans to create the most ambitious rock 'n' roll project of all time. Because they had been ignored for the single, Queen did not consider themselves an obvious choice for the concert line-up. That seems an irony now. Despite their fifteen-year career, a matchless back catalogue of albums, singles and videos, royalties into the multimillions, and having landed most music awards going thanks to musicianship which embraced rock, pop, opera, rockabilly, disco, funk and folk, Queen's star appeared to be in the descendent. The band had been away from home for a considerable period between August 1984 and May 1985 promoting their album, *The Works*, during which they took part in the Rock in Rio festival in January 1985 – performing live for 325,000 fans. But the tour had been beset by problems. There was talk of them going their separate ways.

'They were obviously drifting,' confirms Spike Edney. 'Times had changed, we were into a whole new musical genre. It was all New Romantics, Spandau Ballet and Duran Duran. There's no accounting for success or failure – and no guarantees. Things had been going a bit awry for Queen for a while, especially in America. There was shit going down with their US label. Their confidence was knocked. Maybe they did take it out on each other a bit. Who wouldn't?'

'Hey, people fight,' reasons their close friend, keyboard maestro and former Strawb and Yes-guy, Rick Wakeman.

'Band members argue. It's understandable: in how many other jobs are you flung together all the time? Out on the road, you eat breakfast together, travel to work together, have every meal together. The only time you are alone is in bed – and not always then. No matter how friendly you all are, there comes the day when you say to yourself, "If that guy scratches his head one more time, I'll stick a knife in him." You have to learn to give each other space. Provided you make the right music, it doesn't matter if one gets

pissed, one goes to a drugs den, one makes it to the arena to practise, another nips off to a football match. Get a band of four or five
people together, extreme creatives who do wondrous things with
their minds, hands and voices, and there's all the potential for fire-
works. In that respect, Queen were no different from the rest of us.'

After touring to promote their bewilderingly dance-y, guitar-
less 1982 album *Hot Space*, Freddie Mercury, Brian May, Roger
Taylor and John Deacon had effectively disbanded to concentrate
on solo pursuits – notably Brian with Eddie Van Halen on the Star
Fleet Project, and Freddie on his own album. In August 1983, they
regrouped in Los Angeles to collaborate on *The Works*, their tenth
studio album and debut CD. 'Radio Ga Ga' was the first single.
The Works also featured hard-rock number 'Hammer to Fall', the
plaintive ballad 'Is This the World We Created . . . ?', and the controversial 'I Want to Break Free' – its outrageous cross-dressing video
loosely based on a domestic scene from British TV soap *Coronation
Street*. While the single proved hugely popular in the UK and other
territories, it had offended conservative Middle America and upset
many fans.

Worse, Queen had recently broken the United Nations cultural
boycott, as had Rod Stewart, Rick Wakeman, Status Quo and others,
to perform in apartheid South Africa. Their October 1984 shows
at Sun City, Sol Kerzner's casino, golf and entertainment resort in
Bophuthatswana, earned the band widespread criticism and saw
them fined and blacklisted by the British Musicians' Union. For an
African-born musician – which Freddie was – this was a travesty.
The situation was not solved until racial segregation fell in 1993, a
year before Nelson Mandela was elected President of South Africa.
Queen would become major and active supporters of Mandela in
later years.

'I stood up for Queen totally when they went to South Africa,'
retorts Rick Wakeman. 'I too performed a concert in the middle of
apartheid, with an orchestra made up of black Zulus, Asians and
whites.

'I did *Journey to the Centre of the Earth* down there, and got cruci-fied by the British press. I tried to explain, but they wouldn't listen. Music isn't "black" or "white", it's just an orchestra, a choir. To play there wasn't supporting the apartheid regime. George Benson went there. Diana Ross went there. How come people of colour could perform, but not whites? That's racist in itself. Shirley Bassey went down, saying, "For fuck's sake, I'm half-black and half-Welsh, how bad can it be?" So when Queen went to South Africa, I thoroughly applauded it. They threw a spotlight on the stupidity of it all, and drew attention to the fact that music has no sexual, cultural or racial barriers. It is for everyone.'

Live Aid's 'global jukebox' would be staged in two vast venues on 13 July 1985. Wembley Stadium and the John F. Kennedy Stadium in Philadelphia were booked. Organisation proved a logistical nightmare.

'When Bob first came in to my office to discuss this event, I thought he was joking,' remembers promoter Harvey Goldsmith. 'In 1985 there weren't fax machines, let alone computers, mobile phones or anything else. We were working on telex and landlines. I remember sitting in my office one afternoon with a big satel-lite map and a pair of old callipers, trying to map out where the satellite was going to be at certain times. Also, when we went to the BBC, Bob was thumping the table and saying, "I want seventeen hours of television" – that was revolutionary. Once the BBC had committed, we could use that as leverage to persuade broadcasters all over the world to do it. It was the first time that had ever happened. It was my job to pick up the pieces and make it work.'

Then came the challenge of persuading rock's biggest names, some of whom had already contributed to the recording of the charity singles, to perform and help raise further money for the dying. This was to prove a fantastically blatant retaliation by the music fraternity at governments around the world that had failed to act.

As Francis Rossi of Status Quo puts it, 'This was the dick-heads in rock 'n' roll, just getting on with it. It does make me angry, when I look back. I believe that if everyone had pulled together – if we'd understood then the magnitude of what could have been achieved – we could have got the oil companies, the BPs and Shells and whoever else, to do their bit. We could have made twenty times whatever it was we raised. Don't tell me the government couldn't have legislated to get round the issues with advertising and so on. All big businesses could have got involved, and the result would have been mega. At the time, it was virgin territory. We think about Live Aid differently today. But still, all credit to Bob. He pulled together something which precious few could have achieved.'

How did Geldof get Queen involved?

'Bob asked me to ask the band if they'd be up for it, which I had the opportunity to do when Queen were on tour in New Zealand,' says Spike Edney. To which they replied, 'Why doesn't he ask us himself?' I explained that he was afraid they would turn him down. They didn't sound that convinced, but said they might be prepared to consider it. I told Bob, and he approached [Queen manager] Jim Beach officially.'

Geldof later explained how he'd persuaded them.

'I traced Jim all the way down to . . . some little seaside resort that he was staying at, and I said, "Look, for Christ's sake, you know, what's *wrong* with them?" Jim said, "Oh, you know, Freddie's very sensitive." So I said, "Tell the old faggot it's gonna be the biggest thing that ever happened – this huge mega thing." So eventually they got back and said OK, they would definitely be doing it, and I thought, Great. And when they did do Live Aid, Queen were absolutely the best band of the day. Whatever your personal taste was irrelevant. When the day came, they played the best, they had the best sound, they used their time to the full. They understood the idea *exactly* – that it was a global jukebox, as I'd described it. They just went and smashed out one hit after the other. It was just unbelievable. I was actually upstairs in the Appeals box in Wembley Stadium, and suddenly I heard this sound. I thought, God, who's got *this* sound together?'

Geldof had no way of knowing, and nor did anyone else at the time, that just ahead of their 6.40 p.m. appearance, Queen's sound engineer James 'Trip' Khalaf went out front to 'check the system', and fiddled surreptitiously with the limiters.

'We were *louder* than anyone else at Live Aid,' confessed Roger Taylor. 'You've got to overwhelm the crowd in a stadium!'

'I went outside,' said Geldof, 'and saw that it was Queen. I looked down over this crowd of people just going crazy, and the band were amazing. I think they were delighted afterwards – Freddie in particular. It was the perfect stage for him: the whole world. And he could ponce about on stage doing "We Are the Champions" and all that, you know? How perfect could it get?'

'We didn't know Bob at all,' remarked John Deacon in a rare interview. 'When "Do They Know It's Christmas?" was out, that was a lot of the newer acts. For the gig, he wanted to get a lot of the established acts. Our first reaction was, we didn't know – twenty minutes, no sound check! When it became apparent that it was going to happen, we'd just finished touring Japan and ended up having a meal in the hotel, discussing whether we should do it . . . and we said yes. It was one day that I was proud to be involved in the music business. A lot of days you certainly don't feel that! But the day was fabulous, people forgot that element of competitiveness . . . it was a good morale-booster for us, too, because it showed us the strength of support we had in England, and it showed us what we had to offer as a band.'

'There was nothing very magical about the way we put the set together,' admits Spike Edney.

'We all sat around discussing which songs to play, and eventually hit upon the idea of playing a medley of hits. No great mystery to it – if you've got a bunch of songs and you can't choose, it's the obvious thing to do. It was all very matter-of-fact, perfect timing notwithstanding, of course. Every member of that band is a night-mare perfectionist . . . and a good thing too. On the day, it turned out to be amazing.'

'Queen had rehearsed really hard at the Shaw Theatre on [London's] Euston Road for a whole week, while others just went on and busked it,' remembers Peter 'Phoebe' Freestone, Freddie's personal assistant.

'That's why they were the best on the day. I remember Freddie being stunned when he launched into "Radio Ga Ga" and saw thousands of hands start going. He was dazzled by that, having never seen anything quite like it before. They had only ever performed that song in darkness.'

Spike Edney remembers things somewhat differently, however, insisting that Freddie was in 'full-blown bring-it-on mode', and that he and the band took proceedings completely in their stride. From what I saw, I have to agree with him. This was Queen's ultimate moment, towards which they had been building their entire career.

'It was all organised chaos behind the scenes,' Spike recalled. 'Everyone backstage was exceedingly engaging and open. No one was being bitchy or trying to outdo each other. Until Queen came on, it was all a bit of a nice summer picnic. Which is not to say that Queen were being calculating and cunning. They just did things the way they normally would, expecting everyone else to do the same. I was stunned to hear certain artists belting out their latest single: that's not your audience out there! Queen didn't do that. They just did what Bob demanded. The "greatest rock perform-ance of all time", as it's often referred to nowadays. What does that really mean? What it was, actually, was a band at the top of their game doing what they did best and surprising the fuck out of everybody.'

'No one was ready . . . except Queen', recalls Pete Smith, the show's worldwide event coordinator, and author of *Live Aid*. 'I saw the set on the monitors backstage. The BBC had installed

TV monitors all around the artist area. With the many clocks that Harvey had ordered, these TVs kept everyone aware of what stage in the proceedings we were at. Queen tore up the rule book and then rewrote it in twenty minutes flat. The effect was palpable. Live Aid was now cooking on gas.'

At their brilliant best both musically and technically – there was no more professional rock band in existence at that point – Queen's reputation on the world stage was confoundedly on the wane. Their popularity had slipped due to a plethora of miscalculations, mishaps and a general, wide-sweeping change in musical tastes. Queen were beginning to feel that they'd had their day. A permanent split was on the cards. They'd talked about it. Thanks to Live Aid, all this was about to change.

Yet why were people so amazed by their electrifying performance? Spike Edney for one couldn't fathom it.

'This was what Queen were about!' he laughed. 'They were well known all over the planet for putting on a terrific show, for giving it all they'd got. They were veterans at stadium gigs, they weren't exactly novices. This was their natural habitat, and the bigger the audience the better. They could practically do this stuff in their sleep. Queen were surprised that everyone else was surprised, frankly! To them, it was another day at the office. Having said that, we knew when we came off that we'd done it. After Live Aid, Queen found that their whole world had changed.'

Bernard Doherty masterminded publicity for the event, taking care of all the media on the day.

'We knew we had to keep the press sweet, to ensure maximum coverage. I had only eight triple-A laminate passes, but hundreds of press. We had to share them around. One by one I said to everyone: "Right, you've got forty-five minutes in there, get what you can, get back out. See you in the Hard Rock Café", of which there was a "branch" backstage. Backstage was a wagon-train-style scenario, with all the artists' Portakabins pointing inwards, and Elton cooking a barbecue somewhere in the thick of it all because he didn't fancy the offerings of the café. David Bailey set his photo studio up in a stinky little corner, he wasn't proud. Nobody's conditions were ideal. It was all thrown together on the fly. But somehow it happened. Everyone got in the spirit of the thing, most people left their egos at home, and it worked.'

At the time, Doherty had David Bowie as a client, and was obliged to take care of his needs too.

'Always a little nerve-wracking when you are looking after your artist and doing two jobs at once. In my case, that day, about eighteen jobs. There wasn't much love lost between David and Elton – they'd obviously fallen out. David came out of his performance OK. Elton did all right. The one musician David was genuinely pleased to see was Freddie. They really were delighted to be together again. They stood chatting, as if they'd only seen each other yesterday. The affection between them was tangible. David was wearing an amazing blue suit, and looked incredibly sharp and healthy. Just before David went on, Freddie winked at him and said, "If I didn't know you better, dear, I'd have to eat you." No wonder David went out on stage with such a big smile on his face.'

All day long, Freddie remained relaxed.

'He sat holding court, in that perfectly camp but quite humble way of his,' agrees Bernard. 'He knew the power he had over people, but it didn't go to his head. If he'd been sitting outside a beach hut in Southend-on-Sea, he'd have taken people's breath away. He was a true star, with that indefinable quality. John Deacon I wasn't aware of, where was he? And I didn't see Brian May or Roger Taylor speak to each other all day. They were like a divorced couple at the same party.'

Quo's Francis Rossi disagrees.

'I don't subscribe to the theory that Queen were on the point of breaking up then. They seemed like they were getting on all right to me, and we knew the boys in the band pretty well. All bands have differences. They were certainly united in their commitment to the Live Aid cause.'

The backstage area was nonetheless rife with rumours about Queen being on the verge of breaking up.

'It showed,' insists Bernard Doherty.

'Not when they went on, though. If there were differences, they were intelligent enough to put them aside to get on with the job in hand. And they went out there and won. Queen had the wow factor. What else do we remember about Live Aid? The sound going down on The Who. Bono getting in the zone, losing the plot and confounding the others by breaking the rules of performance that day – none of the rest of U2 would talk to him after that.'

Despite Live Aid turning out to be the performance that estab-lished U2 as a stadium group with a superstar future, it almost went horribly wrong. Not only did they play a self-indulgent four-teen-minute version of their 'heroin song' 'Bad', from the 1984 album *The Unforgettable Fire*, but Bono punctuated it riskily with blasts of Lou Reed's 'Satellite of Love' and 'Walk on the Wild Side', as well as by bits from The Rolling Stones' 'Ruby Tuesday' and 'Sympathy for the Devil'. This left room for only one other song, causing their finale 'Pride (In the Name of Love)', an eventual global mega-hit, to be ditched. Then Bono spotted a young girl being crushed in the crowd when the audience, reacting to the singer's charisma, surged forwards. Although he signalled desper-ately to stadium stewards to save her, they failed to understand. So Bono took a leap of faith thirty feet down into the throng to pick her up himself – and wound up dancing with her. What emerged from the experience was how brilliantly Bono connected with an audience. That brief dance, sealed with a kiss, became an indelible image of Live Aid, resulting in all of U2's albums re-entering the UK charts.

'On the day, though, they really thought they'd blown it,' said Doherty. 'Simon Le Bon did blow it, with the bum note of all time.

Then there were the critics drooling over Bowie. Phil Collins, playing both Wembley and JFK courtesy of Concorde – though I think a lot of people wished he hadn't bothered, not least the hastily re-formed Led Zeppelin, who he drummed for at JFK. As for Queen, they did exactly what Bob had asked them to do. I watched from the wings and I was blown away. I was behind Freddie, looking over his shoulder onto the piano, just a couple of feet away from him. I stood watching the audience with some trepidation. You never know: even the greatest acts in the world bomb, and you don't know why.'

We needn't have worried. Queen drew from every influence, every which way. They gave it all they had. So many other supreme performers flooded back into my mind at that point: Alex Harvey, the great glam rocker of the Sensational Alex Harvey Band. Ian Dury and the Blockheads. Mick Jagger. Ziggy Stardust and the Spiders. What Freddie displayed better than on perhaps any other occasion was instinctive star quality, as well as a phenomenal grasp of what makes a must-watch show. He conjured up all the genius of Vaudeville. It was as if he had studied and absorbed the best-kept secrets of every definitive artist who had gone before him, and sorcered a little of all those greats into his own act. It was quite a formula. The ultimate peacock, Freddie seduced us all.

Not, admits Doherty, that he knew Queen were making history that day.

'Not on the day, no. I had headphones on, and a walkie-talkie – no mobile phones back then. I was worrying about Dave Hogan and Richard Young in the pit. I had Bob and Harvey to fret about. It was all going on, I had a lot on my mind. I knew the band were going down well, sure. The crowd was going nuts. Everyone backstage stopped talking to watch them. That was bizarre. Never normally happens . . . Who came on before or after Queen? Hardly anyone remembers. What do I remember? That Freddie Mercury was the greatest performer on the day. Perhaps the greatest performer ever.'

David Wigg, the veteran journalist then writing for the *Daily Express*, had long been a close personal friend of Freddie's.

'I was the only journalist allowed to join Freddie in his dressing room as he prepared for Queen's performance at the biggest show in the world,' he says. 'He was very relaxed, and looking forward to getting out there to do his bit.'

'We are playing songs that people identify with, to make it a happy occasion,' Freddie had explained.

Freddie and David discussed the reasons behind Live Aid, and talked about Freddie's own experiences in childhood.

'He said that he first became aware that he was luckier than a lot of children when he attended an English boarding school in India, and discovered through a boy's eyes the plight of the country's poor.'

'But,' Freddie had insisted, 'I'm certainly not doing this out of guilt. I don't feel guilty just because I'm rich. Even if I didn't do it, the problem would still be there. It's something that will sadly always be there. The idea of all this is to make the whole world aware of the fact that this is going on. By making this concert we are doing something positive to make people look, listen, and hopefully donate. Neither should we be looking at it in terms of us and them. When people are starving, it should be looked upon as one united problem.'

Freddie openly admitted to 'Wiggie' that when he saw TV film of Africa's starving millions, he had to switch off his set.

'It disturbs me so much, I just can't watch it. Sometimes I do feel helpless, and this is one of those times I can do my bit. Bob has done a wonderful thing, because he actually sparked it off. I'm sure we all had it in us to do that, but it took someone like him to become the driving force, and actually get us all to come together.'

For one concert-goer, that day was the more overwhelming for the fact that this was his first rock experience. Jim Hutton, the humble hairdresser who became Freddie's partner shortly before

Live Aid, went on to share the rest of Freddie's life. Little could he have known that day that, just six years later, he would be helping to prepare his lover for burial. Conveyed to the concert in grandeur as Freddie's other half in the star's own limousine, it was the first time Jim had ever attended a gig of any kind, let alone watched Queen play live.

'Talk about chucking me in at the deep end,' laughed Jim. 'I was a bit blown away by all the glamorous superstars to be honest. Every member of the band had his own trailer. All the wives were there, as well as Roger's and Brian's children. Freddie knew everyone. He took me to meet David Bowie, who I'd actually met before, when I cut his hair. He even introduced me to Elton John as "my new man". Freddie didn't need time to get ready, he was just going on stage in what he was wearing when we left home – a white vest with a pair of faded jeans. He also had on a pair of his favourite trainers, a belt and a studded amulet. When it was their turn to go on, he knocked back another large vodka tonic and said, "Let's do it."

'I walked with him to the stage, and kissed him good luck. Not that he needed it. To hear them playing those songs live – a bit of "Bohemian Rhapsody" with Freddie on the piano, "Radio Ga Ga" with the crowd clapping wildly in unison, "Hammer to Fall", then Freddie on his guitar for "Crazy Little Thing Called Love", and "We Will Rock You", and "We Are the Champions", thundering away . . . to a simple guy like me, this was all just mind-boggling. Then later on, once it had got dark, Freddie and Brian back on stage together, just the two of them, performing that wonderful ballad "Is This the World We Created . . . ?". They had recorded it quite a while before Live Aid, hadn't they, but it was as if they had written it especially for the occasion. The words were so right, and the way Freddie sang them was just magical. It moved me to tears, as Freddie often did.'

At last, Jim, who died from cancer in January 2010, nineteen years after Freddie's death, had seen his rock-star lover at work.

'He gave it everything up there. He amazed me. Then, when he was off, he seemed glad it was done. "Thank God that's over," he laughed. Another large vodka, and he was calm. We did stay until the end to catch up with everyone, but Freddie didn't want to bother with the after-show party at Legends nightclub. Instead, we went home to Garden Lodge like an old married couple, to watch the rest of the American leg on television.'

Conspicuous by their absence that day were Freddie's own parents. Although often in attendance at Queen's UK concerts, they chose instead to witness this spectacle at home.

'It was such a huge event, it would have been too complicated,' recalled Freddie's mum Jer, suggesting that she and Freddie's father Bomi would have been overwhelmed by both the crowds and the logistics of getting to and from the stadium. So I watched it on television. I was so proud. and turned to me and said, "Our boy's done it."'

From the viewpoint of professionals charged with transmitting and recording the event, Freddie's contribution had been little short of sensational. Mike Appleton, former executive producer of *The Old Grey Whistle Test* – the influential BBC television rock series – remembers Mercury's performance as 'fascinating'.

'For a start, he was not even supposed to go on. Doctors had already said that he was too ill to perform. His throat was terrible, from a cold or something. He wasn't well enough, but he absolutely insisted. It happened that he and Bono of U2 wound up as the most successful performers of the day.

'It was so interesting to see Freddie through the monitors – I was shut away in a sweltering OB truck all day long. We were literally building a programme live on air as we went. Come five o'clock and we were flipping live to JFK – alternating twenty minutes here, twenty minutes there, let's put an interview in here, a live bit from earlier there, some highlights of the first hour in this slot . . . it's actually very exciting television, and the only way I like to work. Freddie simply came on, took immediate possession of the stage, coolly and calmly, and then proceeded to take possession of the audience.

'Queen had at that point been off the boil for a while, having made no significant impact with an album for some time. The Live Aid experience wound up putting them back on the map, and had the same effect on the music business as a whole. Overall, sales went up. Live Aid proved to be a tonic for the entire industry. As Freddie was the out-and-out star of the day, he was undoubtedly the main ingredient of that tonic. He was more dominant that day than I'd ever seen him before. The day may have belonged to Bob emotionally. It definitely belonged to Freddie musically.'

Mike later received the BAFTA Award for Live Aid as Producer of the Best Outside Broadcast.

Dave Hogan, who captured the show in stills, shares Appleton's opinion.

'Only six of us were chosen as Live Aid's official photographers', reveals the fabled *Sun* lensman known as 'Hogie' (who is no stranger to a splash headline himself – 'Maimed By Madonna' was his Warholian moment).

'We were shooting for the Live Aid souvenir book, so we weren't stopped from going anywhere,' he recalls.

'It was obvious to everyone on the day that Freddie was the main man – but not until he actually got on stage. Freddie wasn't a limelight-grabber when he wasn't on. His behaviour was gentlemanly and low-key, compared to most. No one realised how powerful he was until he went out there. At that point, we knew, this is it. I remember him launching into "Radio Ga Ga". It wasn't even dark, he was whipping up all this magic in daylight. That ocean of fans clapping and stamping together just sent shivers down your spine. For us, it was heaven. This is the moment you want. He stole it. The day was full of fantastic moments – Bono leaping into the crowd, McCartney's first live performance since John Lennon was assassinated. But what I saw Freddie do that day took my breath away. He engaged with every single person present. Total unison. Nobody has done that, before or since. I think he was the only one who *could* do it.'

Thus, the cream of rock sang and danced to feed the world. It has been repeated ad nauseam that Queen's performance was the most thrilling, the most moving, the most memorable, the most enduring – surpassing as it did the efforts of their greatest rivals.

'By far the most extraordinary,' agrees radio presenter Paul Gambaccini. 'You could sense a frisson backstage as heads rose towards the monitors like dogs hearing a whistle. They were stealing the show, and they would regain a stature they would never lose again.'

The other members of Queen were the first to praise their front man.

'The rest of us played OK, but Freddie was out there and took it to another level,' said Brian, with typical modesty. 'It wasn't just Queen fans. He connected with everyone.'

As he later elaborated to me in an emotional interview at Queen's Pembridge Road offices, 'Live Aid *was* Freddie. He was unique. You could almost see our music flowing through him. You couldn't ignore him. He was original. Special. It wasn't just our fans we were playing to, it was *everyone*'s fans. Freddie really gave his all.'

Of all Queen's 704 live performances fronted by Freddie, it remains their most iconic, their finest hour. Live Aid gave the band the perfect opportunity to demonstrate that, stripped of props and trappings, of their own lighting rig and sound equipment, of fog and smoke and other special effects, without even the natural magic of dusk and with fewer than twenty minutes in which to prove themselves, they were unchallenged sovereigns who still had what it took to rock the world. They would now embrace the unequivocal fact that Queen were greater than the sum of their parts. They had no way of knowing that their finest hour was already behind them. United in exultation, recommitted to the cause, all thoughts of solo careers shelved – for the moment, at least – they were soon to discover that their glittering, second-chance future with Freddie would be tragically short-lived.

2

Zanzibar

I'd be woken by the servant. Clutching an orange juice, I'd literally step out onto the beach.

Freddie Mercury

He was very secretive about his background. He never even told me his real name. He was fairly dark-skinned, a cross between Oriental and Asian, so there was no disguising the fact that he came from somewhere off the beaten track, or at least had exotic parents. He must have been in denial about it. Not for sinister reasons, or that he was racist in any way. Not when you consider how he hero-worshipped Jimi Hendrix.

Tony Brainsby, Queen's first publicist

Perhaps Freddie believed that music fans of the 1970s were not ready for a rock star with African and Indian roots. It would not matter now. On the contrary, many would see it as an advantage. The more blended and obscure an artist's cultural and musical heritage today, the more desirable. Back then, things were different. It is not hard to imagine that he regarded the facts of his life as out of kilter with the image he yearned to create. A rock star, by definition, was ideally American, and hailed from California (The Beach Boys), New York (Lou Reed), Florida (Jim Morrison), Mississippi (Elvis Presley) or Washington State (Jimi Hendrix). Liverpool was also cool, thanks to The Beatles, as was London, courtesy of Mick Jagger and Keith Richards of The Rolling Stones. White Anglo-Saxon was favourite, Black American almost as good. It was common in those days for musicians to blur the detail of their backgrounds, as this facilitated glamour and mystery: the kind of thing that publicity people were paid relative fortunes to invent. There was so much by way of conflicting information about Freddie's birth and childhood that I realised I would have to go looking for myself.

I flew to Dar es Salaam via Nairobi, and hitched a boat to Zanzibar Town across a harbour rocking with dhows and simple fishing canoes. Everything about the place felt exotic. To someone like me, born in the dullest of backwaters, Freddie's dismissal of Zanzibar began to seem puzzling. The thought of him camping it up in front of his dinner party guests with stories of Ali Baba and Sinbad, of wild Arabian princes and Eastern promise galore is irresistible. Why didn't he? There had to be a reason. An 'enchanted past' was so quintessentially Freddie.

Zanzibar, no more than a speck in the atlas, lies just south of the Equator off Africa's east coast. Peer closer and it's actually two specks: the main island, Unguja, and the more remote Pemba, a destination popular today with European honeymooners. Together with neighbouring former German and subsequently British colony Tanganyika, they now form the United Republic of Tanzania. For a tiny territory, Zanzibar has suffered more corruption, disruption and massacre than perhaps it was due. Invaded down the centuries by Assyrians, Sumerians, Egyptians, Phoenicians, Indians, Persians and Arabs, as well as Malays, Chinese, Portuguese, Dutch and British, its history reads like *One Thousand and One Nights*. Some, notably the Shirazi Persians from what is today Southern Iran, the Omani Arabs and much later the British, stayed on to settle and rule. The Swahili civilisation here dates back to the earliest awakenings of Islam. When the clove tree was introduced in 1818, Zanzibar's spice industry was born. Ginger, nutmeg, vanilla, cloves and cardamom began to be exported around the world. Thanks to missionaries and explorers passing through its portals en route to the Dark Continent, tales of harems, palace intrigues and royal elopements all added to its romance. As a flourishing trade centre of ivory and human trafficking, it acquired an awful notoriety. Until abolition in 1897, some 50,000 Africans a year, drawn from as far away as the continent's central lakes, were dragged through its barbaric market to be flogged, in both senses, as slaves.

On Unguja's shores stand imposing sultans' palaces, an ancient Arab fort with rusting cannons, colonial buildings and merchants' mansions, some in a state of lingering renovation, some delapidated beyond repair. Behind these lie labyrinths of bazaars and narrow streets crammed with dwellings. For the first eighteen years of Freddie's life, a Stone Town flat overlooking the sea was home.

His mother Jer was little more than a child herself when she gave birth to him in Zanzibar's Government Hospital, on Thursday 5 September 1946 – which happened to be the Parsee New Year's Day. That the tiny eighteen-year-old's first-born was male was a blessing. When the news reached her husband at work, Bomi rejoiced. The family name would continue. At least, they assumed that it would, blissfully ignorant of lifestyle choices that lay distantly ahead. The couple mused together on what they might call their baby. As Parsees – adherents of the monotheistic Zoroastrian faith dating back to early sixth century BC Persia – their options were limited. They settled on Farrokh, the name duly registered by Bomi according to legal decree at the Government Records Office.

'I remember very clearly when Freddie was born,' Perviz Darunkhanawala, née Bulsara, told me, when I visited her at home in Shangani district. Perviz was Bomi Bulsara's niece. Her father Sorabji and Freddie's father Bomi were two of eight brothers.

'Freddie's father and mine were born and brought up in Bulsar, a small town north of Bombay [known today as Mumbai] in the Indian state of Gujarat,' she explained.

'That was how they got the name Bulsara. The brothers all came to Zanzibar one after the other to look for work. My father got a job with Cable and Wireless. Bomi took a job in the High Court, as a cashier for the British Government. When Bomi came to Zanzibar he was not yet married. It was only later that he returned to India and married Freddie's mother Jer in Bombay. After that he brought her here, and Freddie was born.

'He was so small, like a little pet. Even when he was a very young baby, he used to come to my home with his parents. They used to leave him with my mother and go out. When he was a bit older, he would play about in our house. He was such a naughty little one. I was much older than him, and I liked taking care of him. He was such a small boy, a very nice child. I loved him so much. Every time he came, I wanted him to stay. But his parents would always collect him and take him back home at the end of an evening out.'

Perviz described how the Bulsaras enjoyed a relatively sophisticated social life within the confines of their rigid religion and culture. On a salary that would have defined him as little more than a modest civil servant in Britain, Bomi was able to support a comfortable home and domestic servants, including Freddie's ayah (nanny), Sabine. The family wanted for nothing and the climate was good. In 1952, when Freddie was six years old, his sister Kashmira was born.

Bomi Bulsara was based at offices in the non-residential Beit-el Ajaib, the House of Wonders, built for ceremonial purposes by Sultan Sayyid Barghash in the late nineteenth century. In its day, it had been the tallest building in East Africa, and boasted lush botanical gardens. It survived bombardment by a British fleet following a brief uprising, and later underwent extensive conversion to become Zanzibar's main museum. Bomi's job necessitated travel throughout the colony and into India, which may well have influenced his decision to send his only son far away to school. But there was also the question of how far the child's education could be taken domestically. While his parents continued to practise Zoroastrianism,

Farrokh attended the Zanzibar Missionary School from the age of five, where his teachers were Anglican nuns. Considered brighter than average, he displayed early aptitude for painting, drawing and modelling.

'He was developing quickly into a delightfully courteous, serious and precise little boy,' remembers Perviz.

'He had a twinkle in his eye and a mischievous streak, which would now and then get the better of him. But I remember him most vividly as secretive and shy. Painfully shy. He would not talk much, even when he came with his parents to see us. That was his nature. As he grew older, we didn't see each other so much, as he would be out playing on the streets and on the beach with all the other boys.'

'As a young boy, he was very happy and loved music,' his mother Jer recalled. 'Folk, opera, classical, he loved them all. I think he always wanted to be a showman.'

Perviz was surprised to learn that my efforts to procure a copy of her cousin's birth certificate from official sources had ended inconclusively. Not even an audience with the chief registrar produced good news.

'So you are here for Freddie Mercury's birth certificate?' he smiled. 'It's not here. It *was* here. An Argentinian woman came some years ago, to look for it. A copy was made out for her, and the original has not been seen since, although it has been asked for on numerous occasions – I presume by his fans. The main problem is that, in 1946, 1947, proper records were not yet kept. Just pieces of paper, which now lie in a jumble all over the place. I will show you.'

Behind the counter in the main office, the registrar rummaged in filing cabinets and returned with handfuls of loose birth certificates. Perhaps a dozen of these spilled onto the floor, and were left there.

'There is one person, a physician by the name of Dr Mehta, who is currently in Oman but returning next week. I know he has a copy of Freddie's birth certificate.' Try as I might, however, I was never able to track Dr Mehta down.

My investigations into the family's roots did not meet with the approval of all concerned. Perviz's beautiful daughter Diana was unimpressed, while insisting that she was not at all interested in 'Freddie *Mercouri*'. Why?

'He went away from Zanzibar when I was only a baby,' she shrugged, her face flushing. 'He gave up his family name. He did not live like us. He was nothing at all to do with us. He never came back. He wasn't proud of Zanzibar. He was a stranger. He was of another life.'

She declined to elaborate. So there was more.

Diana's attitude was in keeping with what I found elsewhere. Although several Zanzibaris now claim to live in dwellings once owned by the Bulsara family, none could offer tangible evidence, and no one, it seemed, really cared. As one Indian shopkeeper explained, 'I don't know anything – and neither does anyone else. Anybody who tells you they do is only guessing. Especially these guides who take you round the island and show you the sights. They just want money. There is no one left here who knows. So many people left suddenly at the same time, a long time ago. But if ever you find out, will you come back here and tell me, please? Because I am heartily sick of people always asking me. Americans. South Americans. English. German. Japanese. Local people don't understand. Who was this person anyway?'

Who was Zanzibar's most famous son? For Queen pilgrims, this island is the ultimate destination. Specialist tour operators run expensive fan-friendly holidays to the singer's birthplace, where a few restaurants with beautiful views and a couple of gift shops cash in on the connection. But Freddie was never in his lifetime accorded star status here. No Freedom of the City. No official archive entry. No acknowledgement, at the time of visiting, at the local museum. No former dwelling converted into personal shrine. No statue, waxwork, or effigy, no mass-produced ashtray nor fridge magnet, not so much as a postcard bearing his likeness – although there are postcards of almost everything else. Perhaps not even thermometers here have mercury in them. If ever one had cause to seek the antithesis of Elvis Presley's Graceland in Memphis, this must be it.

The mystery of the missing birth certificate reared its head again when I got home. Out of the blue, Marcela Delorenzi, an Argentinian – *that* Argentinian – made contact. She was, she told me, on her way to London with a gift for me. What the Buenos Aires-based broadcaster and journalist brought me was a copy of Freddie's birth certificate. I hadn't asked for it. We'd never spoken. I hadn't tried to track her down, she asked for nothing in return. If there was guilt, this was not discussed. At the time that she obtained it, she insisted, the original handwritten document was still in place in the Records Office. She'd seen it. Perhaps, in the end, it changed hands for vast profit, and is tucked away in a private collection somewhere.

In 2006, the Association for Islamic Mobilisation and Propagation (UAMSHO), a Zanzibar Muslim group, protested vociferously against plans to celebrate Freddie's sixtieth birthday on the island. Claiming that he had violated Islam with his openly gay, flamboyant lifestyle until his untimely death in 1991 from AIDS, the angry group called for a 'gay-tourist' beach party to be scrapped, and for thousands of fans heading for the celebration from every part of the world to be sent packing.

It hardly came as a surprise. When Zanzibar officially outlawed gay relations in 2004, the move attracted criticism from gay communities everywhere. But UAMSHO head Abdallah Said Ali insisted defiantly that the event would 'send out the wrong signals'.

'We do not want to give our young generation the idea that homosexuals are accepted in Zanzibar,' he said. 'We have a religious obligation to protect morals in society, and anyone who corrupts Islamic morals should be stopped.'

Islamic morals notwithstanding, there had long been the faith of Freddie's own family to consider. He loved and respected his parents and sister with all his heart. He also knew too well that orthodox Zoroastrians support the suppression of homosexuality – perhaps the primary reason why Freddie tried for so long to suppress his own inclinations. In the sacred Zoroastrian text the *Vendidad*, it is stated: 'The man that lies with mankind as man lies with womankind, or as a woman lies with mankind, is a man that is a Daeva (demon): this man is a worshipper of the Daevas, a male paramour of the Daevas.'

For Parsees, homosexuality is not only sinful, but a form, unimaginably, of devil-worship.

Let's set this in context. Consensual homosexual activity between adults remains illegal in some 70 of the 195 countries of the world. In 40 of these, only male–male sex is outlawed. Sexual acts between two adult males became legal in England and Wales in 1967, but not until 1980 in Scotland, and 1982 in Northern Ireland. During the 1980s and 1990s, gay rights organisations lobbied for the age of consent for heterosexuals and homosexuals to be equalised. Today, the age of consent in England, Scotland, Wales and Northern Ireland is sixteen.

'Freddie did not live like us,' his cousin Diana had said. 'He was of another life.'

Naked truth, better than the best-dressed lie. Freddie had apparently forsaken his African homeland for the most fundamental of reasons.

Perhaps what he felt in his heart was '*hiraeth*'. No single word translates its ancient Welsh meaning. What it evokes is melancholy, a deeply rooted sadness for what is lost. Did Freddie, like most of us, secretly mourn his spent innocence, longing for chapters of his past he could no longer reach?

Sometimes we go back. We revisit. We console our adult selves with quiet remembrance. Freddie never could. He would always have to fill the void elsewhere. Some believe he made peace with his past in 'Seven Seas of Rhye' – the band's first hit, in 1974. A hard-rock anthem on an otherwise progressive album, its lyrics were based on a fantasy realm created by young Freddie with his little sister Kashmira. Could it have been the mysteries of their Persian roots, and in particular the prophet Zarathustra's epic journey, which fuelled their flights of fancy and inspired their fairytales of Rhye? It seems likely, according to Radio 2 producer, music archivist and renowned record collector Phil Swern.

'It has always been my impression, from remarks he made in interviews over the years, that "Seven Seas of Rhye" was about his life in Zanzibar,' says Phil. 'It was where he escaped to – in his mind, at least. He always had that, when reality got too much.'

In one radio interview, Freddie described the song's subject as 'a figment of my imagination'.

'My lyrics and songs are mainly fantasies,' he said. 'I make them up. They are not down to earth, they're kind of airy-fairy really. I'm not one of those writers who walks out onto the street and is suddenly inspired by a vision, and I'm not one of those people who wants to go on safari to get inspiration from wild animals around me, or go up onto mountain tops or things like that. No, I can get inspiration just sitting in the bath.'

Whatever else, Rhye proved to be a recurring theme. Other early Queen songs also featured the fantasy land, such as 'Lily of the Valley', 'The March of the Black Queen' and 'My Fairy King'. Its allure was to prove ever further-reaching and enduring. In Queen's futuristic jukebox stage musical *We Will Rock You*, which debuted in London in 2002, the Seven Seas of Rhye is a place to which the rebel Bohemians are transported after being brain-wiped by Khashoggi, commander of the Globalsoft police.

As the final bars of 'Seven Seas of Rhye' fade, an old English bucket-and-spade ditty crooned by a raucous saloon bar crowd echoes fleetingly: 'Oh, I do like to be beside the seaside'. Further allusion to Freddie's once carefree beach life, to the palm-fringed, pristine coral reefs of youth?

We can't know. What we know is that there could never have been a welcome in the hillside for the man who fractured the code of his family's faith.

3

Panchgani

I was ... a precocious child, and my parents thought boarding school would do me good. So when I was about seven, I was put in one in India for a while. It was an upheaval of an upbringing, which seems to have worked, I guess.

Freddie Mercury

Freddie's parents sent him away to school in India, and it saddened me greatly to see him go. But here in Zanzibar at that time, the standard of education for boys was not so good. Also, I believe it was about the same time as his parents were transferred for work to the island of Pemba, and there was certainly nothing of a high enough educational standard there. They felt that the best solution was to send him to Bomi's sister, also called Jer – my auntie, in Bombay – where he could study properly.

Perviz Darunkhanawala, Freddie's first cousin

In November 1996 I was invited to a cocktail party and private preview of the Freddie Mercury Photographic Exhibition at London's Royal Albert Hall. It was to commemorate the fifth anniversary of his death. Everyone in the room that night had a direct link to Freddie and Queen – from Marje, Freddie's cleaning lady, and Ken Testi, the band's first-ever manager, to Denis O'Regan, a regular Queen photographer. Freddie's frail old parents were also there. When I introduced myself, they greeted me warmly. His father Bomi Bulsara held my hand.

'It is wonderful to see all these photographs displayed, and to see all these people here in honour of our dear son. We feel very proud,' he said.

The exhibition would tour the world, visiting numerous relevant cities including Paris, Montreux and Mumbai. After the London opening, a number of fellow journalists chose to 'out' the Great Pretender for having 'hidden his Indian roots'. Under headlines such as 'Bombay Rhapsody' and 'Star of India', Freddie was 'exposed' as Britain's first Asian pop star. Despite the fact that there was less than a sentence of truth in it, the yarn made several sensational page leads. Freddie's Persian origins were thus disputed. Widespread discussion ensued. This caused offence within London's Persian Parsee community. Not that Fleet Street's finest gave a toss about that.

'Just because our people have not lived in Persia since the ninth century, that does not make us any less Persian,' declared a spokesman for the Parsee community in London.

'While Parsees are described as "Indian Zoroastrians", we descend from the Persian Zoroastrians who fled to India in the seventh and eighth centuries to escape Muslim persecution. The fact that we migrated to India does *not* make us Indian. If you are a Jew, but your family have not lived in Palestine for the past two thousand years, does that make you less Jewish? There is a great deal of difference between race and nationality. Between roots and citizenship. The Persian Parsee may not have a place to call home [the land which was once their territory being modern-day Iran]. Nonetheless, he remains Persian in his heart.'

As far as Freddie was concerned, you only had to look at him. His classic Persian looks were indisputably at odds with what is commonly considered 'Indian'. Every picture, those extra teeth notwithstanding, tells the tale.

Born pre-independence in colonial India, Freddie's parents Bomi and Jer were both British subjects, their nationality British-Indian. This was recorded officially, both at the time of their own births, and at that of their son. Significantly, they declared their race to be Parsee. Freddie was born in Zanzibar, so was considered Zanzibari. It must be mooted that he was more African than Asian. 'Britain's first Asian pop star' was stretching it: yet another new hook from which to dangle old frames. Why did his family not object to this blurring of their past, to such dismissal of their sacred heritage? Their behaviour has often seemed puzzling.

Quiet, diligent and homely people, un-materialistic and content with their lot, the Bulsaras did things at a measured pace, observing the rituals, rules and restrictions of their religion and culture. Both were physically small, almost delicate in build. Freddie took more after his mother in terms of looks, inheriting in particular her full lips, open smile, and unusual teeth. Keeping themselves politely to themselves in public, Bomi and Jer were always kind and convivial behind closed doors, if a little on the restrained side. While they were dutiful family members with a strong sense of tradition and who knew their place, Bomi was neither a dominant role model nor macho hero to his son. More comfortable among the matriarchs of the family, Freddie never showed a shred of inclination to follow in his father's clerical footsteps. While his mother has said that she was keen for him to study Law, the thought of working in an office left him cold.

Being so reserved and undemonstrative, there was little in the way of physical contact between the Bulsaras and their children, as Freddie would later reveal to his lovers Barbara Valentin and Jim Hutton. When the family still lived in Zanzibar, their children were cared for day to day by a nanny, Sabine. While neither Freddie nor Kashmira was chastised with beatings, they were never cuddled much either. According to Jim, Freddie would ponder from time to time whether that lack of affection during his early childhood was what led to a 'disproportionate obsession with physical love in adulthood . . . a craving which all too often manifested itself in meaningless sex, because he generally couldn't get the one without the other. Sex was never a substitute for the thing he wanted most, which was affection . . . proof that he was loved. He was quite childlike about it. All the petting and stroking which he lavished on the cats, for example: it was what he wanted for himself.'

On 14 February 1955, according to the official school records, when he was only eight years old, Freddie – then still Farrokh – was enrolled as 'Farookh Bomi Bulsara' (note the change in spelling compared to that on his birth certificate) at St Peter's Church of England School in Panchgani, where he was admitted to 'Class Three'. He would remain there for a decade, seeing his parents only once a year, for a month each summer. Little wonder that his relationship with his mother and father became distant, as evident from the respectful but unemotional letters he wrote to them. Despite the stiff upper lip and brave face that he was encouraged to maintain, it is impossible to imagine that Freddie did not feel vulnerable and lonely so far away from home, without even the luxury of a telephone to enable him to speak to his parents whenever he missed them, which was often.

'He was six when I was born, so I only had a year of him, yet I was always aware of my proud older brother protecting me,' recalled his sister Kashmira in an interview with the *Mail on Sunday* in November 2000.

'He didn't always come home for the holidays – sometimes he'd stay with my dad's sister in Bombay, or with my mum's sister, and it was she who got him started on playing the piano and drawing. He was talented in all areas. It made me feel sick, of course. Mum and Dad kept all his school reports.'

For the eight-year-old Freddie, the journey from home to his new school was an arduous one. 'He went by ship with his father before taking the train up to Poona [now Pune],' recalls Freddie's cousin Perviz.

'It was a very long and tiring journey. There were regular ships from Zanzibar to Bombay' – already the busiest, most industrialised and most progressive city in India – 'and we went often because we had relatives there. Freddie would go to my auntie Jer, Bomi's sister, during school holidays. She was a very good, kind lady who also used to take care of the small children of another of my father's brothers in India.'

A typical British Raj hill station in Western India, 184 miles from what was then Bombay, Panchgani ('Five Hills') is renowned for its quaint old bungalows, public buildings, ancient Parsee dwellings and lush strawberry fields. The tranquil colonial town was founded during the Raj as a sanatorium and rest resort. It is not hard to see why. Looking out across coastal plains, dense forest and the River Krishna, its high-altitude, iron-rich waters and dense, volcanic red soil make it a popular haven with tourists. Many make the four- or five-hour drive from Mumbai for 'Monsoon getaways'. Here, they walk, ride and unwind away from the dust and heat of the Indian plains. Some also send their children here, to its English-style boarding schools.

St Peter's School stands to this day. Founded in 1904, it contin-ues to uphold traditional Indian values and culture, and to promote tolerance of faiths as diverse as Catholicism and Zoroastrianism. The school's motto is '*Ut Prosim*' ('That I may profit'). Its crest, 'a symbol of hope and rebirth', features a phoenix rising from flames, the olive branch of peace held in its beak. Freddie's headmaster, Mr Oswal D. Bason, arrived in 1947, the year India was granted independence. He remained principal until 1974, just as Queen were tasting the *amuse-bouche* of fame. While the school does not flaunt its rock 'n' roll connections, it is rarely reluctant to open its doors to the curious. Staff there have even assisted in research and filming for Freddie Mercury documentaries. Together with his friend and contempo-rary Victory Rana – later Lt General Victory Rana of the Nepalese Army – and Ravi Punjabi, philanthropist and businessman, Freddie numbers among the school's most famous Old Boys.

By the time he arrived on this pleasant, sprawling fifty-eight-acre campus, Freddie had been indoctrinated into the family faith and was a fully-fledged Zoroastrian. At eight, he experienced the Naojote ('Navjote') ceremony. In common with Christian Confirmation, this embraces girls as well as boys, while resembling more closely in style the male Jewish Bar Mitzvah. The ritual involves a cleansing bath, symbolising purification of mind and soul; the wearing of a symbolic white shirt and wool cord, and the chanting of ancient prayers over a flame said to be both sacred and eternal. Such fires are a core feature of the Zoroastrian faith. In some fire temples, it is claimed that flames have burned continuously for thousands of years. The Zendavesta, or sacred scriptures, contain no formal commandments, but simply the 'Three Good Things' by which Parsees have long tried to live. '*Humata, Hukhta, Huvareshta*': 'good thoughts, good words, good deeds'.

In Freddie's day, St Peter's was widely considered to be the best boys' public school in Panchgani. It offered a full English education leading to Cambridge University O-level and A-level examinations, and maintained consistently excellent results. Attracting families from the USA, Canada and the Gulf as well as from all over India, its school year ran from mid-June to mid-April. With concessions to India's climate, the main eight-week holiday fell between April and June, with an additional fortnight break at Christmas. Discipline at St Peter's was strict, and conditions were on the severe side. While there was hot water for baths on Wednesdays and Saturday lunchtimes, the rest of the week it was cold. Bathing routines were supervised by Matron, who also ran the school hospital with the help of a resident nurse and on-call doctor. The school had its own church, with a when-in-Rome stance: while boys of all religions attended the school, and their faiths were respected, Sunday Mass was compulsory for all. No pupil was allowed off campus unless accompanied by a member of staff. For all this, St Peter's was well-known as being a caring establishment with a gentle and fun family atmosphere, which nurtured the strengths of pupils to bring out the best in the individual. Whatever he felt about it at the time, Freddie admitted in later life that he felt privileged to have been sent there, knowing the sacrifices his parents had made.

Not only was it a struggle to find the school fees – Freddie's father was modestly-paid as a government clerk, and there was not much money to spare, it was painful for Bomi and Jer to part with their only son, and for his sister to be separated from her only sibling.

That sense of privilege was not enough to dispel separation anxiety. Having grown exceptionally close to his mother and to his sister Kashmira as a small boy, being sent thousands of miles away to school at such a tender age must have been a terrible wrench. It is impossible to imagine Freddie feeling anything other than alone and afraid, longing for a cuddle and a bedtime story as he tucked up at night. Those close to him in later years have told how Freddie harboured a deep resentment towards his parents for 'sending him away', even though he was never less than a respectful and loving adult son. He clearly tried his hardest to overcome his feelings of rejection.

Jer and Bomi must have felt that they were doing the right thing at the time. Giving their son the best start in life undoubtedly caused financial hardship. But sending a shy little boy like Freddie so far away to school was probably their biggest mistake. Some young children appear to deal better than others with prolonged separation from their families. For Freddie, a sensitive child and by his own admission a little clingy, that wrench, at just eight years of age, was initially unbearable. He would cry himself to sleep at night in his narrow dormitory bed, surrounded by a quivering bunch of nineteen other new boys. Deprived of daily one-to-one affection and attention at the most crucial stage of his development and at a deeply impressionable age, Freddie's outlook and expectations inevitably changed.

He would seek solace in the company of like-minded lads. As well as Victory Rana, he befriended Derrick Branche, who later moved to Australia to become an actor. In 1985, just as Freddie was stealing the show at Live Aid, Branche had a part in the movie *My Beautiful Laundrette*, a comedy drama starring Daniel Day-Lewis which explored relationships between White and Asian communities, and which tackled, poignantly, such issues as homosexuality and racism.

Freddie's circle also included Farang Irani, later to become a restaurateur in Bombay; and Bruce Murray, last heard of working as a porter at London's Victoria railway station. Over the next few years these five boys would become inseparable, sleeping close to one another in their dormitory, and collaborating on endless schoolboy pranks. Packed off to either his paternal aunt Jer or his maternal aunt Sheroo during the term and half-term breaks, Freddie was rarely reunited with his parents during his time at St Peter's, even during school holidays.

'You had to do what you were told, so the most sensible thing was to make the most of it,' said Freddie, years later. 'I learnt to look after myself, and I grew up quickly.'

So began the moulding of the personality of the 'real' Freddie, which would stay true until the end of his life.

The realisation that he would have to hold his own and stand up to the school bullies proved a steep learning curve for Freddie. It also dawned on him that the name would have to go. 'Farrokh' was a mouthful, pronounced as it was the Persian way: 'Far**och**', as in 'loch', as opposed to the African 'Far**ouk**'. He was relieved when teachers and friends adopted the diminutive of a respectable English name. 'Freddie' he became. Thankfully, it stuck. His parents and family raised no objections, and refer to him as 'Freddie' to this day. The change of surname would come much later, for different reasons.

When Freddie was about ten years old, he began to display an aloof, somewhat condescending streak, which he would retain for the rest of his life. While waspish on occasion, he was neither unkind nor malicious.

He was simply not the typical team player. In sport, he excelled at solo and one-to-one activities such as chess, sprinting, boxing and table tennis. He became school table tennis champion before he turned eleven. While rugby and football were not his thing, he was said to have enjoyed cricket, although he denied this later. Whether he felt that an open love for the game would harm his hard-rock image, who can say? In 1958, aged almost twelve, he won the Junior All-Rounder prize, and the following year took first prize for Academic Prowess. He assumed lead roles in a variety of plays, and sang a solo in the Seniors' production of 'The Indian Love Call'. His favourite subject was Art. Much of his free time was spent sketching and painting, particularly for his aunt Sheroo and grandparents in Bombay. He also began to indulge enthusiastically in extracurricular music.

Even during the late 1950s and early 1960s, Bombay enjoyed a cosmopolitan East-meets-West culture which allowed Western pop and rock to take hold. While Freddie loved the classical music he studied, particularly opera, he adored the contemporary even more. He took up the piano, passing exams up to and including Grade IV in both Theory and Practical, and joined the choir. With his close friends, he formed his first band, The Hectics. Thanks to his lively boogie-woogie piano-playing style, Freddie was soon the talk of the town. The Hectics started performing at school concerts and at the annual fete. Girls from local schools would stand at the front and scream their lungs out, having heard that this was the way to behave in front of a group. The pop idols of the day included Elvis Presley, Cliff Richard, Fats Domino and Little Richard, and it was from these artists that Freddie drew inspiration. He practised hard to emulate their styles. He was not yet front man material, however, and took a willing back seat to his friend Bruce Murray, who played guitar and sang lead vocals.

'There was also, of course, a school choir, which sang all the traditional choral works and hymns, and which practised regularly in order to lead the singing at the school's church services,' remembered Freddie's former school chum and Hectics band mate Derrick Branche.

'The choir was about twenty-five-strong, and we would often be mixed with girls from one of our sister schools in the town. Not only did Freddie love the choir, but I believe he also loved one of the girls, too – fifteen-year-old Gita Bharucha, if I'm not mistaken!'

Although it has been reported that Freddie was sexually active at St Peter's from the age of about fourteen, and that his encounters were mainly with other boys and even a couple of hired school hands, Freddie's first-ever girlfriend is not so sure.

'I never thought Bucky was gay,' Gita told me. 'Not at all. Never saw any evidence of that. Maybe his masters knew, and were discreet. We his friends were certainly not aware of it. He was quite the flamboyant performer, and absolutely in his element on stage. Invariably he had the roles of girls in plays!'

Having married, changed her name to Choksi and moved to Frankfurt, where she worked for an Indian tour operator, Gita was not easy to trace. When I found her, she was at first reluctant to talk about Freddie. Eventually she agreed, and we met in London.

'I first met Freddie in 1955, when I started at the Kimmins School in Panchgani,' she told me.

'It was run by Protestant missionaries from England. I left there in 1963. For most of the ten years that Freddie was in "Panchi", we were friends. I was from Bombay, but I lived with my mother and grandparents in Panchi. I was a day scholar. The way it worked was that the boys from St Peter's would attend the Kimmins kindergarten, then continue from Standard Three at St Peter's proper. A group of us were in the same class together for years. Victory Rana and I were together right through school. And Bucky – that's what we used to call Freddie, because of his teeth. Derrick Branche was another one.

'Bucky and I were particularly close – but just good friends. Nothing intimate. Holding hands, that's all. We used to rent bicycles at three rupees a day and go cycling. We'd also go out in rowing boats on Mahableshwar Lake. Mum would let me have a party, or a few friends over to lunch, after which we would go for walks or play games. Bucky often came during the holidays, and spent time at our home. He was extremely polite and well-mannered. My mother and grandparents liked him enormously.'

Janet Smith, a Panchgani schoolmistress who lived at St Peter's during Freddie's tenure because her mother taught him Art, was in no doubt about Freddie's homosexuality.

'He had this habit of calling one "Darling", which seemed a little fey. I just knew that he was homosexual when he was here. It was unusual in those days, admittedly, but almost accepted in a boy like Freddie. Normally it would have been just ghastly. But with Freddie, somehow it wasn't. It was OK. Not a phase: it was very much inside him, a fundamental part of him. I couldn't help feeling sorry for him, as the others would make fun of him. Funny thing was, he didn't seem to mind.'

Despite the fact that Gita Bharucha and Freddie had been insep-arable, she never heard from him again after he left Panchgani.

'Very sad, I know, but that was it. As if he wanted to divorce himself from life in India and get on with the next stage.'

By the time he reached Class Ten, Freddie's grades had begun to slip. He failed the end-of-year examination, and left the school ahead of year eleven. Freddie never actually sat his O-levels. Possibly distracted by confusion over his sexuality, and by the more creative pursuits of Music and Art, he lost interest in his studies and set his sights on more glamorous goals. While previous biographies report that he left St Peter's with a string of O-levels and with exceptional grades in English Language, History and Art, he did not. Quite why the facts were distorted by early publi-cists only becomes clear when set against the incredible academic achievements of his fellow band members. Brian May studied Physics and Maths at Imperial College London, and graduated with a BSc Hons in Physics. The PhD he began in Astrophysics would be completed thirty years later. John Deacon achieved a first-class Honours degree in Electronics at Chelsea College, now part of King's College London, while Roger Taylor won a place at the London Hospital Medical College to study Dentistry, later abandoning the course to focus on music.

'Freddie didn't want to come across as a ... dimwit, compared with the other members of Queen who had achieved so much,' commented Jim Jenkins, official Queen biographer and co-author of *As It Began*. Perhaps that's why he said he had passed O-levels which he hadn't really. It is understandable in the circumstances.'

Freddie's maternal aunt Sheroo Khory spoke to me about her beloved nephew from her home in Bombay's Dadar Parsee colony. Bombay became Mumbai in 1995, when the former name was declared to be an unwanted legacy of British colonial rule.

'Even when Freddie would stay with Jer, he would always come to me after breakfast, and would spend entire days with me. He was very good at drawing, and I encouraged him. When he was eight, he drew an excellent picture of two horses in a storm, which was signed "Farrokh". It used to hang in his mother's house. I don't know if she still has it.'

But once Freddie was in England, 'That was it,' she said. 'He never wanted to come back to India. He called himself British, he liked the more civilised lifestyle there, and most of all he liked the justice system – especially in comparison to all the corruption here in India. But he did keep in touch with me regularly. He even sent me money for an eye operation which I badly needed, and wanted to take me on a tour of Europe. He never forgot his old auntie.'

Years later, Sheroo revealed, she fell into regular correspondence with her nephew's former girlfriend Mary Austin, trading photographs of Freddie in boyhood and Freddie the famous rock star. She also touched on the subject of Freddie's 'enemies' in England, and how she used to fear for his safety. Discussion about religion upset her, she said, especially rumours that Freddie had converted to Christianity shortly before his death.

'The whole family was extremely distressed by this news,' she said.

'It was a great blow. We were all fed up with so many heartbreaking things being said about our Freddie, all the lies being told, particularly things about him becoming a Christian. Which I am sure that he did not. Certainly not to my knowledge, and I'm sure I would have known.'

Despite reports to the contrary, Freddie returned to Zanzibar in 1963, and completed the final two years of his education at the Roman Catholic St Joseph's Convent School. Bonzo Fernandez, a former Zanzibar policeman who later worked as a taxi driver, knew Freddie well at this school.

'I remember he had a very good relationship with his family, and had a good sister. Freddie was very well brought-up. They were good, well-mannered people. We used to play hockey and cricket together. He was especially good at cricket,' he said.

'I knew that he had been away at school in India, but he never spoke about his years there. Sometimes after school we used to jump out of the window and swim in the sea, which Freddie loved to do. We also used to swim at the Starhe Club on Shangani Street, which had a very clean beach. We'd cycle to Fumba in the south, Mungapwani in the northwest, the site of the old slave caves, or to Chwaka on the far southeastern peninsular. Sometimes a whole group of us would go. We'd swim, eat snacks, climb coconut trees. We were mischievous, but not bad. No alcohol, drugs or cigarettes, not in our day.

'I can still see that slim and happy young boy in his short blue pants and white shirt. He was always smartly-dressed, especially for cricket, when his immaculate whites would always seem whiter than everyone else's.

'After the Revolution we all departed from the island. I never knew where Freddie went, nor what became of him. Only later did I find out that we were living in the UK at the same time. Only after his death did I discover that my former classmate and close friend had become that world-famous rock singer.'

Gita Choksi's experience was similar.

'Years later, when I found out who he became, I bought some of his recordings and enjoyed his music immensely,' she said.

'I never saw him perform live, however. I have always been disappointed about that. Another of our good school chums did go once to a Queen concert, and tried to go backstage to see Bucky. But when he managed to put himself face to face with him, Freddie just looked right through this poor fellow and said to him, "I'm sorry, but I'm afraid I just don't know who you are."

'That was when we all knew for sure that he wanted nothing more to do with us. The past was something he was determined to leave behind.'

4

London

I'm a city person. I'm not into all this country air and cow dung.

Freddie Mercury

Many people are drawn to London because of the relative anonymity. You can lose yourself in a crowd, meet large numbers of like-minded people. There's a critical mass. London was swinging in those days. Zanzibar would have been constraining to a personality like Freddie's, to someone with a restless spirit.

Cosmo Hallstrom, Consultant Psychiatrist

The 1950s saw a marked rise in nationalist advances against British rule. Britannia's loss of India and Pakistan in 1947, the independence of Burma and Ceylon in 1948, and China's social revolution of 1949, all impacted strongly on nationalist struggles in North, Northeast and East Africa. Zanzibar was not immune. Trade unions there had begun to reinvent themselves as political parties in order to effect change. The Zanzibar National Party, founded in 1956 by the minority Arabs and Shirazi, was succeeded by the Afro-Shirazi Party, its leadership mainly of African mainland origin. Labour militancy was on the increase, and strikes were disabling many industries. Pro-Arab election results, and frustratingly poor clove and coconut harvests, incited the masses to riot. Although independence was achieved in December 1963, imbalances in electoral representation infuriated the black African majority, and their anger flared in a radical left-wing coup. The violent Zanzibar Revolution of 1964 saw the new Sultan Jamshid bin Abdulla deposed, and Sheikh Abeid Amani Karume, President of the Afro-Shirazi Party, installed as first President of Zanzibar. Thousands were slaughtered in bloody street battles. The Bulsaras and many like them ran for their lives. Leaving Zanzibar with a few suitcases between them, Freddie's family headed for England, where relatives had offered them refuge. They never looked back.

'That was that, as far as our family relationship was concerned,' remembers Freddie's cousin Perviz, sadly.

'When I heard, much later on, that Freddie had become a famous musician, I was very happy that we had such a genius in the family. How proud we were of him. But he did not communicate with any of us. He never even sent us a cassette.'

Following the Revolution, Zanzibar agreed a union with Tanganyika in April 1964 in which it would remain semi-autonomous under the new name Tanzania. Zanzibaris today are laid-back, peaceful, and tolerant people – with the exception of their almost universal abhorrence of homosexuality.

The Bulsaras were not prepared for the culture shock when they arrived in Feltham in the London Borough of Hounslow, a nondescript town about thirteen miles southwest of the capital and a couple of miles from Heathrow Airport.

'My dad had a British passport,' explained Kashmira, 'so it seemed the obvious choice to come to England.'

'Freddie was so excited', remembered his mother, Jer. '"England's the place we ought to go to, Mum"', he said. 'But it was very hard'.

The dull, grey orderliness of flight-path suburbia, not to mention the cold climate, were in stark contrast to what they had known in Zanzibar and Bombay. In London, they found themselves without status, salary, servants or mansion. Despite his government connections and track record, no official accountancy job awaited Freddie's father. Bomi eventually found employment as a cashier with the Forte catering group, while his mother took a job as an assistant at a local branch of Marks & Spencer. Even after her son found fame, she stuck with the job for some time.

'I was struck by how conspicuous we were,' recalled Kash, who was then about twelve years old.

'Freddie was very fastidious about his appearance. Whereas he looked neat and tidy, and his hair swept back, everyone else wore their hair long, and looked scruffy. I used to walk behind him because I didn't want people to think I was with him.

'But he changed his appearance very quickly,' she went on. 'He always used to take hours in front of the mirror looking after his locks.'

At eighteen, Freddie found himself in a quandary. Although anxious to spread his wings, he was still financially dependent on his parents, and therefore obliged to live at home. Well aware of all that the metropolis had to offer, remaining trapped under their roof cramped his style.

'People in small towns find it difficult to accept anything or anyone who differs from the norm,' observes James Saez, producer, writer, multi-instrumentalist and former engineer at Record Plant, Los Angeles.

'There's a lot of Jesus and guns in West Virginia. Growing up in Zanzibar and India, Freddie knew all about that. If you come from such places, and you're this whole other person inside who might not find acceptance, you have *got* to get to the city. Lucky Freddie for having to move to London when he did.'

While many his age were already out there earning their own money and leading independent lives, Freddie's parents were keen for him to continue with his education. No career in Law or Accountancy for their son, however. By his own admission, Freddie was simply 'not clever enough' for academic pursuits. Opting instead to develop his artistic talents, he attended Isleworth College in 1966 to obtain an A level in Art, moving to Ealing College of Art that autumn to embark on a course in Graphic Design and Illustration. He would graduate in the summer of 1969, aged twenty-three, with a Diploma in Graphic Art and Design. Far from being 'the equivalent of a degree', it failed to match the scholarly brilliance achieved by his future fellow band members.

'I went to art school with the intention of getting my diploma, which I did,' Freddie said, 'and then becoming an illustrator – hoping to earn my keep as a freelance.'

'He'd go out a lot, too,' remembered Kashmira, 'and stay out all night. My mum and he used to argue about it constantly. And she was always going on at him to make sure he got a degree, but he was determined to do what he wanted. There was quite a lot of door-slamming. But when Freddie made it, Mum was very proud.

'I only really got to know him during this period,' she added. 'He would help me with my homework, and I'd pose for him when he was doing his sketches.'

During college holidays, Freddie earned pocket money in Heathrow Airport's catering department, and also worked in a container warehouse on the Feltham trading estate. Dismissing jibes from his co-workers, who teased him for his 'feminine hands and camp, flamboyant ways', he retorted that he was really a musician, marking time.

London, the Mecca of youth culture, was by now in full swing. With the pop boom on the turn, the singles market was beginning to fade in favour of LPs. Ballroom managers, finding that rock 'n' roll 'beat' nights no longer drew the crowds, began switching to straight dancing sessions. The Beatles were still the most popular group in the world, with chart competition from The Rolling Stones, The Animals, Manfred Mann and Georgie Fame. Tom Jones, a beefy singer from the Welsh valleys, was the latest pop discovery. Sandie Shaw and Petula Clark were Britain's most popular girl singers, and the folk boom of the previous year was on the rise. Joan Baez

Freddie's birth certificate, verifying that his arrival was registered 15 days after his birth, and that his race was recognised as 'Parsee'.

Freddie's 4th birthday in Zanzibar. He wears the white Zoroastrian prayer cap and celebration garland.

Freddie's father's workplace.

Freddie's first band, The Hectics, formed at St. Peter's School in the early 1960s (Freddie, centre). The group's name was said to have been inspired by Freddie's frantic playing style.

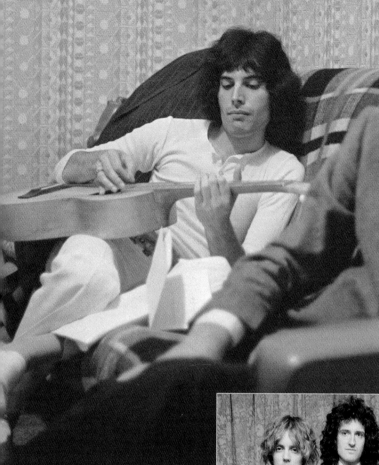

Freddie relaxing in a
Shepherd's Bush flat,
1969.

Queen – drummer
Roger Taylor, guitarist
Brian May, bassist John
Deacon and Freddie –
photographed early 1974,
as they embarked upon
their first major tour of
the United States.

Freddie on the verge of
superstardom in 1975:
the year of 'Bohemian
Rhapsody'.

Promoting *A Day At The Races*,
at Kempton Park race course,
October 1976. From left,
Mary Austin, Freddie and
John Reid. Brian May's bride
Chrissie Mullen May, Roger
Taylor and Brian May can be
seen behind them.

Hallowe'en 1977: Freddie celebrating with Elton John and Peter Straker. Queen's album *News of the World* had just been released.

January 1978, as Brian, Roger, Freddie and John embarked on a major European tour. Freddie sports his favourite footwear: ballet pumps. Brian sports his: white wooden clogs.

New Year's Eve 1978, Maunkberry's Club, London. From left, actress Britt Ekland, Freddie, a friend, Ronnie Wood and his wife Jo.

Freddie, 1974. © Mick Rock 1974

Freddie poses for the camera as Mary looks on: the loving couple relax after hours, 1974.
© Mick Rock 1974

Brian and Freddie listening to playback in the studio, 1974. © Mick Rock 1974

Freddie and Brian, 1974. © Mick Rock 1974

Freddie reclining on the pink
satin sheets and pillows of his
bed at his Holland Road flat.
© Mick Rock 1974

Freddie backstage with John Deacon
and make-up artist as Queen close
their first UK headline tour, at the
Rainbow Theatre London, 1974.
The lavish costumes are by Zandra
Rhodes. 'You had to be very careful
with his make-up', said Rock. 'He
was very conscious of his overbite,
and the way his chin would look'.
© Mick Rock 1974

Brian and Freddie at the console with a
studio engineer, 1974. © Mick Rock 1974

Freddie and John Deacon backstage
during Queen's support of Mott the
Hoople, 1974. © Mick Rock 1974

Freddie with Mick Rock, 1974: 'Freddie's teeth were his prime concern when taking photos … He had too many teeth: 4 extra at the back of his palate, which pushed the others forward. When I pointed out that this was a relatively easy, if painful, thing to correct, he told me he couldn't. "I'm frightened it will affect my voice", he said. "I need the extra teeth".'
© Mick Rock 1974

Bright-eyed Roger in the lap of a bleary-eyed Freddie at an after-show tour party, 1974. © Mick Rock 1974

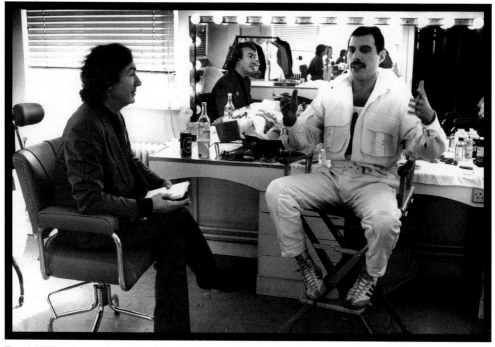

David Wigg interviews Freddie in his dressing room on Queen's 1979 European tour.

and Bob Dylan weighed in with political messages about Vietnam. Donovan befriended Dylan. Elvis Presley, Peter, Paul and Mary, The Byrds, The Righteous Brothers, and Sonny and Cher and other Americans, held their own in the British hit parade. Television was taking hold, its pop programming dominated by Cathy McGowan on *Ready, Steady, Go!*

Fashion, too, was booming. Mary Quant and Angela Cash ruled the design scene, while John Stephen became the 'King of Carnaby Street', at that time the Mod centre of the world. Young fashion had acquired its own voices. The Who popularised 'Op Art' designs, wearing T-shirts adorned with bull's-eyes and Union Jacks. John Lennon did the same for the tweed peaked cap, while Dave Clark, of The Dave Clark Five and later a close friend of Freddie's, made white Levi jeans a must-have. A lean and snake-hipped Freddie favoured tight hipster trousers in crushed velvet and cord. Leather and suede jackets, satin, silk and floral shirts and ankle boots completed the look.

Living on the fringes of the world's most exciting city made Freddie restless and rebellious. He wished more than ever that he could afford to leave home, and soon took to dossing on a series of friends' floors.

'Fred lived like a gypsy,' Brian May would recall.

He wanted it all and he wanted it now, right on his doorstep: the fashion boutiques, the record stores and bookshops, the music venues, pubs and clubs. Trendy Kensington Market and the celebrated Biba emporium would soon become his stamping ground.

Ealing College of Art boasted several famous alumni, not least The Who's Pete Townshend and Ronnie Wood of The Faces, later a Rolling Stone. Former student Jerry Hibbert remembers the place as both progressive and practical, the kind of college that produced graduates ready for the workplace. Arriving there from Oxford, he started two years below Freddie in 1968, but got to know him well through shared musical interests.

'Ealing College was going through many changes at that time,' Jerry remembers.

'New York's advertising centre Madison Avenue was the big thing. It influenced our lifestyle, right down to the way we dressed. We wanted to look like New York ad execs. We cut our hair short and came to college in suits and ties, because hippies were everywhere and art students like to do something different. It was all pretty stylised. We even had a thing about the way we walked. We were definitely not your Union Bar-type students, all rugby-playing and beer-swilling. The college restaurant was our social centre and gathering place. Freddie – he was still Freddie Bulsara in those days – used to hang out there with us all. He was definitely one for style and clothes. He was always very conscious of the way he looked.'

'Art school teaches you to be more fashion-conscious,' Freddie would later remark. 'Always that one step ahead.'

Bored by course work, and lacking both discipline and diligence, Freddie quickly lost interest in his studies. He enjoyed, however, the more hedonistic aspects of college life. During lessons, he spent most of his time sketching portraits of his classmates and of his new idol Jimi Hendrix, whose influence was to change Freddie's life. The African American from Seattle, just four years Freddie's senior, had been discovered in New York by Chas Chandler, The Animals' bass player. Persuading The Beatles, Pete Townshend and Eric Clapton to turn up at the 'in' clubs to watch his outrageously talented protégé play, Chandler quickly built a huge following for The Jimi Hendrix Experience, which also comprised drummer Mitch Mitchell and bass player Noel Redding. The American left his rivals speechless. Performing tricks he'd picked up from a string of nameless musicians, Hendrix played his white Fender Stratocaster upside down, behind his neck and with his teeth, displaying a breathtaking range of techniques. Although many subsequent rock guitarists would take the instrument in other directions, few would ever equal Hendrix's brilliance.

'Jimi Hendrix was just a beautiful man, a master showman and a dedicated musician,' Freddie would later remark.

'I would scour the country to see him whenever he played because he really had everything any rock 'n' roll star should have: all the style and the presence. He didn't have to force anything. He'd just make an entrance and the whole place would be on fire. He was living out everything I wanted to be.'

Freddie's ambition was crystallised. While still as enthusiastic as ever about the musicians who had thrilled him at school – Cliff Richard, Elvis Presley, Little Richard and Fats Domino – he was bowled over by Hendrix, and set about reinventing himself in the American rocker's image. Just as Jimi's guitar work challenged conventional expectation, Freddie's future songwriting, arranging and vocal techniques must do the same. Hendrix's stage presence and outrageous style left them gasping in the aisles. Freddie knew he had to do likewise. Hendrix was wildly original, performed innovatively, and was so energetic that he exhausted his audiences. Freddie was determined to have the same effect on his own fans some day. Hendrix could take any song, even something mundane, and make it sound as if it were his own unique composition. In 1986 I was to witness Freddie do likewise, live on stage in Budapest, when he brought tears to the eyes of thousands with his rendition of a simple Hungarian folk ballad. The foreign lyrics scrawled on his hand could not have meant less to him. The melody sounded nothing like a rock song. But Freddie performed it as if he meant it, from the heart. The audience was spellbound.

Back in Kensington, the drab walls of his tiny flat plastered with images of his idol, Freddie applied himself assiduously to perfecting the Hendrix style. Brightly coloured floral jackets over black or multicoloured shirts, skinny coloured pants, Chelsea boots, chiffon scarves knotted at the Adam's apple, chunky silver rings. According to fellow student Graham Rose, 'What he wore was no different from what we were all wearing at that time. On the whole, Freddie was a quiet guy, although he was prone to fits of giggles. When that happened, he would put his hand right over his mouth to cover up those huge teeth of his. I remember him as a terrific bloke, very sweet and considerate. There wasn't a nasty streak in him. A lot of us were very pleased when he went on to become such a great success.'

Jerry Hibbert agrees that Freddie did not stand out at college.

'Except that he was very keen on singing. He used to sit at his desk and sing. He was in the next room from me, and a year or two above. He sat opposite his mate Tim Staffell, and they used to sing together, in harmony. That was very strange, since at that time we were all into blues stuff. John Mayall and Eric Clapton, pre-Cream. We became quite obsessed with all the underlying influences. For example, we no longer wanted to see Eric Clapton play 'Hideaway', we were more interested in seeing Freddie King play it. Freddie Bulsara definitely had an interest in all that, along with the rest of us. So sitting in class singing harmonies made him look a bit ridiculous. It was out of kilter with what everyone else was doing. That didn't appear to bother him or Tim. They'd sit there working away, and they'd be singing together.'

'Music was always a sideline, and that sort of grew,' remarked Freddie later.

'When I'd finished with the illustrating course, I was sick of it. I'd had it up to *here*. I thought, I don't think I can make a career of this, because my mind just wasn't on that kind of thing. So I thought I would just play around with the music side of it for a while. Everybody wants to be a star, so I just thought that if I could make a go if it, why not?'

As for Freddie's personality, Jerry refutes the idea that he was any kind of attention-seeker.

'No, he wasn't like that. He was the nicest possible guy. Nor did I have any idea that he was gay. He showed no signs of that at all. He was quiet, friendly. Always polite, always nice. The sort of lad your mum might say was "well brought-up". He used to lark about and sing, using a ruler as a pretend microphone, but that was just for laughs.'

After both had left college, Freddie broke his usual rule of not keeping in touch with people once he had moved on from a stage in his life. He and Jerry maintained their friendship for quite some time.

'It was because of the music,' Jerry explains. 'I used to play blues: at college, at parties, at other people's flats. Freddie would come down and join in. This was in the days before people played records at parties. If you wanted music, you'd get a band in.'

Freddie would eventually confide in Jerry about his dream to pursue a career in music.

'After Freddie left college, I was in a band for about two years. He came round one day and told me that he was going to concentrate on getting a band together. I told him, "Don't do it, stick to graphics. There's no money in music. Stick to what you know."'

But Freddie had made up his mind.

'I did see him after that – I bought some equipment, or sold him some, I can't remember which. He came back to play at college with a group called Wreckage. I didn't think much of them to be honest. After that, we just lost touch.'

Jerry went into animation, joining one of the many outfits who worked on The Beatles' full-length feature, *Yellow Submarine*.

'I completely lost interest in music,' he admits. 'I found myself hating everything. Never bought any records, never went to see any bands. About four years later I heard a DJ on the radio talking about a band called Queen. 'Seven Seas of Rhye' was their first hit. Not bad. But I simply didn't associate the name Freddie Mercury with my mate Freddie Bulsara from Ealing College. Suddenly there was a lot of publicity. You couldn't miss him. I was walking past a newsagent's one day and I happened to see his photo on the front page of *Melody Maker*. A huge picture, with a screaming headline. I stared at it and thought: "Bloody hell, that's Freddie Bulsara."'

Quite by chance, Jerry would later collaborate on a project for Queen towards the end of Freddie's life, but he was never to set eyes on his college friend again.

5

Queen

The idea of Queen was conceived by me whilst studying at college. Brian, who was also at college, liked the idea and we joined forces. The very earliest traces of the band go back to a group called Smile. I used to follow Smile a lot, and we became friends. I used to go to their shows, and they used to come to see mine.

Freddie Mercury

To begin with, he was this absolute nerd. A toothy nerd, who grew into his own fantasy. The classic cygnet who turned into a swan. Any band would give their bass and drum away for a singer like Freddie. No one could really match him. Bowie was the only one who came close.

David Stark: publisher, Songlink International, rock aficionado and drummer

The two-part classroom harmonies had graduated to three-part when Freddie and fellow college crooner Tim Staffell took to hanging out with another student, Nigel Foster. Spending much of their spare time perfecting versions of 'Hey Joe', 'Purple Haze' and 'The Wind Cries Mary', all British Top Ten hits for Jimi Hendrix, these private jam sessions, held ostensibly for their own amusement, would soon bring them to the attention of the boys who would be Queen.

For a while, Tim and Freddie were inseparable. Tim and their other college mates were only vaguely aware of Freddie's background, and of the circumstances that had brought the Bulsaras to England. Since Freddie never took friends home, they were left with the impression that his parents were aloof, and reluctant to integrate or adapt. It was even rumoured, erroneously, that they barely spoke English, and that they were determined to keep their culture, religion and language untainted and separate. In fact, Freddie had spoken English since toddlerhood.

By this time, Tim was playing regularly with a semi-professional band called Smile. Freddie started tagging along to rehearsals. Smile's lead guitarist was Brian May, a gangly Physics, Maths and Astronomy student at lofty Imperial College. Unbeknown to either of them, he and Freddie had been virtual neighbours in Feltham, Brian having grown up in a modest home not unlike Freddie's, just a few streets from the Bulsaras' house on Gladstone Avenue. Brian, a studious only child, had been playing guitar since the age of six. While still at school and with the help of his father Harold, he had carved his own Red Special guitar from a discarded mahogany fireplace and some cuts of oak. He played this with silver sixpenny pieces in place of the conventional plectrum. The guitar would later accompany him all over the world.

Brian, like Freddie, had dabbled in amateur bands with schoolfriends.

'None of the groups really got anywhere, because we never played any real gigs or took it that seriously,' Brian said.

It was at a local dance one evening that he and his pals spotted Tim Staffell, a lad from their school, who stood singing and humming on a harmonica at the back of the hall. They asked him to join their group, and he fronted '1984' at their first official gig in St Mary's Church Hall in Twickenham. Showing considerable promise, they were hired, in May 1967, as support act to Jimi Hendrix at an Imperial College gig. A few months later, they won a competition at Croydon's Top Rank Club. A professional career looked half-set.

'1984 was purely an amateur band, formed at school, although perhaps at the end we got fifteen quid or something,' was the way Brian would later remember it.

'We never really played anything significant in the way of original material – it was a strange mixture of cover versions, all the things which people wanted to hear at the time. This was about the time the Stones were emerging, and later we did Stones and Yardbirds things . . . I was never happy about it. I left because I wanted to do something where we wrote our own material.'

Explaining to his band mates that his studies must come first, Brian withdrew and the band broke up. Brian and Tim Staffell, by now a student and cohort of Freddie's at Ealing College of Art, kept in touch. Suffering musical withdrawal, they were soon discussing the logistics of starting another band. Together with Chris Smith, another Ealing undergraduate who was also a useful keyboard player, they agreed to have another go, deploying Smith on organ, Staffell on lead vocals and bass, and May on lead guitar. The only thing missing was the drummer.

With his baby-blond hair and deep blue eyes, Roger Meddows Taylor was almost too beautiful to be male. Norfolk-born but raised in Truro, heart-throb Taylor had already made a name for himself as a drummer in Cornwall with an outfit called Johnny Quale and The Reaction. The group won fourth prize in the local Rock and Rhythm Championship, and attracted quite a following on the Cornwall circuit. When Quale ditched his band, Taylor was elected lead vocalist. Tightening their name to The Reaction, their popularity continued to swell, with a musical style based primarily on soul until they discovered The Jimi Hendrix Experience in 1967. Roger headed for London that autumn to begin his Dentistry degree at the London Hospital Medical School. He soon became the fourth flatmate in rented lodgings in Shepherd's Bush, where his friend Les Brown from Truro already lived. Les was a year older, and like

Brian May was a student at Imperial College. Already hooked on the dream of becoming a rock star, but removed from his old band mates in The Reaction – with whom he would re-engage for a few ad hoc gigs during the summer break in 1968 – Roger needed to find himself a new band. Despite his Don Juan-ish reputation, he was shy, engaging and popular with other guys. Eventually, with Les Brown on the lookout on his behalf, an opportunity arose at the start of the autumn term. Scouring the Imperial College notice-board one day for something that might suit his friend, Les found a postcard advertising for a 'Ginger Baker/Mitch Mitchell-type drummer'. This showed that Brian and Tim meant business: Baker had attracted a cult following with the Graham Bond Organisation, a 'musicians' group' who had recorded with The Who, before jumping ship to join Eric Clapton's Cream. Mitchell drummed with The Jimi Hendrix Experience.

Brian May's was the contact name on the card. Roger called him immediately. Brian outlined what he and Tim were looking for, and soon the pair found themselves heading over to Roger's flat for a jam session on acoustic guitars and bongos, because Taylor's full drum kit was still at home in Cornwall, gathering dust. Shortly afterwards, the trio began rehearsing in earnest in the jazz club room at Imperial College. Not only did they play credible covers of other artists, Brian and Tim were now composing their own songs. More metal than minstrel, this early music rippled with classical undertones and borrowed from an astonishing range of influences. Part Elizabethan troubadour, part monster rock, Smile's sound featured dramatic drums, insistent guitars, strong lead vocals and intelligent harmonies, while their lyrics plundered the works. The overall effect was multilayered, embellished and breathtaking. It was nothing if not the shape of things to come.

This was the true genesis of Queen.

'I could play you tapes of Smile which have the same general structures as what we're doing today,' Brian said in an interview in 1977.

Queen chemistry was already being created, by very different personalities who complemented each other brilliantly. Brian, the quiet and gentle type off stage, was tall, lean and angular. Irresistibly snake-hipped in his velvet loons, his unruly dark curls fell sexily into his eyes as he played. Tim was more rough and ready, and, in his torn denims, not exactly fashion-conscious. Neither was fun-loving Chris, the only member of the group who was studying privately on the side for a Music degree. Blond Roger, described as 'a drummer both by name and by nature' and as 'sex on legs', was too pretty for his own good. It was his energy, enthusiasm, unfailingly upbeat and cleverly humorous attitude that drove the band. Those were happy, hopeful, carefree days.

'Brian May's mum and I would ask each other, "Are they going to make it?"', remembered Freddie's mother Jer.

In October 1968, Brian was awarded his BSc Honours degree, the diploma presented by Her Majesty the Queen Mother at the Royal Albert Hall. He had already elected to stay on as a post-graduate tutor at Imperial College while working on his PhD thesis on the movement of interplanetary dust, with a long-term plan to become an astronomer. There was an ulterior motive: remaining at Imperial made gigs and rehearsals easier. Tim Staffell and Chris Smith were still at Ealing. Roger, meanwhile, dropped out of medical school after completing only half of his degree. Just two days after Brian's graduation ceremony, the boys supported Pink Floyd at Imperial College, which is both remembered and disputed as Smile's debut gig. They would go on to open for T. Rex, Yes and Family. In February 1969, Smile asked Chris Smith to leave the group – which Smith himself has denied on the grounds that he had decided to quit, citing musical differences. A couple of nights later, the remaining members took their places at their first charity line-up at the Royal Albert Hall. A fundraising event for the National Council for the Unmarried Mother and Her Child, it was presented by the late DJ John Peel. Performing on the same bill as Joe Cocker and Free, little could Brian and Roger have known that, thirty-five years later, they would be collaborating with Free's lead singer Paul Rodgers (who in the meantime would front Bad Company, The Firm and The Law) on two acclaimed world tours, on *The Cosmos Rocks* – Queen's first studio album for almost fifteen years – and on a live album and two live DVDs.

Early in 1969, Tim pitched up at a Smile rehearsal with his art college pal Freddie Bulsara in tow. The attraction was instant and mutual. Freddie was in his element among accomplished and experienced musicians. More than ever, he was convinced that this was how he wanted to spend his life. Brian and Roger were equally entranced, falling irrevocably for Freddie's image, dry humour and razor wit.

As Roger's friend Les Brown later recalled, 'I don't think I've ever met someone so outrageous since. He was very enthusiastic about everything. He once physically dragged me into a room and made me listen to a soul record he really liked. No one admitted to still liking soul at the time; it was all rock. I suppose he was showing his catholic taste.'

Soon a regular fixture at Smile gigs, Freddie took to making candid comments about how they should style themselves, passed remarks about their performance, and even started telling them how they should sit, stand, walk and talk.

'He offered suggestions in a way that couldn't be refused,' remembered Brian. 'At that time, he hadn't really done any singing, and we didn't know he could. We thought he was just a theatrical rock musician.'

When Freddie graduated from Ealing College in summer 1969, he did not have a full-time job to go to. Nor did he have any intention of getting one. He and Roger Taylor (who had by now discarded the middle name 'Meddows') would run a tiny ten-pound-a-week 'Kasbah' stall within three-storey Kensington Market, on the antiques trading alley known as 'Death Row'. Most of the stallholders were flamboyant, jobless artists and writers. Their customers included Michael Caine, Julie Christie and Norman

Wisdom. To begin with they sold artwork by Freddie – mainly fashion sketches and drawings of Jimi Hendrix – and the work of fellow Ealing College students. They even sold Freddie's college thesis on Hendrix. Although this would undoubtedly be worth thousands today, none of it was valuable at the time. They needed to make more money. Unashamed clothes horses themselves, they decided to have a go at selling fashion. Dandy paraphernalia became their stock in trade: everything from exotic scarves and cloaks to jackets and fur stoles, all of which was little more than tarty tat and jumble sale junk, flogged at shamelessly inflated prices. They even started having garments made up out of old fabrics and trimmings, and became expert at acquiring 'job lots'. On obtaining a box of moth-eaten fur coats for £50 from a Battersea rag merchant, they sold them on at £8 each.

'Roger and I go poncing and ultrablagging just about everywhere, and lately we've been termed as a couple of queens,' Freddie wrote to student friend Celine Daley during that period.

Tim Staffell would later recall that Roger and Freddie revelled in their narcissistic 'Del-Boy-esque' market-trader profile.

'They really enjoyed being outrageous,' he said. 'Freddie developed the camp side of his nature – he regarded it as an amusing part of his personality. At no time was it suggested that he was gay. He was never overtly sexual.'

Freddie, now an accepted part of their entourage, had started to travel with Smile on the road.

In April 1969, the band performed at London's Revolution Club, where they met the head of Mercury Records' European division, the late Lou Reizner. Lou had brokered David Bowie's American deal, and would later achieve fame for having produced Rod Stewart's first two solo albums. He also produced the orchestral version of The Who's rock opera *Tommy*, and Rick Wakeman's *Journey to the Centre of the Earth*. A Chicago-born former singer himself, he offered Smile a one-single deal for the US only, which they signed on the spot. Nothing much happened until June, when the label booked Smile into Soho's Trident Studios.

It was an auspicious beginning. Trident Studios, at 17 St Anne's Court, a Soho alleyway in the heart of London's West End, was the brainchild of Normal Sheffield, former drummer with Sixties group The Hunters, and his brother Barry. The Sheffield brothers' 'relaxed attitude to audio-engineering' and the studios' state-of-the-art recording equipment made it a magnet to many top artists. At other facilities such as EMI's Abbey Road Studios, engineers still went about their business in white coats. Another, not inconsiderable Trident attraction was its already legendary Bechstein piano, at which Rick Wakeman had laboured lovingly for many a session, and the keys of which still echoed with the chords of Paul McCartney's 'Hey Jude'.

Offering the most advanced technology then available, the studios' first major hit had been Manfred Mann's 'My Name Is Jack' in March the previous year. The countless beloved albums recorded at Trident include Lou Reed's *Transformer*, produced by David Bowie, who recorded his own masterpieces there, not least *The Rise and Fall of Ziggy Stardust*. Rick Wakeman was the in-house session keyboard player in those days: he features on Bowie recordings such as 'Changes' and 'Life On Mars'. Trident exists to this day, and has welcomed many revered artists in its time, including James Taylor and Harry Nilsson. Legendary status was conferred for having hosted The Beatles in July 1968, for the recording of 'Hey Jude' – more than seven minutes long and at the time the longest single ever to top the British charts. Tracks for the 'White Album' and *Abbey Road* were also cut at Trident.

Despite recording several tracks in St Anne's Court, not a single release date was set. A deal with the Rondo talent agency kept them in gigs throughout the summer. That August, Mercury Records released the single 'Earth/Step on Me' in the States, where, due to lack of promotion, it sank without trace. The label being reluctant to waste a band with potential, and aware that Brian and Tim had co-written a wealth of material, a possible album or EP was discussed. The band were despatched to De Lane Lea Studios at Engineers Way, Wembley – not to the De Lane Lea branch at 129 Kingsway, as stated elsewhere. At De Lane Lea, founded in 1947 and famous for its work during the Sixties on albums by The Beatles, The Stones, The Who, Pink Floyd, ELO and The Jimi Hendrix Experience, Smile worked with late producer Fritz Freyer on two original songs and one cover. But the EP was not released, and the recordings were consigned to the vaults. They would not resurface until around fifteen years later, by which time Queen were superstars. The EP was eventually released in Japan, where fans can never get enough of curiosities.

By the end of the year, the band were dejected and on the verge of walking away. Indeed, Tim Staffell did so: weary of the drudgery and poverty of life on the road, he quit, giving the excuse that Smile were not the right group for him.

'I was beginning to get a rather jaundiced view of the music we were doing,' he later said. 'Then I heard James Brown and thought "God!" . . . Basically, I had changed musical tracks completely.'

Tim joined Colin Petersen, a former Bee Gees drummer, in a line-up dubbed Humpy Bong. One single, one TV appearance, and the band were has-beens. Tim settled eventually for a career in special effects, and would enjoy fleeting limelight as creator of the model trains for television's *Thomas the Tank Engine*.

Without their lead singer, their label concluded that Smile were no longer a band. Roger and Brian were released from their contracts. Although dejected, they were not ready to give in. A further recording session came their way when Smile met former Blackburn club DJ Terry Yeardon through a friend who may have been Christine Mullen, Brian May's first wife-to-be. Yeardon was now a maintenance engineer at Pye Studios in London's Marble Arch, famous for having nurtured Petula Clark and for the work, particularly for television themes (*Crossroads*, *Neighbours*) of husband-and-wife composing team Tony Hatch and Jackie Trent. Pye also produced

Hendrix's 'Hey Joe' and the Troggs' 'Wild Thing' in 1966, and had welcomed The Kinks, Richard Harris and Trini Lopez. The studios had even boasted Jimmy Page and John Paul Jones as session musicians, before they teamed with Robert Plant and John Bonham to form Led Zeppelin.

Would-be producer Yeardon arranged a late-night studio session at Pye for Smile. Acetates of the tracks 'Polar Bear' and 'Step on Me' were cut, giving Smile professional audition material which they were free to take to other labels. Not that Yeardon expected to see so much as a grin of Smile again.

Brian, Roger, Tim and a couple of musicians from a northern band called Ibex were by now living in a one-bedroom flat in a semi called 'Carmel' in Ferry Road, Barnes. Two sisters, Helen and Pat McConnell, had seen Smile play in their local pub, and had also fallen in with the gang. That cramped, damp flat would be remembered with myopic hindsight as 'bohemian'. In fact the flatmates had lived in stinking squalor, most of them sleeping on filthy mattresses on the floor. To make matters worse, they had recently acquired yet another room mate: Freddie Bulsara. What did *he* think they should do?

6

Front Man

I was saying to Brian and Roger, "Why are you wasting your time doing this? You should do more original material. You should be more demonstrative in the way you put the music across. If I was your singer, that's what I'd be doing!"

Freddie Mercury

You play better when you ham it up a bit. You are different from the guy who goes out on stage. The trick is making sure you are not still the performer when you come off stage. Bowie had it down to a fine art. He was a completely different person every week, practically. Freddie took that ball and ran with it. I'd lay odds that he never choreographed a single move. His showmanship, everything he did, was instinctive. That's an art form in itself. I have no idea what he might have done had he not been a performer.

Rick Wakeman

Still obsessed with Jimi Hendrix, and inspired by Brian's guitar-playing, Freddie had obtained a second-hand guitar which he got Tim to re-fret and modify to suit his needs. Then he went out and bought some Teach Yourself manuals, and started to learn to play. Freddie must have known that he would never make an axe hero. This was not, however, his objective. Suddenly anxious

73

to write and compose original songs, he simply needed to know enough guitar to be able to work out the chords. Those initial attempts at composition were like everyone else's: raw, clumsy, excruciatingly personal. He would soon learn to take a more abstract approach, to delve beneath the surface of his emotions and to look beyond his own experiences, experimenting with universal themes.

The Ibex boys living at Ferry Road were soon joined by the rest of the group from Liverpool, who had convened in London to seek a record deal. Guitarist Mike Bersin, bass player John 'Tupp' Taylor and drummer Mick 'Miffer' Smith were road-managed by young Ken Testi. Ibex were occasionally joined by Geoff Higgins, who would take a turn on bass so that Tupp could play the flute. Ibex played cover versions of hits by Rod Stewart, The Beatles and Yes, and usually kicked off their show with 'Jailhouse Rock', a mega-hit for Elvis Presley some twelve years earlier. Impressive though they were, Freddie couldn't help but notice that they lacked a decent vocalist. Just as he would do with Smile, he had taken to turning up at their rehearsals and gigs, and would occasionally get up and sing with Mike Bersin.

'He gave the same kind of performance he did at the peak of his career,' remembered Ken Testi. 'He was a star before he was a star, if you know what I mean. He'd strut around the stage like a proud peacock.'

The band were still based in Liverpool, where Freddie became the short-term lodger of Geoff Higgins's family. The Higginses lived above a pub called Dovetale Towers on Penny Lane, a street immortalised by The Beatles. Freddie slept on the floor in Geoff's bedroom, but he never complained, determined as he was to honour his own parents by being the perfect house guest. Geoff's mother Ruth is said to have adored him.

'My mother liked him because he spoke properly, because he was from the South', Geoff explained to Mark Hodkinson, author of *Queen: The Early Years*. 'Freddie was very, very kind to her.'

Although the band played as much as they could around the UK throughout 1969, no record deal was forthcoming. Eventually they talked about calling it a day. Miffer had family problems, and needed to earn a regular wage. Friend of the band Richard Thompson replaced him as drummer. The new line-up played a single disastrous gig. Everything that could go wrong – lights, sound, equipment – did go wrong. Even the microphone fell short of expectations. Whenever Freddie did a turn as front man, he would twirl his mic around like a majorette's baton. This one came complete with a cumbersome heavy stand. At one point he seized the mic and attempted to swing it, but the bottom part fell off. Unfazed, Freddie carried on with the top half. A trademark was born.

The strange contradictions of Freddie the performer and Fred Bulsara the person were becoming too extreme to ignore. Even on a makeshift stage, and without ever having been appointed official lead singer, Freddie projected supreme confidence, every gesture and movement flamboyant and melodramatic. Offstage, he would cower in kitchens and cupboards, the make-do dressing rooms of the pub and club circuit, where he'd struggle coyly into handmade skin-tight outfits so skimpy that, once on, he could barely breathe in them, let alone sit down. Relatively small, slight and not conventionally handsome, Freddie knew that he stood out thanks to his dark skin and swarthy looks. His features at times embarrassed him. He took to hiding his dark eyes behind a floppy fringe, and his buck teeth behind his hand whenever he felt the urge to smile. His inherent shyness would get the better of him when he attempted to chat to fans after a gig. He could never think of much to say. Worse, although he enunciated English beautifully, his speaking voice was whispery and hesitant. He also lisped a little, probably because of all those teeth. Of these, he was painfully self-conscious. Only when he felt relaxed among friends did his humour and 'real-life' personality shine through, and would he let himself laugh openly. The rest of the time, when not on stage, he tried his hardest to blend into the background. Not yet in the habit of getting blindly drunk or out of his head on drugs – he couldn't afford to, so would make do with the odd 'girlie' port and lemon in pubs – Freddie never mastered the art of projecting confidence among strangers. However happy and at ease he felt at his own parties, he was a fish out of water at anyone else's.

Freddie grew tired of hacking up and down to Liverpool, of never making ends meet, of crashing out on other people's floors in whichever town the band found themselves. He quit Ibex just after his twenty-third birthday, headed back to London for good with Mike Bersin, and applied himself to scouring the ads.

As Ken Testi would later put it, 'I think Ibex filled a gap for Freddie. He wanted to be singing in a band, and Ibex benefited enormously from having him. It was a marriage of convenience for all parties. We were all very naïve . . . to Freddie, it was like his first second-hand car, the sort of thing you buy when you can just scrape a bit of money together. Eventually, you want a better one.'

No one blamed Freddie for the band's demise. They all adored him regardless, touched as they were by his ambition, abandon and exhilarating appetite for life. Ken Testi spoke for everyone when he commented: 'It was an education knowing Freddie. He was very committed about everything. He had a certain tenacity, a single-mindedness, a desire for excellence.'

Bersin and Taylor returned to Liverpool. Thompson evaporated into the London music scene. The rest of them continued to cram into their overcrowded West London flat. Freddie without a band, and Roger and Brian without a lead singer. Why didn't they simply snap him up?

'The Smile people thought of Freddie as a little bit of a joke,' their friend Chris Dummett later admitted. 'They used to send him up, take the piss a bit . . . in an affectionate way, I suppose.'

Often the solution under our noses is the one we notice last.

As if he didn't have enough to worry about, Freddie had started to struggle with his sexual orientation. Despite the fact that he'd already had girlfriends, in particular a young woman on his course called Rosemary Pearson, some remember him showing a passionate interest in meeting gay men, but never having the confidence to act on it.

As one former art college associate puts it, 'He thought he liked women, but it took him quite a while to realise he was gay . . . I don't think he could face up to the feeling it caused inside him. He was obviously terribly interested in homosexuality, but was afraid of it as well. I suppose he was squeamish, and frightened of accepting himself as gay.'

Another friend remembers Freddie paying regular visits to a bunch of gay flat-sharers in Barnes. He concealed these visits from his own flatmates, at a loss to explain to his friends what he couldn't comprehend himself. Worrying constantly about the impression he was making, Freddie would from time to time retreat into his shell and become quite reclusive. At around the same time he began to reveal less attractive traits. He could be self-centred and egotistical, not to mention petulant and sulky, as if an overwhelming internal struggle was getting the better of him.

We all have our dark side. Freddie was fundamentally a kind, generous and considerate human being. Averse to using others to get what he wanted, he rather seemed happy to allow himself to be used, expecting nothing in return. Perhaps his worst characteristic was his vanity. He would fiddle endlessly with his hair and his clothes, and obsess about his appearance ad nauseam. His endless declarations that he was going to be 'a legend' could get on people's nerves.

His preoccupation with keeping up appearances didn't help:

while living hand to mouth, as most of his cohorts did, Freddie refused to use public transport, preferring to spend the last coins in his pocket on taxis home when he should have been feeding himself. Friends began to despair of him. What would become of Freddie, they wondered, should he fail to make it in the music business? Despite his graphic design qualification, they knew he'd never hold down a nine-to-five job.

Lacking stability and direction in every aspect of his life, no wonder he felt insecure. Freddie knew that he was not like most people. He also knew that he had to pay the bills. While he still had a bedroom of his own at his parents' Feltham house, to which he could return any time he wanted, he was reluctant to admit defeat and slink home. He knew that his family would struggle to understand the life he was leading now, and never took friends home to meet his parents or sister.

'As a parent, you worry – but you have to let your child get on with their life,' his mother Jer said.

Freddie continued to go home for dinner once a week or so, and his mother would always cook his favourite meal, Dhansak: a delicious if laborious Indian dish popular in the Parsee community, which marries aspects of both Persian and Gujarati cuisine. The recipe comprises vegetables and lentils, garlic, ginger and spices, with meat – usually mutton – and pumpkin or gourd. It seems likely, given his poverty-stricken status at the time, that this was the only square meal Freddie ate all week.

The first cold weeks of 1970 saw him trudging around the London agencies with his art portfolio. Austin Knight, in Chancery Lane, Holborn, agreed to represent him, and to pitch for design work on his behalf. But Freddie ran out of patience, unable to bear all the sitting around waiting for the phone to ring. He went freelance, and started placing ads. But he spent so much time hanging out with Smile at rehearsals and gigs that his focus was distracted, his heart not in finding himself regular work. There was only one thing for it: he would have to get his own band together. Pulling in Ibex's sometime drummer Richard Thompson, Mike Bersin and Tupp Taylor, Freddie reinvented Ibex as Wreckage. Their first live gig was at Ealing College of Art, attended by a bemused Brian May, Roger Taylor, his flat-mates, and a loudly encouraging Kensington contingent. Brian and Roger, who hadn't altogether twigged that camp, opinion-ated Freddie really did 'have something' as a front man, were completely taken aback. If the band was musically underwhelm-ing, at least Freddie was an eyeball magnet. The gig was a success, and Wreckage were booked to play Imperial College, with a string of rugby club dates to follow.

Freddie remained frustrated. He knew he had what it took, but sensed that something was wrong. Whether he had been expecting an instant three-album deal with a major record label, or whether he simply felt out of tune with Wreckage's general musical style and ambition, he couldn't say. He soon quit the band, resolved to wait for Brian's and Roger's pennies to drop, and auditioned for a band called Sour Milk Sea.

'Sour Milk Sea' was a song written by George Harrison during sessions for The Beatles' so-called 'White Album'. Recorded by Apple artist Jackie Lomax and released as a single in 1968, it was one of the few non-Beatles songs to feature at least three of them. With George Harrison and Eric Clapton on guitar, Paul McCartney on bass, Ringo Starr playing drums and Nicky Hopkins on piano, it so impressed Chris Dummet (who later changed his surname to Chesney) and Jeremy Gallop, a pair of public school friends from St Edward's, Oxford, that they changed the name of their common-room band Tomato City to that of the song. Sour Milk Sea's line-up also featured drummer Robert Tyrrell, who had played at Charterhouse School with Mike Rutherford and Anthony Phillips in pre-Genesis group The Anon. Sour Milk Sea's debut took place at Guildford City Hall, where they opened for emerging acts Deep Purple, Taste, Blodwyn Pig and Junior's Eyes – whose everlasting claim to fame would be for having acted as David Bowie's backing band during 1969. Junior's Eyes founder member and guitarist Mick Wayne would join Rick Wakeman as a guest musician on Bowie's breakthrough, 'Space Oddity.' Sour Milk Sea turned professional in June 1969, well aware that they lacked *je ne sais quoi*. It arrived in the form of Freddie Bulsara, who rocked up to a Dorking church crypt to audition as lead singer and front man. With his flowing black hair and sporting dandy velvet clobber, he oozed nonchalance and style. He was several years older than the Sour Milk Sea boys, and it showed. He introduced himself as 'Fred Bull'.

'He had an immense amount of charisma, which was why we chose him,' remembered Jeremy 'Rubber' Gallop, who subsequently became a guitar teacher, and died of pancreatic cancer in January 2006, 'although we were actually spoiled for choice that day. Normally at auditions you'd get four or five guys who were rubbish, but we had two other strong contenders. One was a black guy with the voice of God, but not the looks of Fred, and the other was folk singer Bridget St John, later known as "the female John Martyn".'

Freddie joined the band, and was in business. Sour Milk Sea soon landed a high-profile gig in the ballroom of Oxford's Randolph Hotel, attended by debutante-types in posh frocks.

'Our sound wasn't great,' admitted Gallop.

'Freddie definitely managed to get what people were there in the palm of his hand, just by sheer aggression and his good looks. He was very posey and camp and quite vain. I remember him coming into my house once and looking in the mirror, poking his long hair about. He said, "I look good today, don't you think, Rubber?" I was only eighteen at the time, and I didn't think it was very funny.'

The only other significant Sour Milk Sea gig featuring Freddie as front man was a benefit for homeless charity Shelter, staged at Highfield Parish Hall, Headington, Oxford, in March 1970. The band gave an interview in the *Oxford Mail*, which also published the lyrics to Freddie's song, 'Lover', with the immortal opening line

'You never had it so good/the yoghurt-pushers are here'. Following this promising start, however, old school friends Chesney and Gallop fell out.

'Freddie very quickly wanted to change us,' explained Gallop.

'On stage, he became a different personality. He was as electric as he was later in his life. Otherwise he was quite calm. I'll always remember him being strangely quiet and well-mannered. My mum liked him. Rather shamefully, I ended the band.'

Jeremy Gallop was Jonathan Morrish's half-uncle. Former CBS Records and Sony executive Jonathan, who became Michael Jackson's publicist and confidant for twenty-eight years, remembers attending that Oxford gig as a teenager.

'At that stage, Freddie, to me, was Martin Peters,' Jonathan tells me, referring to the 1966 England World Cup soccer legend described by manager Sir Alf Ramsey as being 'ten years ahead of his time'. Peters was blessed with such versatility that he was deployable in every position at West Ham United, including goalkeeper.

'Freddie was this flamboyant showman at a time when bands went on stage dressed in whatever they'd been wearing all day,' says Jonathan.

'That Freddie understood showmanship was plain for all to see, even then. It's hard now for people who weren't there to understand what developing rock music was like. You were in it to be a musician. You were "musician-ly". You lived the life. What Freddie knew, intuitively, was the golden rule of showbiz: you make a show. It was what Epstein did with The Beatles. "*Mach Schau!*", the German promoters used to yell at the boys in Hamburg's Star Club. In other words, it was not just about singing. It was also about the lapel-free jackets, the hairstyles, the bashful grins. The Beatles then spent the next eight years rebelling against all that, as if trying to prove that music was the only thing that mattered. Freddie, even as an embryonic performer, knew otherwise.'

Jonathan knew Michael Jackson intimately until the end of his life. The reasons behind the eventual bond between Freddie and Michael, he says, were obvious to those who knew them both.

'Neither one was simply a musician or a singer. What Freddie did with "Bohemian Rhapsody", Michael recreated with "Thriller". The point being that the great artists just get it. They know instinctively how to be multimedia. Freddie's genius was understanding, not just the song he had written the words and melody to, and how it all sounded, but how you deliver it in a contemporary fashion which the audience will comprehend and absorb. How you record it, how you present it on stage, how you style the video, how you dress. You can just picture him on the shoot: "Guys! Make-up, frocks, action!" Who the fuck wore make-up? Men didn't. In 1970, if you wore moisturiser you were dismissed as "queer" – the word of the day. Yet all these years later, the men's cosmetics industry is worth billions. As I said, he was way ahead of his time. Even in 1970, Freddie was saying "NO, guys, *this* is what showbiz is about!"'

For as long as Queen have existed, an error has prevailed regarding alternative names that the band considered calling themselves.

'Brian and Roger had both read the same trilogy of books by C.S. Lewis during their childhood – *Out of the Silent Planet* – from which the phrase the Grand Dance had come', explained Jacky Gunn and Jim Jenkins in Queen's 'official biography' *As It Began* (1992). This information has been repeated in so many Queen and Freddie Mercury books that it has become 'fact' – even appearing as such on Queen's official website, where Queen expert Rhys Thomas, in 'A Review' (7 March 2011) discusses The Grand Dance, The Rich Kids (later picked up by Sex Pistol Glen Matlock as the name of his new group), and Build Your Own Boat as other names that Queen had discussed. In an interview with *Q* magazine, March 2011, Brian said, 'We had a list of suggested names, and Queen had come from Freddie. One of the others was the Grand Dance, which I don't think would have been very good . . .'

In fact, the reference is erroneous. *Out of the Silent Planet* is the first novel of the Lewis sci-fi trilogy referred to as 'the Space

Trilogy', 'the Cosmic Trilogy' or 'the Ransom Trilogy'. The other two volumes in the collection, which was itself inspired by David Lindsay's *A Voyage to Arcturus* (1920), are *Perelandra* and *That Hideous Strength*. In the *second* novel, *Perelandra*, Lewis introduces a new Garden of Eden on the planet Venus, an alternative Adam and Eve, and a new serpent figure to tempt them. The author explores what might have come to pass had Eve resisted temptation and avoided the Fall of Man. It is in *Perelandra* that we find our Queen reference: a description of the mystical experience of seeing directly into 'the GREAT Dance' – not 'Grand' – of the multi-dimensional space-time-consciousness continuum that is the time cosmos: 'So with the Great Dance. Set your eyes on one movement and it will lead you through all patterns and it will seem to you the master movement. But the seeming will be there . . . there seems no plan because it is all plan: there seems no centre because it is all centre. Blessed be He!'

One-word titles work better, Freddie argued. They are infinitely more memorable. They have more punch. Freddie's own outrageous suggestion was 'Queen'. The others resisted with snorts and scorn, primarily because of the word's homosexual connotations. 'Gay' was a word rarely heard at that time. It probably emerged eventually in defiance of 'queer', its disparaging predecessor. Although Freddie had not 'come out' – nor would he ever officially do so – he was used to being called 'an old queen'. He rather liked it. He swooned at its androgyny and adored its regal whiff. Even better, the name would give him the perfect excuse to camp it to the hilt on stage. Brian and Roger soon came round, having seen the funny side. The point being that no male could be more macho, more straight nor more besotted by women than those two. In their terms, to be called 'Queen' was ironic, and it worked.

Having agreed the band's identity, Freddie set about renaming himself. Bulsara was dropped in favour of Mercury, the ancient Roman messenger of the gods. Like Hermes, his Greek counterpart,

Mercury was represented with winged sandals and a staff entwined with snakes. Also the name of the common liquid metal long ago familiar in Chinese and Hindu culture and found in ancient Egyptian tombs, 'Mercury' identifies the planet closest to the Sun as well, which has no moons.

Many theories have arisen over the years as to why Freddie chose that surname. According to Queen fan and author Jim Jenkins, 'Freddie told me himself in 1975, that it was after the messenger of the gods. I remember it as if he's just said it to me. People have said since that it was after Mike Mercury in TV's *Fireball XL5*, but I can tell you for sure that it was nothing to do with him.'

According to Brian May's memory: 'Freddie had written this song called "My Fairy King", and there's a line in it that says, "Oh Mother Mercury what have you done to me?" [The lyric actually reads: Mother mercury mercury/look what they've done to me/I cannot run, I cannot hide.]

'And it was after that that he said, "I am going to become Mercury as the mother in this song is my mother." And we were like, "Are you mad?"

'Changing his name was part of him assuming this different skin,' adds May. 'The young Bulsara was still there, but for the public he was going to be this god.'

Although it has been widely assumed that Freddie changed his name by deed poll in or around 1970, nothing exists to prove this. While they were able to supply Elton John's, there is no official entry for Freddie at the Public Records Office, now the National Archives, in Kew, West London. As an official there told me, 'Only ten per cent of name changes are registered through the Supreme Court and therefore appear on our records. These days, in fact, it's about five per cent. It is not a legal requirement: you can call yourself whatever you like. Chances are that Mr Mercury changed his name through his solicitor. When the documentation is drawn up, he'd keep half and the solicitor would keep half.'

Freddie later revealed his fascination with mythology and astrology, by designing Queen's now legendary logo. Its principal figure is a spread-winged phoenix, the symbol of immortality remembered fondly by Freddie from the crest of his alma mater, St Peter's in Panchgani. The logo also incorporated the zodiac signs of each band member: two lions, for the Leos, Taylor and Deacon, a crab for Cancerian May, and a couple of fairies for Virgoan Mercury, complete with a stylised 'Q' and elaborate crown.

Other commitments notwithstanding, the band were ready to play their debut gig as Queen: a Red Cross benefit at City Hall, Truro in Cornwall, Britain's most southwesterly point. The show, which took place on 27 June 1970, was co-arranged by Roger's mother Win Hitchens, and the line-up featured Mike Grose on bass (he lasted only three shows). Their opening number was 'Stone Cold Crazy', based on an energetic Wreckage number. But it fell a bit flat in that half-empty venue. Observers remembered that the band were not yet 'tight' enough, nor Freddie coordinated enough.

'Freddie was not like how he became,' commented Roger's mum Win. 'He had not got his movements off properly.'

But: 'Freddie had real ambitions for the band,' remembers his sister Kashmira. 'He had this complete determination to succeed.'

A show at Imperial College on 18 July followed, their set made up almost exclusively of cover versions – everything from James Brown and Little Richard to Buddy Holly and Shirley Bassey – and just two original compositions: 'Stone Cold Crazy', which featured the whole group as co-writers, and 'Liar'.

'We did more heavy rock 'n' roll with the Queen delivery to give people something they could get hold of – get on, sock it to 'em, get off,' commented Brian.

Mike Grose was replaced by bass player Barry Mitchell, who performed with Queen at eleven shows from summer until Christmas, in London colleges, Liverpool's famous Cavern Club and a couple of church halls. Queen still hadn't found the one they were looking for.

Now that Roger had enrolled at North London Polytechnic to study Biology, he would get a grant to supplement his meagre income. This left Freddie the only Queen member not engaged in tertiary education. Not that it bothered any of them. Queen threw themselves at the live circuit with renewed vigour. That September, Brian arranged a showcase at Imperial College and invited a number of top London booking agents. Although several turned up, none was impressed enough to offer Queen a tour. Hungry for fame and success, they took this badly.

Tragedy struck in Freddie's life (and many shared the sadness) on 18 September 1970, when his idol Jimi Hendrix died. The definitive rock musician who had famously performed the Star-Spangled Banner at the Woodstock Festival the previous year, who had just opened his own state-of-the-art recording studio, Electric Lady, in Greenwich Village, New York, and who had only the previous month played for his biggest-ever audience – 600,000 people at the Isle of Wight Festival – was found dead in a pool of red wine vomit at girlfriend Monika Dannemann's Samarkland Hotel apartment in Notting Hill. While insiders would claim for years that Hendrix was murdered, the most likely cause of his death was an overdose of the sedative Vesparax, ingested with excess alcohol. Dannemann later committed suicide.

Freddie was inconsolable. Too devastated to work, he and Roger closed their stall as a mark of respect. Later that day, while rehearsing at Imperial College, virtually on the doorstep of the scene of Hendrix's death, Brian, Roger and Freddie played their own personal tribute in a jam session of 'Voodoo Chile', 'Purple Haze', 'Foxy Lady' and other now immortal Hendrix hits.

The perfect bass player continued to elude the trio. Not until February 1971 did they run into John Deacon by chance at a London disco. Leicester-born Deacon, who had been involved with bands since the age of fourteen, was an Electronics undergraduate at Chelsea College. A man of few words, he made up for it with an acute sense of rhythm and a restless brain. He was also a dab hand with amplifiers and other music equipment, and was looking for a band to join.

More than that, says Roger: 'We thought he was great. We were all so used to each other, and were so over the top, we thought that because he was quiet he would fit in with us without too much upheaval. He was a great bass player too – and the fact that he was a wizard with electronics was definitely a deciding factor.'

From February 1971 until Queen's final gig on 9 August 1986, the band line-up remained exactly the same.

Six months of intense rehearsal ensued as Brian, John and Freddie set about teaching John their repertoire. At the time, John was still a student, while Brian was working on his thesis. They still regarded Queen as an extracurricular hobby. Only Roger and Freddie could devote their time totally to Queen, and had set their hearts on a full-blown rock 'n' roll career. On 11 July 1971, Queen began an eleven-date tour of Cornwall, culminating in the outdoor Tregye Festival of Contemporary Music on 21 August. Further gigs followed throughout the Michaelmas term, including another at Imperial College on 6 October, an appearance at Epsom Swimming Baths on 9 December, and a New Year's Eve show at Twickenham's London Rugby Club.

Roger, meanwhile, had lost interest in the market stall. The novelty had worn off, but worse, it had started to feel 'undignified'. He quit the 'Kasbah', leaving Freddie to team up with fellow stall-holder Alan Mair. Freddie remained as enthusiastic as ever about the Kensington scene. Not just because he was a deep-dyed mover and shaker. He had fallen in love.

7

Mary

All my lovers asked me why they couldn't replace Mary, but it's simply impossible. To me, she was my common-law wife. To me, it was a marriage. We believe in each other, and that's enough for me. I couldn't fall in love with a man the same way as I did with Mary.

Freddie Mercury

The self-realisation process would have been so important to him ... Freddie came from a culture in which you are not supposed to love men. So you try and conform, even though you are tortured within. It's not uncommon. Elton did it twice. On the route to self-discovery for a gay man from a repressed background, there is often an interlude of having a girlfriend. This is sometimes about need, and sometimes a case of one trying to do what is expected of one.

Paul Gambaccini

With her apricot hair, green eyes and Bambi lashes, Mary Austin was the embodiment of a Hulanicki Biba poster. When the fashion designer founded the Kensington emporium from which a flourishing fashion movement arose, Barbara Hulanicki might have chosen Mary as her muse. Petite and fine-boned, what Mary lacked in terms of stature and confidence she more than compensated for with almost textbook Seventies style.

★   ★   ★

Mick Rock, a London-born Cambridge Modern Languages graduate and alumnus of the London Film School, got into professional photography when the late Syd Barrett (former lead singer of Pink Floyd) asked Rock to shoot him for the cover of his solo album *The Madcap Laughs*. Rock – his real name – tumbled into Seventies drug culture and befriended David Bowie, becoming his official photographer. He is credited not only with documenting the music scene – 'The Man Who Shot the Seventies' – but with having helped to create it. He took some of the first publicity pictures for Freddie and Queen, going on to produce iconic album artwork for *Queen II* and *Sheer Heart Attack*. Rock has lived in New York since 1977, after becoming immersed in the underground scene created by The Ramones, Talking Heads and David Bowie.

'Freddie was already living with Mary when I met him, so I got to know and love them both equally,' Rock tells me. 'I was always popping round to their little flat to hang out with them at teatime. Freddie was big on tea. At the height of the Glam Rock scene, Mary was a really cute-looking lady who could have had anyone, done anything. But she never saw herself as anything special. She never wanted to put herself forward in any way. She was self-effacing, sweet and charming. You just wanted to give her a cuddle.'

Pale, coy, and peering through shiny tresses, she had the demeanour of an earlier namesake, Mary Hopkin – the fresh-faced prodigy of Paul McCartney who'd had a hit with 'Those Were the Days'. The Marys shared a chaste, untouchable, ethereal quality, which complemented the bohemian fashions of the day. What would later be dubbed 'the Stevie Nicks look' after the Fleetwood Mac singer was already common on Kensington High Street: midi dresses, maxi coats, suede platform boots, chiffon scarves, velvet chain chokers, purple lips and smoky eyes.

'She'd had a tough background,' remembers trusted journalist David Wigg. 'Her parents, who were deaf and dumb, and who communicated through sign language and lip-reading, were poor. Her father worked as a hand-trimmer for wallpaper specialists, and her mother was a domestic for a small company. But that wouldn't have bothered Freddie. He wasn't interested in toffs. He somehow preferred people a little below his own level. An insecurity thing, I always thought. He did like people in his life who were artistic, or who had come from nothing. Artistic and amusing were the key: he loved to laugh. Mary was shy, but she could make him giggle.'

A nineteen-year-old trainee secretary when she landed her job at Biba, she has been described variously as having been a 'PR', 'secretary', 'sales girl', 'floor manager' and 'manageress'. Whatever her role, or roles, at the famous fashion emporium, retail seems an odd career choice for a shy young woman who found conversation challenging, having grown up in a largely silent home. The incense-filled, fern-adorned store was a noisy, busy Aladdin's Cave, stuffed with clothes, shoes, make-up, jewellery, bags and beautiful sales girls. The many music and movie stars attracted to the joint mingled freely with the merely fashion-conscious, plenty of whom were 'just looking' for a Jagger or a McCartney.

Despite her shy demeanour, Mary found herself caught up in London's rock scene. Brian May was the first to notice her at an Imperial College gig one night, in 1970, and the pair got chatting.

In many ways, she was precisely his kind of girl. Tall, dark, dishy Brian wasted no time in asking Mary out. They got on, but their encounters lacked spark. Brian soon saw that things were not going to develop beyond friendship. Freddie, on the other hand, saw otherwise. Having pestered Brian for an introduction, Freddie landed the girl of some of his dreams.

The attraction between them was immediate, mutual, and would last a lifetime. Puzzling, then, that Mary spent the next six months trying to avoid him, to the point of dating other men – though no one serious. Only years later did she explain that it was because she believed Freddie was interested in her friend, not in her. One night, after one of the band's gigs, she left him at the bar with her girl-friend, excused herself to pop to the Ladies, and vanished into the night. Freddie was dumbstruck, but would not be deterred. When he asked her on a date for his twenty-fourth birthday, 5 September 1970, Mary pretended that she was busy that night.

'I was trying to be cool,' she told David Wigg. 'Not because there was any real reason I couldn't go. But Freddie wasn't put off. We went out the next day instead. He wanted to go and see Mott the Hoople at the Marquee Club in Soho. Freddie didn't have much money then, and so we just did normal things like any other young people. There were no fancy dinners – they came later when he hit the big time.'

The pair became inseparable and almost immediately began a sexual relationship. Their relationship would take precedence over every affair, with man or woman, in which Freddie would later indulge.

In many ways, Freddie and Mary had much in common. Each had felt estranged from their parents, and had responded to the urge to assert independence. Each had a 'tip of the iceberg' personality, and tended to reveal little of their true selves. Each could give the impression of being shallow, flippant and frivolous, with materialistic tendencies and a live-for-the-moment style, particularly in their younger day. But most of this boiled down to image, and to deliberate concealment of innate shyness. Both were highly sensitive, naturally reserved, and deeper than they appeared. That they recognised themselves in each other became the foundation of a fascinating and everlasting bond. As they matured, the more contrasting and contradictory aspects of their personalities began to weld them. Mary might look like a gentle soul who couldn't hurt a fly – but her fragile image concealed an inner strength and serenity that Freddie admired deeply, perhaps because he feared that the 'Great Pretender' in him did not really have those qualities himself. Although Mary knew that Freddie had family living in Feltham, it would be some time before he took his girlfriend home to meet them. It is not difficult to see why: Mary was everything the Bulsaras could have wished for in a daughter-in-law. Chances are that they would all too soon have been putting pressure on their son to marry her, and give them the grandchildren they craved. Freddie was not yet ready for anything like marriage. Little did his family know at that stage that he never would be.

Over the years, Mary became Freddie's rock. He would rely on her to be strong for him. Whenever Freddie felt his sex/drugs/rock 'n' roll lifestyle spiralling out of control, and was unable to cope with the pressures of recording and touring, it was to Mary that he turned. Solid and reliable, ever-forgiving, all-accepting, she was the mother figure to whom he would always cling.

'Mary Austin *was* Freddie's mum, in a way,' reasons music publicist Bernard Doherty.

'She was there for him every moment of every day, putting her own life on hold to do so. Where he went, she went. She hardly ever left his side. No wonder he was devoted to her. She evidently filled that great hole that was left by what his parents should have been to him when he was small. Instead, they stuck him on a ship and sent him to school thousands of miles away, a voyage which back then took about sixty days. He was eight years old. Can you imagine? In his deepest psyche, he would never have resolved that. Then there was Mary. "Mother Mary comes to me", sang McCartney on "Let It Be" in 1970, didn't he?: coincidentally, the year Mary and Freddie met.

'It could have been their theme tune, with its matriarchal Blessed Virgin Mary connotation. Mary was the Mary in that song. She was pure. Not even Freddie was sleeping with her in the end . . .'

Because by this time Freddie had chosen to be gay, rendering Mary a born-again virgin?

'The myth was preserved,' nods Bernard. 'In his mind she was perfect, and all for him. For Freddie's benefit only did Mary exist.'

'Mary was undoubtedly a mother figure,' agrees consultant psychiatrist Dr Cosmo Hallstrom.

'More to the point, the *idealised* mother figure: representative of precisely what he considered a woman should be. Freddie was highly sexual, and not too bothered about who he had sex with. He could have loving sex with her, but also rush off out there and have a lot of clandestine and raw encounters elsewhere. Those relationships were notoriously fragile and ephemeral. It was to her that he always returned. And she of course was always waiting for him' – keeping herself only unto her man.

'She looked after him, mothered him, dealt with the good side of Freddie. She was his base and his strength. What he had with her enabled him to go off and have his flirtations. She thus became the long-suffering wife as well as the matriarch, putting up with all kinds of nonsense. But she served a fundamental purpose: the misery his guilt caused him, at the way he behaved when not with her, was the key to his creativity. A happy person doesn't feel the need to do anything, to create anything. Happy people are content with their lot, with the way things are. Freddie was perennially anguished. The way he felt about Mary was the cause of that, but was also an inspiration for his work.'

Some described Mary's feelings for Freddie as 'Mother Love'. No surprise that this would eventually become the title of a plaintive track sung by Freddie and Brian on Queen's *Made in Heaven* album, released four years after Mercury's death in 1991.

'I'm a man of extremes', was how Freddie once described himself. 'I have a soft side and a hard side, with not a lot in between. If the right person finds me I can be very vulnerable, a real baby, which is invariably when I get trodden on. But sometimes I'm hard, and when I'm strong, no one can get to me.'

Mary also knew that Freddie had suffered, since childhood, something to which he rarely admitted: a persecution complex. That is, he worried that people were making fun of him behind his back, and that he was indeed ridiculous. It was to remain one of his fiercest inner demons until his death.

The fear may not have been so irrational, either. According to Peter 'Ratty' Hince, a long-serving Queen roadie who works today as a photographer: 'To be honest, everyone thought that Freddie was a bit of a wally. Even though it was glam, Freddie was over the top even for that. All that flowing costume stuff. I didn't think he was particularly the strongest then. They were all very much a unit.'

Perhaps frustration at this complex was what caused him to boil with rage at times. Freddie would flare in inexplicable bouts of bad temper, which could cause him to be unkind and even cruel, uttering withering put-downs and gratuitously spiteful comments. While it has been suggested that Mary developed a defensive streak to protect first Freddie and then herself from the media and hangers-on, and that she could be untrusting and suspicious, could she really have been protecting them both from Freddie himself?

As much as their union was a meeting of heart, mind and soul, the body in the equation could not be ignored. Freddie's sexual relationship with Mary lasted for six years. That is a relative life-time in one's early twenties, and demonstrates true commitment. They soon began living together, in a cramped, shabby £10-a-week bedsit in Victoria Road, just off Kensington High Street – the London neighbourhood to which Freddie would always return. Today, the street is officially the most expensive for property in England and Wales, the average residence having an estimated sales value of £6.4 million.

Two years later, the couple would move to a larger, self-contained but ruinously damp apartment in Holland Road, costing £9 a week more.

'We grew up together. I liked him and it went from there,' Mary would recall. 'It took about three years for me to really fall in love. I've never felt that way before or since, with anyone ... I loved Freddie very much, and very deeply.

'I felt very safe with him,' she later told David Wigg.

'The more I got to know him, the more I loved him for himself. He had quality as a person, which I think is rare in life these days . . . We knew we could trust each other . . . and that we would never hurt each other on purpose.

'One Christmas he bought me a ring, and put it in the most enormous box. I opened the box, and inside was another box, and so it went on until I got to this very tiny box. When I opened it, there was this beautiful Egyptian scarab ring. It's supposed to bring good luck. He was very sweet and shy about giving it to me.'

'Whatever else was going on,' says Mick Rock, 'Freddie was living this sweet little domestic life with Mary and it was all very cosy and charming. Freddie was always in his dressing gown and slippers, whenever I went round there. We'd sit and talk for hours.'

Mary has mostly made a point of declining to discuss even mundane aspects of their life together. In occasional interviews, however, private details have emerged. For example, during their years living together, whenever Freddie felt the rush of songwriting inspiration in the middle of the night, he would pull his piano next to the bed and carry on composing. The average woman would not have put up with that for very long.

If she had her misgivings about Freddie's sexuality, Mary tried to dismiss them at first.

'I once said to her "surely you must have questioned that Freddie might be gay",' said David Wigg. "But everywhere we went, girls were going crazy for him," she said. "When he came off stage, they were all over him." After one particular concert when he was mobbed by women, she actually started walking away, thinking, "Freddie doesn't need me any more." He spotted her leaving, and ran after her. "Where are you going?" "You don't need me," Mary said to him, "you have all this." "I do need you," Freddie told her. "I want you to be part of it."'

'Later he started coming home quite late in the evenings, and I started thinking "this is it",' she told David.

'Mary told me that at first she thought he was seeing another woman. She said, "I thought he doesn't want me any more. He'd always have an excuse: 'we've been recording, darling', or 'we got carried away, sorry I'm so late'." Nothing else seemed to be wrong between them, she said, except that he kept coming home so late at night. Well eventually he came in one evening and said, "Mary, there's something I have to tell you." She was still convinced there was another woman, and braced herself. But to her great relief, he simply said, "I think I'm bisexual."

'"No Freddie, I don't think you're bisexual," she said to him. "I think you're gay."

'Freddie was mortified in a way, she told me. But he did accept it from her, almost immediately. He told her "I want you always to be part of my life." When eventually he moved into Garden Lodge in Kensington, he bought her a little flat round the corner, where she could see his huge house from the bathroom window.'

She then became, in a way, the matriarch of Freddie's 'family', a largely gay entourage of employees who doubled as friends.

'Freddie had the open and honest relationship with Mary which, because of the family religion, culture and so on, he could never have enjoyed with his birth mother,' affirms Wigg.

Mick Rock remembers Freddie being 'beside himself' over his issues with sexuality.

'This was before he finally came out of the closet. He definitely was gay, but not exclusively gay, and that screwed him. He was torn. It was almost as if he had to know whether he was one thing or the other for sure, but he was caught in this middle ground, in a kind of no man's land. He loved women. He enjoyed their company immensely. Later in life it may have been predominantly men for sex . . . he may have been more promiscuous with men, but he loved to get with the girls. Mary, of course, was the love of his life . . . the closest emotional bond he had ever known. The greatest irony of Freddie's life is that, though he was essentially gay, his most mean-ingful relationship was with a woman. Perhaps that had more to do with the woman in question than sexual preference. There was a real true love there between him and Mary. The sexual thing wasn't nearly so important as their emotional and spiritual bond.'

Freddie was soon taking male lovers, though he never took them home to the bedsit he shared with Mary. He behaved discreetly at first, maintaining the façade of his heterosexual domestic relationship. Hoping that it was just a 'phase', Mary indulged him, and turned a blind eye. As time went on, however, it became obvious that he preferred his own gender. In the end he could conceal the truth no longer, and confessed.

'I could see that he felt uncomfortable about something,' Mary told David Wigg. 'So it was a relief to hear it. I liked the fact that he was honest with me. I don't think he thought I'd be supportive, but I couldn't deny Freddie the right to be at one with himself.'

It says much about the woman that she parked her personal grief over broken dreams and allowed their relationship to metamorphose into a deep, platonic friendship. From then on, she was Freddie's Girl Friday, and spent at least part of every day with him. She described herself as his 'general dogsbody'. Freddie called her 'Old Faithful'.

Mary was now free to seek another partner. It would be a long time before she did so.

She couldn't let go, even allegedly suggesting to Freddie that they have a child together – to which he reportedly retorted that he would 'rather have a cat'. Mary would later give birth to two sons: Richard, to whom Freddie was godfather, and Jamie, born just after Freddie died. But many of her relationships with men seemed doomed to failure: perhaps because Freddie cast long shadows and was forever under her skin. Even the boys' father, interior designer Piers Cameron, came and went.

'He had always felt overshadowed by Freddie,' Mary explained.

As for Freddie, there would be other affairs with women, despite the endless stream of boyfriends. Because she had chosen to remain an integral part of Freddie's life, Mary could only accept this. Most people who knew them both believe that no other woman ever replaced Mary in Freddie's affections. The fact that he left her his home and most of his fortune probably proves this.

'Mary's nothing short of a saint,' explains Mick Rock. 'She's fabulous. Terrific. Very loyal. Unpretentious. Unintrusive. A good person. One of the best people I have known in my life. After Queen had made it and I'd moved to Manhattan, I'd often see Freddie in New York. We'd hang out and talk. On one occasion years later when I was in London, I had tea with Mary, and she said a very strange thing. I didn't understand it at the time, but I think I do now. She said: "First my father, then Freddie, now my sons. It would seem that I was put on this earth to nurture men." She seemed to be saying that's her lot in life. A strange life, when you think about it. But it makes sense.'

Rock was relieved that Freddie treated her decently.

'He was unique, a one-off, and anybody would have had trouble dealing with that. Also, he was more into his work than anything else. To compound the problem, he'd have these inexplicable crazy moments. He must have been a nightmare to work with and to live with. He knew that. He wasn't stupid. What Mary had to put up with was more than most people could take, but she never stopped loving him. Not to this day. You could say that she gave her life for him, and what she's got in return is nothing to what she gave, believe me.'

As Mary would later explain, 'He widened the tapestry of my life so much by introducing me to the worlds of ballet, opera, art. I've learned so much from him, and he's given me personally so much. There was no way I'd want to desert him, ever.'

None of which made him any easier to be with. Not only did he make a drama of every crisis, but things had to be exact. Even vases of flowers around the home had to be arranged just so, or he would throw them outside in disgust.

'This was all to do with his style,' Mary said. 'He wanted things done his way, and he could be very difficult. We quarrelled a lot. But he liked a good row.'

Years later, long after his death, Mary would come to terms with the fortune Freddie left her, and found happiness again in his magnificent Georgian home. This was with Nick, the London businessman whom she married quietly on Long Island in 1998, with only her sons as witnesses.

'I think Nick was very brave to take me on really,' she said to David Wigg. 'I come with a lot of baggage . . . As life unfolds . . . I can appreciate what I had, and what I now have, and move on with my life.'

Adds her friend Mick Rock, 'Some people criticised her for the way she hung in there, and they all questioned her motives. But I can tell you she was not there for the fucking money. I'd stake my life on that.'

People could say what they liked. Those who counted knew the 'his' and 'hers' of the scenario (there being at least three sides to every story). For twenty-one years, Mary kept her own counsel. As far as Freddie was concerned, her loyalty spoke for itself. Why did she never face the truth, leave town and start a new life? Could her deepest fear have been that without him she was nothing?

'That she hung on in a situation from which most women would have bowed out to find a heterosexual milieu . . . is a feat both of perseverance and, it has to be said, of acting,' commented Freddie's close friend and confidant David Evans.

'I honestly believe that she never was at ease in the gay company with which Freddie surrounded himself,' he revealed in his 1995 memoir *More of the Real Life*.

'I could sense her unease, and – as far as I could – compensated for it, consciously toning down some of my own behaviour to accommodate her essentially heterosexual femininity. Mary was never "one of the boys" as so many of the women were in Freddie's life. She appeared not to have that glorious, ebullient self-confidence of a Barbara Valentin . . . or Anita Dobson or Diana Moseley . . . all wonderfully talented and strong women who were not threatened by Freddie's outrageousness one bit. In fact, they were validated by it.

'Mary was always remote, removed in spirit and in flesh from The Real Life [as Freddie's household set-up was referred to by insiders].'

While Freddie and his friends were genuinely delighted when she took up with Piers Cameron and became pregnant by him with the first of their two sons, none was surprised that the affair did not last. 'That she remained part of The Real Life is undeniable,' said Evans. He had hoped Mary would remove herself 'from what I always considered the unhealthy clinging-on to a situation that could only ever compound the initial grief and heartbreak, from which it is obvious that she had never recovered.'

8

Trident

It's very difficult to put your trust in others, especially with the kind of people that we are. We're very highly strung, very meticulous and fussy. What we went through with Trident took a lot out of us, so we became very careful and selective with the kind of people that worked with us after that, and became part of the Queen unit.

Freddie Mercury

Queen's sessions have always benefited from technology. In the very beginning, on that very first record, they were gifted downtime at Trident Studios. So they were in the unique position of having A-list studios right at the start of their career. They were able to use the very latest equipment available, which was sixteen-track at the time. A band often develops their sound in the studio, where they can take advantage of the multitrack guitar techniques that are prevalent in a lot of rock music. Having that studio time meant that Brian May could take it to the next level. That was really important for them.

Steve Levine, legendary record producer and owner, Hubris Records

1971 was almost over and still Queen were going nowhere fast, despite performing as many gigs as Brian's and John's academic timetables would allow, and despite the assiduous efforts of all concerned to get them signed. As Brian remarked, 'If we were going to drop the careers we'd trained hard for, we wanted to make a really good job of music. We all had quite a bit to lose, really, and it didn't come easy. To be honest, I don't think any of us realised it would take a full three years to get anywhere. It was certainly no fairytale.'

Said Freddie, 'At one point, two or three years after we began, we nearly disbanded. We felt it wasn't working, there were too many sharks in the business, and it was all getting too much for us. But something inside kept us going, and we learned from our experiences, good and bad.'

On another occasion he would contradict his earlier assessment with the declaration: 'There was never a doubt, darling, never. I just knew we would make it. I told everyone who asked just that.'

Roger also remembered those days with optimism.

'For the first two years nothing really happened,' he agreed. 'We were all studying, but progress in the band was nil. We had great ideas, though, and somehow I think we all felt we'd get through.'

Queen had work to do. Confident in their talent as musicians, and convinced they blended well as a group, they continued to badger every record label in London. They also played live at every opportunity, accepting all the college gigs they could land. Some were well-attended, others less so. Tony Stratton-Smith, head of the Charisma label, showed early interest in Queen, and made them the substantial offer of £20,000. They could have done worse than sign with the football-mad Brummie, an eccentric after Freddie's own heart. A heavy drinking, racehorse-owning, homosexual former journalist, Strat had narrowly avoided death in the 1958 Munich air disaster, which claimed twenty-three lives including eight of Manchester United's 'Busby Babes'; he had decided at the last minute to cover a World Cup qualifier. In the late Sixties he became a rock manager and label owner, operating out of a tiny office in Soho's Dean Street. He signed Genesis in 1970, and backed the Monty Python albums, as well as Peter Gabriel, Lindisfarne, Van der Graaf Generator, Malcolm McClaren and Julian Lennon. Adored by his artists, Strat was 'the man who made dreams come true'.

Queen were not to be wooed by the late, great Strat – even though they were made for each other. Queen suspected they would always play second fiddle to Genesis, according to rumour. Figuring that, if they were worth twenty grand to Strat, they must be worth more elsewhere, they used Charisma's offer and enthusiasm to attract interest from other labels.

'The moment we made a demo, we were aware of the sharks,' recalled Freddie in 1974. 'We had such amazing offers from people saying "We'll make you the next T. Rex," but we were very, very careful not to jump straight in. Literally, we went to about every company before we finally settled. We didn't want to be treated like an ordinary band.'

'We're basically very big-headed people,' Brian later admitted, 'in a sense that we're convinced of what we're doing. If somebody tells us it's rubbish, then our attitude is that the person's misguided, rather than that we are rubbish.'

'We aimed for the top slot,' Freddie would explain. 'We were not going to be satisfied with anything less.'

Queen did not think that they were good, in other words. They *knew* that they were.

What has elsewhere been reported as a chance meeting with John Anthony, in those days one of London's brightest young record producers, was in all probability less happy accident, more a typically Freddie deliberate confrontation. Well known around Kensington and Chelsea for his diverse musical and sartorial influences, Freddie continued to dress up in exotic garb and cruise 'Ken High' and the King's Road on Saturday afternoons, usually after having sweet-talked a pal into minding his market stall. He would swan about in his element, spouting to all who would listen about his idols – at that time Liza Minnelli, The Who, Led Zeppelin and David Bowie's Ziggy. He justified the outrageous amounts of time he spent on his increasingly eccentric appearance with the retort 'you never know who you might meet'. Freddie meant to be noticed, and by someone in particular.

His perambulatory perseverance paid off. John Anthony and Freddie came face to face eventually during a typical weekend strut. In no time, Freddie had charmed an invitation to bring the band to Anthony's apartment in order to discuss their career.

This was some coup, given Anthony's reputation. A former London club DJ at venues such as The Speakeasy, The Roundhouse and UFO, Anthony turned to producing after recording demos for Yes in 1968. As an associate of Strat's, he had worked with Genesis, Van der Graaf Generator and Lindisfarne. His mantra for making records was 'There's one right way to do an album, and four hundred wrong ones.'

The encounter resulted in Anthony persuading Barry Sheffield, co-owner with his brother Norman of Trident Studios, to join him at a Queen gig at Southeast London's now defunct 'Forest Hill Hospital' on Friday 24 March 1972. Until then, the Sheffields had only heard Queen's five-song demo, but had never actually watched them perform. Barry wanted to see for himself what they were like as a live act before committing his company to a deal. So impressed was Sheffield by Queen's performance that he wanted to sign them on the spot – especially after their camp rendition of Shirley Bassey's immortal 'Hey Big Spender'.

'Trident was the best studio in the world,' said John Anthony, 'which was why it was booked twenty-four hours a day.'

The Sheffield brothers had recently launched a subsidiary of their company, called Trident Audio Productions, with a ground-breaking master plan to sign acts, put them in Trident's own state-of-the-art studios, then negotiate pressing and distribution deals with mainstream record companies for the actual recordings. Although aware that beggars could not be choosers, this was not what Queen had been looking for. The Sheffields were a pair of clever and canny businessmen who had shivered many a timber in their time. Acutely business-minded, they sat bouncing ballparks at the band until their eyes glazed. What Queen failed to spot among the small print was that the prospective deal was not exclusive, but a package, involving two other unrelated acts: Irish singer-songwriter Eugene Wallace, and a group by the name of Headstone. Equally alarming were the Sheffields' references to managerial control. What they were offering – a one-stop management and recording deal in which Trident would manage, produce, record and song-publish Queen, as well as negotiate a record company deal on their behalf – was not common practice. All Queen could see were conflicts of interest. Despite their insistence on sub-contracts for each aspect of the deal, Queen remained unsettled by the thought of Trident controlling every facet of their career.

They took their time before signing the contract, dithering for almost eight months, until November 1972, during which time they played not a single live show.

'I told them to lie low,' explained John Anthony. 'I wanted them to concentrate on getting their sound together, and then they could come back and play bigger gigs'.

Given that no one of significance really remembers, the reasons behind their prolonged procrastination remain unclear. There having been no drawn-out legal wrangles, perhaps the band were up to their old tricks again, wielding the Trident offer to attract better ones. If they were holding out for a more lucrative deal from the Sheffields, they were disappointed. What Queen eventually signed was a poor excuse for a contract. They would not discover for quite some time how unfavourable it was.

In fairness to Trident and the Sheffields, their reputation was sound. Not only did they run one of the finest studios in London, used regularly by A-list artists, but they were not known for dishonourable business dealings. Having invested time and money in Queen, they expected and were entitled to a return. Only Brian would bring himself to acknowledge their contribution to Queen's success in later years. The rest of the band didn't want to know by then.

As Freddie would say after the eventual demise of their relationship with Trident, 'As far as Queen are concerned, our old management is deceased. They cease to exist in any capacity with us whatsoever . . . we feel so relieved!'

To the outside world, the deal seemed too good to be true: the best recording studios in the world giving an unbroken band use of the studios and all facilities. Queen could record their entire debut album under the wing of producers John Anthony and his friend Roy Thomas Baker, who would then do the legwork and tout it around the labels. Not as good as it looked: the band, already humiliated by the fact that no record company seemed interested, would now suffer the indignity of having access to a recording studio only during 'down-time', when it was not required by paying clients such as Bowie or Elton John.

'They would call us up and say David Bowie had finished a few hours early, so we had from three a.m. until seven a.m. when the cleaners came in,' Brian admitted. 'A lot of it was done that way. There were a few full days, but mainly bits and pieces.'

The arrangement was hardly conducive to creativity. Ironic, then, that a notable recording from the Trident era and a highly collectible item today was created by accident. Hanging about in the studio waiting for access one day, Queen were invited by producer Robin Cable to record cover versions of the Phil Spector/Ellie Greenwich composition, 'I Can Hear Music' – with which The Beach Boys had scored a Top Ten hit in 1969 – and 'Goin' Back', written by husband-and-wife songwriting team Gerry Goffin and Carole King, and first recorded by The Byrds. Freddie provided vocals while Brian and Roger played and harmonised. Each Queen member received a modest fee. None of them could have imagined then just how infamous and eventually how valuable those recordings would become. Queen had signed

nothing and had agreed to nothing, but by default, and in innocence, had relinquished their right to control over the finished
product. The recording was released by EMI the following year
under the made-up name Larry Lurex, in both homage to and
as a send-up of Gary Glitter. But the gag backfired. Most high-
profile British DJs were offended by the dig, fiercely protective as
they then were of The Leader (long before Glitter's spectacularly
shameful fall from grace). Thanks to negligible airplay, the record
sold few copies and was relegated to the bargain bins. Years later
it would be re-released to become the coveted disc it is today,
changing hands for relative fortunes. Growing wise to the ways of
the cut-throat record industry, Queen would eventually acquire
the rights to the record themselves.

Queen bit the bullet and got on with the disjointed business of
recording their first album that summer. Not with John Anthony,
however. Day-job commitments to recording with Al Stewart, and
unable to withstand round-the-clock pressure indefinitely, Anthony
collapsed in the studio one night. After his doctor signed him off
with EBV, a debilitating illness causing chronic fatigue, Anthony
disappeared on extended holiday to Greece and left Queen in the
capable hands of Roy Thomas Baker.

Thomas Baker, a former trainee classical engineer at Decca,
had joined Trident in 1969, where he'd already contributed to such
hits as Free's 'All Right Now' and T. Rex's 'Get It On'. His relationship with Queen was challenging, and the eventual 'finished'
album lacked shape. On his return from Greece, and during
Thomas Baker's absence, Anthony went to Trident to listen to it,
and described what he heard as 'schizophrenic'.

'So Freddie, Brian and I came in, and we remixed most of it . . .
I wanted it to show the balls and the energy of Queen's live show,'
Anthony said.

The remixes and fine-tuning exhausted all concerned – as one
engineer involved in the project remarked of Freddie, 'it was quite
nerve-racking working with a born superstar'. Thomas Baker and

John Anthony then started doing the rounds of labels. Still nobody wanted to know. It was baffling. A common criticism was that Queen's sound was too obviously reminiscent of bands such as Yes and Led Zeppelin, despite the fact that those who had actually worked on the album agreed that the Queen sound was unique. The band still lacked a record company to press their efforts onto vinyl and release their LP into the market. They fared better with regard to their song publishing, a deal for which was secured with B. Feldman & Co. The Sheffields, meanwhile, had brought in Jack Nelson, a vigorous American record industry executive who had honed his act at the sharp end, to help find Queen a record deal and a manager. Excited by what he heard, but puzzled by the lack of interest from labels and managers, Nelson would assume the role of Queen manager himself.

'It took me over a year to get Queen a deal, and everyone turned them down,' said Nelson. 'I mean everyone. I won't name names . . . but they know who they are, every one of them.'

Nelson himself was blown away by Queen's talent. As he would later remember, 'Queen reminded me of the make-up of The Beatles. Each guy was so totally the opposite of the others, the four points of the compass. Freddie . . . composed on keyboards, and was classically trained. Very complex guy. Incredibly talented. Brian was a rock 'n' roll guitarist and he brought that influence. Incredibly talented. Scatter-brained. Focused. He had a degree in infra-red astronomy. John was the bass player. He brought the solid bit, as bass players do. Grounded them. He had a first-class Honours degree in Electronics. Roger, the drummer, had a double degree. They were probably the smartest band in the business. And totally diverse personalities – we could get into an airport and one would stop, one would go right, one would go left, and one would go straight ahead. But it made a great creative force. When they got together in the middle, with the stacked vocals, that centre was amazing.'

Each was first among equals. No one would ever emerge as

leader of the pack. Too intelligent to gang up on the others, Freddie and Roger remained partners in crime in terms of their friendship, although Roger would later remark that he felt he had more in common with Brian when the band first got together.

'We haven't always got on, but we've come to realise that we need one another', he told *Q* magazine in March 2011.

'Brian is my enduring mate, but I was very close to Fred. I think we were the naughty ones.'

Brian took almost everything too seriously, was long-suffering, introspective and stubborn, and rarely conceded control.

'We had quite a complex, sort of multi-way interaction', he told *Q*. 'That's why it worked, really. I was very close to Roger in some ways because we'd already been in a band together. We were – and we are – kind of brothers. We were so close in our aspirations and the way we looked at music, but of course so distant in so many other ways. Like any pair of brothers, we sort of loved and hated each other ... in a way, I was very close to Freddie, particularly in the song writing area. Some of my best times were producing a vocal out of Freddie, sort of coaxing him in various directions'.

What did he and Roger argue about most?

'Anything you care to name. Once we got into details with the music, it was in there as well. We would argue for days over one particular note.'

John commented little but contributed much, in particular to supervision of Queen's financial affairs. Not for some years, however, would bad humour over songwriting credits subside. Whoever's name was on the single (including whoever had written the B-side) got the royalties. Only when all four musicians agreed to credit all songs to the band as a whole , so that everyone would earn equally from every release, did animosity on that subject evaporate. They wished that they had thought of this much earlier. Freddie later commented that it was one of the best decisions the band ever made. Not only is this the most democratic method, but it resolves conflicts before they arise. Many a band and a friendship has been destroyed by squabbles over who gets how much – as Freddie's old friend Tony Hadley discovered to his cost. In 1999, he and fellow Spandau Ballet members John Keeble and Steve Norman decided to sue main songwriter Gary Kemp, for what they said was their fair share of past royalties. They lost, and the band fell out of touch for ten years. They put their differences aside eventually to regroup on a major comeback tour in 2009.

Each member of Queen brought diverse and complementary influences to the table. Each was musically gifted. While Freddie and Brian were regarded as the 'main' songwriters, with what appeared at times to be colliding styles, Roger and John would also write some of the band's greatest tracks. Uniquely for a rock band, all four would compose Queen hits (Freddie's included 'Bohemian Rhapsody', 'Killer Queen', 'Somebody to Love', and 'We Are the Champions'; among Brian's were 'Tie Your Mother Down', 'We Will Rock You', 'Hammer to Fall' and 'Who Wants to Live Forever'; Roger wrote 'Radio Ga Ga', 'One Vision', 'It's a Kind of Magic' and 'These Are the Days of Our Lives', and John contributed 'You're My Best Friend', 'I Want to Break Free' and 'Another One Bites the Dust').

'Most bands are a front man and the rest,' comments music publicist Bernard Doherty. 'There are not many bands in which four guys hit the stage and you go "wow, wow, wow and wow".'

'Freddie and Brian were completely complementary,' explains Paul Gambaccini. 'They didn't overlap, so there was no cause for jealousy within the group. Just admiration. They also freed each other from any responsibility of having to do what the other did. Brian May was not a showman. Not in the way that Freddie was. So how convenient for him that Freddie was. Brian could just stand there, do his job, and let Freddie do the rest. At the same time, Brian doesn't just stand there thinking "I'm a guitar god." He focuses on what he's doing, and it's incredible to see. Brian was also very good-natured about the relative popularity of the singles that Freddie, Roger and John had written. Compare that to a group such as Bread, in which David Gates had all the hits and the other writers didn't happen with the public (antagonism between Gates and the late Jimmy Griffin caused Bread to disband in 1973). But with Queen, Brian seemed nothing but grateful that Freddie's songs were successful. It made for balanced albums, and from that perspective alone was genius.'

In November 1972, having signed their contract with Trident, Queen showcased for the industry at The Pheasantry, a trendy hang-out on Chelsea's King's Road, from which Bob Geldof would later mastermind his Live Aid campaign, and which, at the time of writing, is a branch of Pizza Express. Everyone involved had called in favours, borrowed and pinched address books, filched numbers, phoned round and begged support from every music business contact they could think of. Despite all this effort, the gig was poorly-attended and a miserable night was had. Equipment sagged, the band flagged, you name it. Not a single A&R man showed up.

Five days before Christmas, Queen played the fabled Marquee Club on Soho's Wardour Street, which in its original incarnation on Oxford Street had staged one of the first live performances by The Rolling Stones, in July 1962, and which had hosted the greats: The Yardbirds, The Who, Jimi Hendrix. An improvement on their disastrous night at The Pheasantry, still it yielded nothing resembling a recording deal. There was one glimmer of hope in the shape of Jac Holzman, MD of Elektra Records in the United States. He had been given tapes of the complete Queen album by Jack Nelson.

'I listened to them first through the speakers, then through headphones,' Holzman later recalled. 'It was so beautifully recorded and performed. Everything was there: like a perfectly cut diamond landing on your desk. I was knocked out. "Keep Yourself Alive", "Liar", "The Night Comes Down" – all great songs in a sumptuous production that felt like the purest ice cream poured over a real rock 'n' roll foundation. I wanted Queen.'

After interminable negotiations, Jack Nelson arranged for Jac

Holzman to attend the gig at The Marquee.

'I flew to London,' Holzman remembered, 'listened to them at the gig Jack had set up, and was dreadfully disappointed. I saw nothing on stage to match the power I had heard on the tape. But the music was there. I wrote them a long memo, four or five pages single-spaced, with my thoughts and suggestions.'

It is true that Freddie's camp performance style was at that point still random and not to everyone's taste. Holzman, an American, may have expected a live delivery that was more macho and more recognisably rock 'n' roll. It is unlikely that he had anticipated ballet shoes, feather boas and leotards. All that balletic posturing and preening was at first glance at odds with how the band came across on tape. It simply did not illustrate Queen's recorded sound the way Jac Holzman had perhaps imagined it would.

Shortly afterwards, however, Holzman had second thoughts. He was beginning to see what he had heard after all. Yes it was different and off-the-wall, but it was growing on him. He agreed to sign Queen to Elecktra in America. Despite the fact that they were about to share a highly respected American label with The Doors, the band still couldn't get arrested by a UK label. Their unsatisfactory arrangement with Trident would rumble on.

9

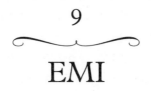

EMI

'Keep Yourself Alive' was a very good way of telling people what Queen was about in those days.

Freddie Mercury

Only two artists spring to mind who, when you first met them, you just knew they were stars from the word go. One was Phil Lynott, the other was Freddie.

Tony Brainsby, Queen publicist

Despite the many frustrations that led to its creation, Queen's eponymous debut album, completed by January 1973, was a masterpiece. The following month, they recorded a session for John Peel's progressive radio show. This was a coup in itself, since it was virtually unknown in those days for Radio 1 to record an unsigned group for broadcast. A further stroke of luck occurred when Queen's song-publishing company, B. Feldman & Co, was bought out by EMI Music Publishing, to which, by default, the band suddenly found themselves signed. This brought them one step closer to the dream.

'EMI was the ultimate record label in the Seventies,' recalls former promotions executive Allan James, who worked for the label during the Seventies before becoming one of the industry's most celebrated record pluggers. In his time, 'Jamesie', known to his artists as 'The Man in Black', has looked after Elton John, Alice Cooper, Rick Wakeman, Kim Wilde, Eurythmics and countless more.

'Warner and CBS were American,' Jamesie points out.

'Pye, Decca and the other UK labels were also-rans. EMI Manchester Square *was* the music business. It was also the British filter for American alternative labels at the time, such as Capitol and Motown. EMI had signed The Beatles, had all the pop hits, and owned every major artist from Vera Lynn to Cliff Richard. It was the greatest record label in the world in those days, and Queen aspired to be signed by them.

'The Chairman, Sir Joseph Lockwood – the only "sir" in the business back then – was this outrageously camp figurehead whom Freddie idolised. It didn't get much better than Sir Joe. As it turned out, he and Freddie were two peas in a pod, they had so much in common. Delusions of grandeur, for starters: whenever Sir Joseph strode through EMI's reception with his entourage, there was always a lift waiting to take them straight up to his penthouse.

'Then there were the Easts.

'Ken East was EMI's MD in the Seventies. He was this big, bold, brassy Australian who'd been a lorry driver before he got into the music business. Dolly, his wife, used to be in PR. Still was, in many ways. She was a large lady, this irresistible Mama Cass figure. Ken adored artists, and was one of the first to come down from his ivory tower to associate with them. EMI was full of queens, so Ken and Dolly embraced that whole scene too.

'We'd all go out for dinner with Cliff Richard, and make mischief around the Soho clubs. They were *Watership Down* days, complete make-believe. No wonder Freddie aspired to all that. It was bloody marvellous. As for EMI, why *wouldn't* they want Queen? That band had EMI written all over them. Why? Because they were so different and intelligent, and had such a creative attitude. They were tuning into the zeitgeist, listening to what music fans wanted, and taking it a step further. They knew what they were doing, and so did EMI.'

The chief A&R man for EMI at the time, and the person who would decide whether the label should sign Queen, was Joop Visser – remembered by former Cockney Rebel front man Steve Harley as 'a lovely great Dutchman'.

'Joop was the guy who found three of EMI's most successful acts of the era, and signed them all at the same time,' Steve tells me.

'One was Queen. The second was Pilot – the band formed by former Bay City Rollers Billy Lyall (who died of AIDS-related causes in 1989) and Dave Paton. The third, by the way, was us. Joop signed Cockney Rebel for three albums, no options. Not one single with options. No messing about. The kind of deal that is unheard-of now. Joop made my career and changed my life.

'I was twenty-two and full of myself. Thank God I was dealing with Joop; anyone else might have knocked my block off. Joop was the man you deferred to, the one you went to for advice.

'I was my own man, something of a gambler, a bit restless, a lot cocky. But you couldn't offend Joop. I loved him dearly. Maybe I made mistakes that Queen were smart enough to avoid. Freddie and I had in common a penchant for the theatrical. Not "Glam Rock" in any sense: you wouldn't have called either my band or Freddie's band that. The thing is, Queen fronted by Freddie Mercury would have been theatrical in any era. It didn't need that "Glam Rock" label to validate it or set it in context.'

It was photographer Mick Rock, Steve agrees, who inspired the theatrical bent in artists like Freddie, Bowie and Steve himself.

'And then he pushed it to the hilt. Mick was the catalyst. He was always putting people together. I remember him bringing Mick Ronson [the late guitarist with Bowie's Spiders from Mars, Mott the Hoople, Van Morrison and many others] round to my flat off the Edgware Road one day, saying that we should meet and that we'd get on like a house on fire. We did, of course. Musos loved

Mick. You wanted him down there in the pit, taking the long shots. He was the rock musician who wasn't.

'Mick photographed me everywhere, and did all that great stuff with Queen. He understood me and Freddie, and encouraged us in our creativity. Bands like Queen and Cockney Rebel knew we had to shake the business up. In my heart and soul I'm a folk singer, but at the time I denied all that. Bugger Woodstock. Wearing make-up and poncing around was of its time. I know Freddie felt the same, because we discussed it over dinner down at Legends a few times. I also know they must have loved Joop as much as I did. Especially Freddie.'

It wasn't love at first sight. Visser was seeking a band to fill the gap left by Ian Gillan quitting Deep Purple after their exhausting 'Machine Head' world tour. But the Dutchman was initially unimpressed by Queen. He too had attended their Marquee Club gig on 20 December 1972, but was underwhelmed. He had watched them in rehearsal, all a bit so-what. He confessed privately that the band members' personalities 'left him cold'. There was work to do.

After another Marquee Club showcase on 9 April 1973, and following three months of complicated negotiations with Trident, during which the latter drove the hardest bargain, refusing to back down, Visser did eventually sign Queen to EMI. It was worth all the agony and the wait. Queen would remain at EMI for the rest of their career . . . almost. (Not until thirty-eight years later, at the end of 2010 and on the eve of remaining band members Brian and Roger entering a year of celebrations for their fortieth anniversary, did Queen abandon the sinking EMI ship to sign with the Universal Music Group. Their recordings have appeared, since January 2011, on the Island Records label.)

Queen's official debut single, 'Keep Yourself Alive' – the opening track of their debut album and written by Brian – was released on 6 July 1973. But they couldn't win. The accompanying promotional blitz was dismissed as 'hype' which, although infuriatingly commonplace in the music business today, was then regarded as opportunistic and in poor taste. Freddie could not have been more frustrated, believing that Queen were doing everything right. Rejected five times by national station Radio 1's playlist compilers, and not yet having the licensed commercial radio stations to fall back on (these only became operational later that year), the single failed to chart. It was both the first and last time in Queen's career that this would occur. The only DJ to give it airtime was the late Alan 'Fluff' Freeman, described by John Peel as 'the greatest out-and-out disc jockey of them all', whose legendary catch-phrase was 'not 'arf', and who played the single on his new Saturday afternoon Rock Show, featuring heavy and progressive sounds.

Undeterred, EMI went into overdrive. Arguably the best exposure for bands at the time was an appearance on BBC TV's cult rock show *The Old Grey Whistle Test*, presented by DJ Bob Harris. Its name was derived from a Tin Pan Alley (community of music publishers and songwriters) phrase of yore: when virgin pressings of records arrived, executives would give a listen to the 'Old Greys', the doormen in grey suits. Songs that made enough impression to have the old boys whistling the melodies after just one hearing were deemed to have passed the 'Old Grey Whistle Test'. Unlike the BBC's *Top of the Pops* weekly chart show, *OGWT* featured only album music. The hit programme had been on air for sixteen years, whereas comparable shows today rarely last a second series.

A 'white label' pressing of Queen's album – a blank LP in a flimsy sleeve – was delivered to *OGWT*'s production department. But the plugger had neglected to write the names of band and record company on the label. No one had any idea who had sent in the disc, nor who the artist was.

'At that time, a lot of the strengths in album music were coming from the States,' remembers *OGWT* producer Mike Appleton. 'Therefore, most of the bands were not available to come into the studio and play live. To get round that, I started this thing whereby I'd pick album tracks and have this talented guy Phil Jenkinson match the tracks with appropriate visuals. Today, many people say that this was what led to the invention of the video. And with hindsight, I can say that it was all rather detrimental to the music industry. It took all the money and emphasis away from the live performance. Rock venues closed down, and ultimately all rock TV programmes began to look the same.'

Creating the visuals proved immensely enjoyable nonetheless.

'Fans began tuning in to *Whistle Test* just to watch those,' agreed Appleton. 'Regular featured artists included Little Feat, ZZ Top, JJ Cale, early Springsteen, Lynyrd Skynyrd – I could have featured their "Freebird" every week and still have been inundated with requests for it; that track was the most popular thing at the time. We showed a broad range – cartoons, abstract films, experimental pieces, the lot. It worked incredibly well. One day I picked up this White Label on my desk and noticed it was unmarked. I might well have ignored it or dropped it straight in the bin, but as it happened I put it on, unaware that this was a first pressing of Queen's debut album.'

Appleton was so impressed by what he heard that he decided to feature the track 'Keep Yourself Alive' on that week's programme.

'I phoned around to try and establish a name and a source. No one knew. In the end I gave it to Phil and said, 'Let's put this on. We'll say on the programme that we don't know what the hell or who the hell, but if anyone out there knows, could they please call us.' Phil pulled in some black-and-white cartoon footage of a super silver streamlined train with F.D. Roosevelt's face on the front, tearing at lightning speed across America. The footage had been used in a political campaign in the 1930s. The next day, EMI called to tell us that the band was Queen, and we planned to inform the viewers on the following week's show. But our audience beat us to it. We got an avalanche of enquiries from enthusiastic fans, which was highly unusual.'

The album was released on 13 July 1973 – coincidentally, twelve years to the day ahead of Queen's triumphant performance at Wembley Stadium for Live Aid. The music press were not amused.

Most were at best dismissive of the record. Some actually loathed it – particularly *New Musical Express* critic Nick Kent, who described it as 'a bucket of urine', thus creating a long-running feud between Queen and the respected rock weekly. At least the public were beginning to listen. The album remained on the chart for seventeen weeks, reaching Number Twenty-Four, and earned them a gold disc.

After a further session at Radio 1 – with the playlisters still snootily ignoring them – Trident booked Queen into Shepperton Studios to develop new songs and rehearse existing material. It was during their spell at Shepperton that Queen found themselves making their first promo film, Trident having recently expanded into video production with another subsidiary company, Trillion. The promo, intended to support the tracks 'Keep Yourself Alive' and 'Liar', would be directed by future film supremo Mike Mansfield.

'The promo video, then in its embryonic stages, was to become such an integral promotional tool of the music industry that soon record companies would be spending countless thousands on top-gun directors, glamorous locations and dazzling special effects in their efforts to push their artists up the charts,' says Scott Millaney, who produced some of the most iconic pop videos in history, including 'Video Killed the Radio Star' for The Buggles – the first-ever video to be shown on music channel MTV in 1981 – 'Ashes to Ashes' for David Bowie, and 'I Want to Break Free' for Queen. In all, his company MGMM would create ten classic Queen videos.

'The promo video business, with all its tricks and techniques, would eventually exhaust itself,' admits Scott. 'The record industry would then remember the human element, and the whole cycle would begin again. But in the Seventies it was still an exciting and fresh new medium which would greatly enhance the careers of dozens of artists, some of whom did little to warrant the hype.'

According to Scott, the successful promo video relies on three essential elements: the music and lyrics of the song; the 'live' performance; and the distinctive imagery of the artist. When the mix of these ingredients is right, a single airing of the video can do more to promote a record and establish an artist than any amount of radio play. As a result, many artists were soon avoiding the live circuit completely, realising that an illusion of perfection can be achieved in a video recording that the live performance can never live up to.

'The downside is that filming is demanding and exhausting,' Scott points out.

'Shoots often begin at sunrise and may not finish until well into the night. Hectic schedules do take their toll on artists. There's no doubt that companies like ours turned video-making not only into a whole separate industry, but into an art form. We mined the philosophy to the point where we were able to say to record companies, "You need to pay a fortune to get the best." I had the best creative partners in the world at that time. We set the standards, and we were operational two years prior to MTV – which came along and changed everything.'

Queen's first experience of the medium was less than encouraging. The band felt uncomfortable in the studio and were at odds with Mansfield, who frustrated them by dismissing most of their 'novice' artistic suggestions in favour of his own 'more experienced' ideas. Freddie in particular felt that Mansfield was missing the point of Queen's music, and that his efforts were dated, predictable and 'full of himself'. The result was pronounced unusable, and was abandoned. When it came to 'Liar', Queen refused to work again with Mansfield. Agreeing that the only way to get what they wanted was to make it themselves, they joined forces with technician Bruce Gowers at London's Brewer Street Studios to create something 'directly in tune with the band's own ideas of how they should be presented. This rare piece was the first to be used to promote Queen, though in these early days there were very few outlets on TV, so it has hardly ever been seen until now', as they later wrote in the accompanying booklet to their DVD collection,

Freddie rehearsing with dancers of the Royal Ballet Company, 1980.

Freddie with Elton John, celebrating the release of the *Flash Gordon Soundtrack*, 1980.

Freddie with Ian Hunter, lead singer of Mott the Hoople, USA, 1982.

Freddie on-set for Queen's 'It's A Hard Life' video, 1984, in a costume designed by Diana Moseley. The get-up became known as 'the Prawn Outfit' – because it made Freddie look like a giant cooked prawn.

Celebrated cartoonist Gray Jolliffe recalls a chance meeting with Freddie in Austria in the late 1980s.

*"Sure I'm Freddie Mercury –
wait till I put my teeth in."*

Journalist, broadcaster and friend David Wigg with Freddie at a Munich dinner party, 1984.

Freddie Mercury on the set of the Queen video 'I Want to Break Free', 1984.

Barbara Valentin,
Freddie and friends in
a Munich nightclub,
late 1980s.

Cliff Richard and Freddie,
New Year's Day, 1985.

Freddie with actress Jane Seymour
as 'bride and groom' at the Royal
Albert Hall for Fashion Aid for
Ethiopia, 5 November 1985. They
are flanked by their costumes'
designers Elizabeth and David
Emmanuel, famous for having
created Lady Diana Spencer's
wedding dress.

Freddie and David Bowie enjoying
a chat backstage at Live Aid,
Wembley Stadium, 13 July 1985.

Live Aid, the finale: From left:
George Michael, Harvey Goldsmith,
Bono of U2, Paul McCartney, Freddie.

Live Aid, the finale:
on stage at Wembley
Stadium, 13 July 1985.
From left: Bono,
Paul McCartney,
Freddie, David Bowie,
Adam Ant, Bob Geldof.

Freddie with Mary Austin at his hat-themed 40th birthday party, held at his Kensington home, Garden Lodge.

Freddie emerging from the lift at London's Roof Gardens nightclub, July 1986. The naked female bell-hop is body-painted to give the impression that she is wearing a uniform.

'Coming out to play?' Enchanted by her amazing personality, Freddie entices Page 3 star Samantha Fox onto the stage for an impromptu duet at Queen's Kensington Roof Gardens party following the band's Wembley show, July 1986.

Freddie, perched on a flight case, relaxes in the sunshine in Hungary before Queen's gig at the Nepstadion, Budapest, July 1986.

Freddie emerges from his dressing room backstage at Wembley Stadium, London, July 1986.

Freddie and John Deacon rehearsing on stage at the Nepstadion, Budapest, July 1986.

Freddie showers his fans with water during Queen's Wembley concert, July 1986.

Freddie performing in the video for 'Who Wants To Live Forever', 16 September 1986.

John Deacon smiles on as Freddie receives a doll dressed in Hungarian national costume, Budapest, July 1986.

Queen fly in over a sea of fans in their customised helicopter for what no one knew at the time would be Freddie's final gig. Knebworth, August 1986.

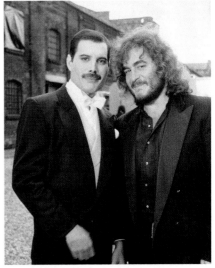

Freddie with the late American composer and, musician Michael Kamen, taking a break during the shoot of the video for 'Who Wants To Live Forever', 1986. Kamen created the track's orchestration.

Freddie in regal cloak and crown, by designer Diana Moseley, Wembley Stadium, 15 July 1986.

Queen Greatest Video Hits 1. The track 'Liar', written by Freddie for the same album, was never released as a single in the UK, only in North America, where it was poorly edited. The version of the track's promo which appears on the DVD had never previously been released.

It had now dawned on the band that, only by retaining close to complete control over their work could they relax enough to take risks with their creativity. This was to set the template for Queen's entire career.

'I wouldn't say that they were control freaks exactly,' Queen's first publicist Tony Brainsby told me in 1996, four years before he died. 'But they always knew exactly what they wanted, and they found it extremely hard to compromise or make do. They had a perfectly clear idea of how they saw something, so it was generally pointless to suggest going with something else.'

Brainsby was brought in by Trident at eye-watering expense to create Queen's public profile. A star in his own right, he cut quite a dash on the music scene, and cruised around London in a Rolls-Royce. Painfully thin, lanky and bespectacled, and usually dressed in a Mandarin-collared black jacket, drainpipe trousers and Chelsea boots, he was precisely the kind of publicist Freddie could relate to. As well as having the requisite post-Swinging Sixties eccentric image, Brainsby came with rock credentials. As a teenager, he had shared a Soho flat with Eric Clapton and Brian Jones of The Rolling Stones. His column in *Boyfriend* magazine took him regularly to rehearsals for pop TV show *Ready Steady Go!*, which inspired him to launch his own PR company. When he met Queen, Brainsby was the most sought-after music publicist in London. He ran his empire from his large, rambling home on Edith Grove, between Fulham Road and the King's Road, which was crammed with dead plants, rock chicks and umpteen television sets. Those of us left can remember pitching up there for Brainsby's parties, and not surfacing thereafter for several days.

Brainsby's close friend Mick Rock had been his wedding

photographer, and his client list featured some of the major artists of the day, from Cat Stevens and Thin Lizzy to Mott the Hoople and The Strawbs.

'The Queen approach came from their American manager Jack Nelson at Trident,' Brainsby remembered.

'It wasn't like me to take on relative unknowns. But Queen were different. I remember going to see them at Imperial College. There was no stage, just a dance floor. There was Freddie doing all his posing in his white cape and what-have-you. That performance was far-removed from the way they ended up. But Freddie certainly had presence and presentation. He already had his act together.'

What impressed Brainsby most was that Freddie did not try to hog the glory.

'What I thought was commendable was that at no time did they style themselves "Freddie Mercury and Queen". It was always a group image. Freddie never tried to project himself as the leader. As far as I could tell, relationships within the band were mostly harmonious. They were unusual for rock musicians in that they were so intelligent. One could feel quite inadequate in their presence.'

At the beginning of their relationship, Brainsby admitted, there was a tendency to use Freddie more than Brian, Roger or John for interviews.

'Then I learned to make sure that they did an equal amount. Later on, we'd save Freddie for the major ones. After that, it was Brian for the major ones. He'd always talk about making his guitar from an ancient fireplace, so that was easy, and got them into the more serious music papers. Roger, who was the pin-up, did well in the teeny girls' mags like *Jackie* and *19*. He was *so* pretty. At least the band weren't precious about where they got coverage, which was just as well, considering so many journalists wouldn't give them the time of day. Although I must say they were rather fussy about photographs. They had to approve every single one personally before I could release anything. Freddie was the most sensitive.

It was all to do with his teeth. He was also such a perfectionist. A typical Virgo. He'd even created a coat-of-arms logo for the band, incorporating all their star signs.'

All of which pre-echoed Rob Reiner's fictional heavy metal band, later the subject of 1984's cult mockumentary *This Is Spinal Tap*.

As cool and laid-back as Brainsby was, he found himself seduced from the outset by Freddie.

'He had many stylish little quirks that would stick in your mind. He'd paint the fingernails of just his right or just the left hand, with black nail polish. Or he'd just varnish one little finger. He'd say "Darling!" or "My *dears!*" every other sentence, and his camp delivery was highly amusing and very endearing. He was great to have around. Never a dull moment. The girls all loved it when he came into the office.

'At the time, of course, he was living with Mary. To start with, his sex life was a complete mystery to us all; we could never quite fathom it. He certainly never spoke about it.'

Not that Brainsby socialised with or got that close to any of the band.

'I never liked to get too involved with clients. Mistaking them for your best pals is the biggest error in PR, because they just take the piss. Artists can become such a pain in the arse if you get too close to them. I left that sort of thing to the girls in my office. That's what they were there for.'

Rock 'n' roll, concluded Brainsby, speaking for all of us, 'is an erratic, unstable, emotional, ego-ridden business. Just like its stars. Work in it as long as I have and you learn not to be surprised by the fact that virtually every rock artist is a paranoid eccentric. It's what it does to them.'

Freddie's saving grace was the fact that he was a *likeable* eccentric.

'I really admired him,' Brainsby said. 'Here was a man bursting with creative powers which were not simply in someone's imagination. They existed. He knew he had it in him, however old he was at the time . . . twenty-seven, I believe. I mean, they were quite old for a band, weren't they, to be starting out. He'd had all this inside him for ever. How frustrating it must have been, knowing that he had what it took, trying desperately to make it big-time and not getting anywhere for so long.'

Freddie gave the impression of being someone who had known exactly what he was capable of since childhood.

'He desperately needed an outlet for his creativity. Success must have been such a relief to him. There were times when he was fighting tooth and nail to get what he wanted, which doesn't always bring out the pleasant side. Having to kick, struggle, scream, punch and shout in order to make an impact and get through to people is always going to take its toll. That's where Freddie was at when I got him.'

The most sought-after publicist in London wasn't the only one with his work cut out.

10

Dudes

I suppose the way we tackled our career sounds clinical and calculating, but our egos couldn't handle anything but the best. I've always thought of us as a top group. It sounds very big-headed, I know, but that's the way it is.

Freddie Mercury

The thing that set Queen apart from other rock bands is that they actively set out to write hit songs. You can be the greatest musician in the world, but writing a three-and-a-half-minute gem that the world can hum along to is incredibly hard. If you can do that, and combine it with great musicianship, then you are truly onto a winner. Therein lies the secret to their success.

James Nisbet, session guitarist

August 1973, and Queen were back at Trident Studios to record their second album.

Tony Brainsby's unflagging efforts having raised the band's profile substantially, the band were at last accorded their own legitimate studio time, during daylight hours if they wanted it.

On 13 September they convened at Golders Green Hippodrome to record an important session for BBC Radio.

Remembers BBC producer Jeff Griffin: 'At Golders Green

Hippodrome we recorded Queen's first live *In Concert* session, compèred by Alan Black [the late, laconic Scottish DJ, cartoonist and animator on The Beatles' *Yellow Submarine* film, who conceived the *In Concert* series]. They didn't do the whole hour. I had Peter Skellern as support. I must admit now that it seems a bit of a bizarre combination. Queen were good on that. Freddie showed some signs of nervousness. Not altogether surprising, because I don't think they'd done a lot of live work. The show went down well, and there was a lot of interest.'

That month, their American record company Elektra launched the first Queen album in the States. After what the band had been through in the UK, they weren't expecting much. They were pleasantly surprised, then, when DJs across America hailed them as 'an exciting new British talent', and began to play their album tracks on air. A surge in requests wafted the record onto the Billboard chart, where it peaked at a respectable Number Eighty-Three – no mean feat for an unknown band. The achievement did not go unnoticed. Brainsby had already introduced Queen to another fabulous act on his roster, the irrepressible Mott the Hoople. Mott were fronted by the sardonic, ringlet-haired Ian Hunter. Despite a staunch following on the London club scene, their album sales were disappointing. They'd called it a day in 1972, only reuniting at the behest of Bowie, who brought them under the wing of his own management. Mott secured a new contract with CBS Records (later Sony), and Bowie wrote and produced their hit single 'All the Young Dudes'. Mott went on to enjoy further Top Twenty hits during 1973, including 'All the Way From Memphis' and 'Roll Away the Stone', which prompted a major UK tour. Comprising twenty prime-venue dates, the tour kicked off on 12 November at Leeds Town Hall, and ended at London's Hammersmith Odeon just before Christmas. Thanks to Brainsby's introduction, not to mention the bung (it was just becoming acceptable for bands to 'buy' their way onto other bands' tour), the support act was Queen.

On 1 November, at the Kursaal, Southend-on-Sea – the world's first-ever theme park, pre-dating New York's Coney Island – Freddie, Brian and Roger sang backing vocals for Mott, on 'All the Young Dudes'.

Maverick Radio Caroline, an unlicensed offshore service operating from a ship anchored in international waters off the coast of England, was founded in 1964. With a self-styled remit to challenge the monopoly of record companies and give the BBC a run for its money over music broadcasting in the UK, it launched the careers of many popular mainstream DJs such as Tony Blackburn, Mike Read, Dave Lee Travis, Johnnie Walker and Emperor Rosko. Caroline's heyday was cut short by the Marine, &c., Broadcasting (Offences) Act 1967, which outlawed the pirates in August that year and shook the BBC from its lethargy to create the new 'teenage station', Radio 1, launched by Caroline favourite Tony Blackburn the following month. Caroline would be back. Meanwhile, as Radio 1 found its feet, Radio Luxembourg came to the fore.

David 'Kid' Jensen joined Luxembourg in 1968, aged just eighteen. The Canadian-born DJ's late-night show *Kid Jensen's Dimensions*, aired between midnight and three a.m., became one of radio's most popular shows, attracting a broad fan base that included British Prime Minister-to-be Tony Blair.

Jensen first met Queen in October 1973, during a promotional tour of European cities set up by EMI. As well as France, Germany, Holland and Belgium, the band stopped off in the Grand Duchy to perform a live show arranged by 'the Kid'.

'From 1968 until 1973, high-profile Radio Luxembourg was "the only place in Europe" to hear rock and pop music,' explains Jensen.

'In those days, Radio 1 closed early evening, and then it would be Radio 2 – at which point, many listeners switched stations to us. We concentrated on what was then called the "progressive" sound. The station was cool, and all the artists of the day wanted to be associated with it. After his death, I met Jimi Hendrix's girlfriend at a party one night, and she told me that Jimi loved my show. "We'd come back from parties and listen to you," she said.

'I was very taken by Queen from the beginning. "Keep Yourself Alive" was the first track I ever heard, from their debut album. I had always favoured guitar-based music, but this was something else. It had such great energy. They had it all: John, the quiet, reliable bass player. Brian, the brilliant guitarist. Roger, the incredible drummer, who enjoyed the rock-star lifestyle to the hilt. And Freddie Mercury, the great showman: perhaps the greatest of them all. Despite their excellent recordings and ground-breaking techniques, they'd got knocked back. I knew they hadn't been able to get airplay on Radio 1. When I heard they were coming over on a promotional tour, I arranged a small gig for them at a venue called the Blow Up Club in the centre of town, with about a two hundred capacity.

'The folks who owned the club fortunately took my word for it that the bands I chose were right, so I had kind of a free rein. The audience were late-teens, early twenties. It was a mixed bill that night: Queen were to play alongside some other seriously good rock acts, including Status Quo, Wishbone Ash, The Grateful Dead and Canned Heat. Radio Luxembourg had planned to record this concert for future broadcast. But the equipment failed, and there is no record of it, sadly. Queen were loud and self-assured. A class above the rest, even in those early days.

'I remember we went back to Freddie's hotel room with their plugger, Eric "Monster" Hall, after the show. We stayed up until very late, talking about everything and anything. Freddie was very chatty and friendly, and a great host. Nothing was too much trouble.

'I liked them as people,' adds Jensen. 'I wrote a piece about them for *Record Mirror*. They flew in the face of some critics, by whom they were not immediately loved, and I admired that. They weren't just sex, drugs and rock 'n' roll, although they did all that. There was an air of intellectualism about them. They would all, I thought, have been successful at almost anything they chose. I remain very grateful to Queen, who actually helped me and my show. I was able to play them late at night on Radio Luxembourg, and they won me huge popularity.'

Their profile rising all the time, the warm-up gigs they played for Mott the Hoople's tour were a smash with fans. At last Freddie had what he had always craved: guaranteed audiences, adulation, crowds baying for more. Rave reviews in the music press were still few and far between, the consensus still being that Queen were little more than 'Emperor's New Clothes'.

'Fuck them, darling, if they just don't get it,' retorted Freddie to a baffled Tony Brainsby.

Tony, so often on the receiving end of Freddie's wrath and frustration when faced with unfavourable reviews, couldn't help but notice the dramatic effect that fan worship was having on his charge.

'In spite of the bad press, Freddie's confidence soared. But I could see that he didn't enjoy doing interviews. In time, we stopped using him more or less altogether, unless it was for an album or a tour. Freddie's deliberate elusiveness only made him appear more mysterious, of course, which rather appealed to him.'

As Freddie saw it at the time, 'I think, to an extent, we're a sitting target because we've gained popularity quicker than most bands,' he said, rewriting history and conveniently forgetting what a long, arduous and frustrating ride to the almost-top it had been. The self-deception was perhaps forgiveable after so much agony.

'We've been talked about more than any other band in the last month,' he went on, 'so it's inevitable. I think it would be wrong if all we got were good reviews. But it's when you get unfair, dishonest reviews where people haven't done their homework that I get annoyed.'

Denis O'Regan, the award-winning rock photographer who made his first forays into the business snapping Bowie at Hammersmith

Odeon with a camera borrowed from his uncle, would one day tour the world with Queen as their official lensman. Watching them open for Mott at the same venue in 1973, he could only marvel at the 'pretentiousness and confidence' of the lead singer.

'Freddie was throwing the shapes and going through the poses even then – as a mere support act,' remembers Denis.

'He talked a bit to the audience between numbers, introducing the songs. Brian May was fantastic. I'd never heard of Queen, but in those days one tended to go along and watch the support as well as the main act. I turned to my friend George Bodnar (who also went on to become a major name in rock photography) and said, "Who does that prat think he is?" I found out why, of course, a year or so later, once the whole world had got used to the idea of Queen. I only got into the music after hearing them on the John Peel show. I've been a big Queen fan ever since.'

'For me,' Joop Visser later observed, 'it was only after Queen toured with Mott the Hoople that they really got it together, and I mean got it frighteningly together. They scared Mott the Hoople at the end of that tour, because they were stealing the shows.'

Meanwhile, the press reviews were improving. 'Atmosphere electric'. 'Band sensational'. Queen concluded a turning-point supporting 10cc in Liverpool.

Asked to comment on the tour which began as Mott's and wound up as Queen's, Freddie responded: 'The opportunity of playing with Mott was great. But I knew damn well the moment we finished that tour, as far as Britain was concerned, we'd be headlining.'

EMI, no longer able to cope with the deluge of Queen fan mail and photo requests, attempted to hand the responsibility to Trident Studios. Trident couldn't, or wouldn't, cope either. There was only one way to solve the problem. By the end of 1973, Queen had launched their own official fan club, run by two old friends of Roger's from Cornwall, Sue and Pat Johnstone. While it has changed hands down the years, the band remained closely involved in the club. Not only does it exist to this day, but the fan club still organises and hosts a well-attended annual Queen Convention.

With album sales healthy, EMI stepped up the international campaign. A promotional trip to Australia was booked for January 1974. Disaster struck when, following a routine travel inoculation, Brian developed gangrene in his arm so acute that amputation was feared. His condition improved rapidly enough for the trip to proceed as planned. Then it was Freddie's turn. During the flight to Sydney, his fear of flying first manifested itself, and he became agitated almost to the point of panic. His anxiety was exacerbated by a painful ear infection, resulting in a temporary loss of hearing. Freddie would remain aerophobic for life. The trip seemed jinxed. Neither Freddie nor Brian was up to performing, and the gigs were lukewarm.

At least things were looking up back in London. In the *NME* Readers' Poll, Queen were voted second most promising newcomers – without a single hit under their belts. In America, Elektra released a second album track as a single, but it sank without trace. Still undeterred, EMI scheduled a further single release; and when a slot became vacant last-minute on *Top of the Pops* on 21 February 1974 – because David Bowie's promo for his new single 'Rebel Rebel' wasn't ready – Queen were rushed to the BBC studios to mime 'Seven Seas of Rhye', before that single had even been released.

'I remember Freddie running along Oxford Street to watch their appearance on a set in a shop window, because he didn't own a telly,' said Brainsby.

The single was rush-released that week, and the tide continued to turn. The band's second album, *Queen II*, was now good to go, and they were planning their first headlining UK tour. Kicking off in Blackpool on 1 March, it would close four weeks later at North London's Rainbow Theatre. The venue, on the corner of Isledon Road and Seven Sisters Road, was built as a cinema in the 1930s, and is now Grade II-listed and used as a Pentecostal church. In the interim, it was an important music venue: where Jimi Hendrix first set light to his guitar in 1967, where the Beach Boys recorded their *Live in London* album, and which echoed with the encores of Stevie Wonder, The Who, Pink Floyd, Van Morrison, The Ramones and David Bowie.

Rehearsals for the tour began in earnest at Ealing Studios. According to Brainsby it was Freddie's idea to get acclaimed young fashion designer Zandra Rhodes to create their flamboyant tour costumes, having seen some of the confections she'd come up with for Marc Bolan. The others agreed readily. EMI, not so readily, to the eye-watering invoice for £5,000, although even they had to concede that Zandra's silk bat-wing tunics were 'very Queen'. Only now did Freddie feel confident enough to kiss the Kensington Market stall goodbye.

'Seven Seas of Rhye' went straight in at Number Forty-Five, four days after the Blackpool show. Three days later, *Queen II* was released, making it to Number Thirty-Five on mixed reviews. The tour was marred by a number of incidents, including violence north of the border, after a fight broke out among Stirling University students and two fans were stabbed. Although the band managed to lock themselves in a kitchen, two roadies were injured and hospitalised. The following night's show in Birmingham was subsequently cancelled, but the damage was done. Queen again found themselves the subject of negative headlines in the music press. The surge of bad publicity continued after their Isle of Man gig at the end of March. Despite all this, that gig was celebrated in dramatic style by both band and entourage, raising the bar for post-Queen-gig revelry for years to come. At another date on that tour, while waiting for the band to come on, the audience began singing 'God Save the Queen'. The serenade would be a given at Queen gigs from then on.

With *Queen II* now at Number Seven on the album chart, increasing numbers of fans were picking up on the first album. That, too, charted for the first time at Number Forty-Seven, about the same time as Elektra released it in Japan, where it was received ecstatically. Little did Trident, EMI or the band themselves realise how big Queen would be in Japan.

There was a price to pay for success. There always is. As Freddie's temper wore thin and he took to flaring at the most minor mishap or inconvenience, Job-like Brian began to lose patience. Their bitchy scraps, exhausting for all, usually resulted in a petulant Freddie flouncing off in a huff, while the others stood around shrugging. As they saw it, time-wasting was pointless when there was so much work to get through. Years later, commemorating Queen's fortieth anniversary in an interview with British music magazine *Q*, Brian and Roger both recalled Freddie as the peacemaker:

'I think that's an odd juxtaposition with Freddie's image of being a prima donna. Actually he was the great diplomat, and if there were arguments between us, Freddie was usually able to sort them out.'

Hindsight, that wonderful thing. According to Freddie, Queen had always 'argued about everything – even the air that we breathe.'

Their confidence boosted by the success of their own debut tour, Queen were pleased but not surprised to receive an invitation from Mott the Hoople to support their upcoming US outing, which would open in Denver, Colorado and take in several nights in New York. Despite Freddie's aerophobia, he was first on the plane on 12 April. They would arrive to news that Elektra had taken advantage of the band's imminent arrival by releasing *Queen II* ahead of schedule. They could not have been more thrilled at the prospect of their first American tour, having worked towards that goal for so many years. By now, the band were attracting the interest of America's own flamboyant artists.

'We thought we were unusual,' commented Brian, 'but a lot of the people that came were surprising, even to us – a lot of transvestite artists, The New York Dolls, Andy Warhol – people that were creative in a way that appeared to trash everything that had gone before.'

It was not to be plain sailing. Disaster struck again when Brian collapsed in New York, having never quite recovered from his infection in Australia. The band were told to forget about playing Boston. When Brian developed hepatitis, it became obvious that they would have to pull out of the rest of the tour. His disappointment and guilt at having to let the band down was immense.

Back home, despite the fact that Brian was still quite ill, Queen relocated to the Welsh Rockfield Studios near Monmouth in the Wye Valley, to start rehearsing songs for their third album. Rockfield was the world's first residential recording studios in the 1960s, and has hosted a huge range of artists over the past forty years, including Mott the Hoople, Black Sabbath, Motorhead, Simple Minds, Aztec Camera, The Manic Street Preachers, The Darkness (who were almost a Queen tribute band) and Nigel Kennedy. It was a studio which would become dear to their hearts. On 15 July 1974, they began recording back at Trident, collaborating again with producer Roy Thomas Baker. Baker, by now referred to as 'the fifth Queenie', had been a Decca engineer in the early Sixties, and had worked with The Rolling Stones, T. Rex, Frank Zappa and Eric Clapton. He had also masterminded recordings by Nazareth, Dusty Springfield and Lindisfarne, among many, making him one of the most respected producers of the day. Recording, which was divided between several London studios other than Trident, namely Air, Sarm and Wessex, was soon halted when Brian was rushed to hospital again: this time with a duodenal ulcer. A further American tour scheduled for September had to be scrapped. Brian became acutely depressed, fearing that Queen would seek a replacement guitarist. He needn't have worried. The rest of the band pushed on, recording what they could and leaving room for Brian's guitar sequences to be added later.

Compensation came in the form of a music industry silver disc, awarded for sales in excess of 100,000 copies of their album *Queen II*. True to form, Brainsby organised a cunning stunt for the presentation ceremony at London's Café Royal, in the form of comely actress Jeannette Charles. Miss Charles made her living doubling for Her Majesty, and had become a national TV institution. She was an inspired choice, especially given that Queen had been perfecting an inoffensive rock rendition of the British National Anthem, with which they planned to close their future live shows.

'Killer Queen', the band's third single, and taken from the forthcoming third album *Sheer Heart Attack*, was released in October 1974.

'"Killer Queen" is about a high-class call-girl,' said Freddie at the time. 'I was trying to say that classy people can be whores as well,' he added, as if alluding to himself. 'That's what the song is about, though I'd prefer people to put their own interpretation upon it – to read what they like into it. People are used to hard-rock energy from Queen, yet with that single you almost expect Noël Coward to sing it. It's one of those bowler hat, black suspender numbers,' he added, in homage to his favourite film, Liza Minnelli's *Cabaret*. 'Not that Noël Coward would wear that!'

'It was the turning point,' Brian later remarked. 'It was the song that best summed up our kind of music, and a big hit, and we desperately needed it as a mark of something successful happening for us. We were penniless, you know, just like any other struggling rock 'n' roll band. All sitting around in London bedsitters, just like the rest.'

'Killer Queen' tore to Number Two, but was kept off the top slot by blue-eyed heart-throb David Essex, whose hit was ironically entitled 'Gonna Make You a Star'. In a bizarre twist of fate, Queen's next UK tour would be promoted by premier rock impresario Mel Bush, who had made a star of none other than . . . David Essex. The tour promised to be more ambitious and elaborate than anything Queen had attempted before. The music papers were now forced to concede that this unique group could not be written off. Not only did *Sheer Heart Attack* receive dazzling reviews, but all three Queen albums to date were now simultaneously on the UK chart.

The album sleeve artwork, another Mick Rock creation, was a departure from the look of *Queen II*.

'We want to look like we've been marooned on a desert island,' was Freddie's instruction to Rock, who took him at his word. Smearing their faces and naked torsos with Vaseline, then spraying them with water, Rock arranged them lying down, in a circle, and shot them from above. The album's musical content was equally surprising, wowing critics and fans alike.

'In 1974 my Dad went out and bought *Sheer Heart Attack*, recalls Eighties pop sensation Kim Wilde, daughter of Fifties rock 'n' roller Marty Wilde. Kim would dominate the music scene herself during the Eighties, her debut single "Kids in America" shooting to number two.

'I was fourteen years old, and a huge pop fan, having just started buying records of my own. I loved Slade, Sweet, Mud, Elton John and Marc Bolan. Not forgetting The Bay City Rollers – well, I *was* fourteen!

'*Sheer Heart Attack* still stands as one of the most exciting albums I have ever heard. It was later the first album I downloaded on iTunes when the world "went virtual". I loved Freddie's soaring vocals, his harmonies and humour. I also loved Brian's guitar playing, with its intense energy and passion, and I had the hots for Roger Taylor. John Deacon seemed to be the glue holding it all together. What a band!'

At the end of October, they ventured out on another UK tour, ending with a single London night at the Rainbow Theatre, which had to be extended to 19 and 20 November after tickets sold out in a couple of days. Both performances were filmed and recorded for posterity and future release. At Queen's debut end-of-tour party, held at the Swiss Cottage Holiday Inn and markedly respectable by future standards, promoter Mel Bush presented the band with a plaque in recognition of them having sold out the whole tour. Their first European dates, in Scandinavia, Belgium, Germany and Spain, were scheduled for the end of November. Continental album sales were through the roof, with most of the gigs a sell-out. In Barcelona, a city with which Freddie fell instantly in love and to which he would return again and again, the 6,000-seat venue was sold out within twenty-four hours.

By December, Queen decided that their position with Trident was untenable. Although their wages had risen from the initial £20 a week to £60 with the success of *Sheer Heart Attack*, it still wasn't enough to live on. Worse, despite projected royalties, Trident refused to give them an advance. John Deacon wanted to buy a modest house for him and his pregnant girlfriend, Veronica Tetzlaff, but Trident declined to lend him the £4,000 deposit. Freddie wanted a new piano, and Roger a small car. All requests for cash were flatly refused. So strained had relations become that it was deemed necessary to appoint a specialist music business lawyer to unravel the mess. Thus began Queen's relationship with Henry James 'Jim' Beach, the senior music partner at law firm Harbottle and Lewis. In 1978 he would become their manager: a position that Beach retains to this day. It would take him nine months to negotiate Queen out of their various signed agreements with Trident, who understandably wanted to hang on to the band. Meanwhile, with both the single 'Killer Queen' and album *Sheer Heart Attack* having broken into the American Top Ten, they were deemed ready to tackle their own major US tour.

On 18 January 1975, John married Veronica, with whom he would go on to have six children. On 5 February the band embarked on their big US adventure. Again, despite enthusiastic backing from their American label Elektra, they encountered problems, with critics comparing them unfavourably to Led Zeppelin. Freddie experienced his first vocal problems, having developed – or not, according to conflicting diagnoses – non-malignant throat nodules. Defying doctors' orders to remain silent for three months – preposterous! – he strode out in full voice in Washington the following night. With his condition improving one moment, worsening the next, Queen had no choice but to cancel many scheduled US shows. What had started to become apparent was that Freddie was giving too much on stage. His performances were more than his body and vocal chords could stand. Time off from touring and recording was vital for him to recover. Some time elapsed before Freddie and the band would take this on board.

There were other lucky escapes. While on the road in the States, Queen agreed a meeting with the fearsome Don Arden, the former Brixton-based, Vaudeville-era nightclub singer and comedian Harry Levy, with a view to him becoming their manager if he could extract them from their crippling Trident deal. They must have felt desperate. The late music manager and agent, who famously masterminded the careers of the Small Faces, ELO and Black Sabbath, was dubbed 'the English Godfather' on account of aggressive and illegal business dealings. Arden was known for resorting to violence when negotiations failed to go his way. Legend had it that he even dangled artists from upper-floor windows to persuade them to sign on the dotted line. When his daughter Sharon married Black Sabbath's front man, Arden became Ozzy Osbourne's father-in-law. To think that Queen could have found themselves under the control of the Al Capone of rock . . . would any of them have lasted as long?

11

Rhapsody

'Bohemian Rhapsody' was something that I'd wanted to do for a long while, actually. It wasn't something I'd given much thought to on previous albums, but I just felt that when it came to the fourth album I was going to do it.

Freddie Mercury

'Bohemian Rhapsody' was ground-breaking on so many levels, and it has never dated – which is true of every milestone track in history. Like 'I'm Not in Love', 10cc: another track which broke all sonic production barriers, and is still as fresh as a daisy. The Beach Boys' 'Good Vibrations': you could put it on right this second, and it would sound as good as when you first heard it. Phil Spector's 'Be My Baby': the moment you hear that opening beat, you want to dance . . . A mark of great record production is that it stands this test of time. Every good record has to start with a good song. But you can't separate the song from the production. To an extent it's that gargantuan production which echoes in our heads, even if we hear the song played without all that.

Steve Levine, record producer

Queen were unprepared for the 'Beatlemania' which awaited them in Tokyo in April 1975. More than 3,000 hysterical fans crammed into the arrivals hall of Haneda international airport, many of them brandishing home-made banners and Queen discs. With *Sheer Heart Attack* and 'Killer Queen' both at Number One, and every Japan gig sold out well in advance, their heroes' welcome should have come as no surprise. Perhaps it didn't, to Freddie, who rose majestically to the occasion, waving and smiling happily. One reporter joked that he probably felt so at home there because he didn't have to hide his buck teeth – so many Japanese fans appeared to have them too. Not only did he warm instantly to their legions of fans, he was intoxicated by the place itself. What better than an ancient, far-flung land to ignite his dormant sense of the exotic – especially to someone removed and estranged from his own? Everything fascinated him, from Japan's history, traditions and culture to its advanced technological lifestyle. He would soon become an avid collector of Japanese porcelain, paintings and other works of art.

The country and the man had plenty in common. Like Freddie, Japan was a mass of contradictions: an old curiosity with a complex, multifaceted personality. To him, the names of her thousand islands echoed like magic spells: Hokkaido, Honshu, Kyushu, Shikoku. He was drawn to the gentle and stoical Japanese, who had survived centuries of feudal oppression to rise with such serenity from the Second World War. Freddie rushed about, soaking up everything. He feasted on sushi and sake, bartered for dolls, silk kimonos and lacquer boxes. He frequented the infamous bath-houses and the *kage-me-jaya* ('teahouses in the shadows', popularised by American GIs), and hung with the geishas – both kinds. He befriended Akihiro Miwa, a beautiful drag queen who produced and directed his own cabaret on the Ginza (Tokyo's equivalent of the Parisian Pigalle or London's Soho). After Freddie's first visit, Miwa (at seventy-five still sporting bright yellow shoulder-length hair), took to performing Queen songs in tribute to his new pal.

'The only place Freddie was ever a classic tourist was Japan,' his PA Peter Freestone would later remember. 'Things Japanese were an all-consuming passion for him, whereas everywhere else he stayed in the world was merely a bed for the night.'

Queen's first and last shows on the tour, at Tokyo's Nippon Budokan Hall, were unforgettable. Not even the bulk of their Sumo wrestler security guards was enough to hold back a 10,000-strong throng of hysterical teenaged girls. At one point during the opening show, Freddie was forced to halt proceedings to beg the fans, for the sake of their own safety, to take deep breaths and calm down. It was the same story in every city they played.

Good news and bad news on their return to the UK. Now the toast of the exasperatingly fickle British media, with an Ivor Novello and a Belgian Golden Lion Award for 'Killer Queen' to their names, the band were still weathering the Trident storm. From the Sheffields' point of view, they had invested more than £200,000 in a new band. *Sheer Heart Attack* alone had cost £30,000 to make – peanuts when compared to today's recording costs, but exorbitant at the time. Now that they were having hits, they had expected to start turning a profit, but to their dismay found that they still owed Trident a relative fortune. That they appeared to the outside world to have made it, but were still broke, Queen found unbearable. Their only option was to knuckle down and get on with writing yet more songs for yet another album. The process was not without tension as they began to take out their frustrations on each other, fuelling rumours that they'd decided to disband. Such gossip was just what Queen needed to make them see sense and call a truce. They were in this together. Agreement with Trident was reached, in which the band would be released from their contracts in return for a compensatory £100,000 one-off payment and a 1 per cent royalty on the next six albums. Not that they had the cash to settle this at the time. They were now, however, able to sign new deals with EMI Records UK and Elektra USA. They'd get by with a little help from their friends.

★　　★　　★

August 1975 saw Queen rehearsing tracks at a rented house in Herefordshire for their fourth album, *A Night at the Opera*. The title was taken from a comedy film by the Marx Brothers, which had been a hit in 1935 and which Queen adored. They then decamped back to Rockfield, which would acquire legendary status as the studios used for the backing track of 'Bohemian Rhapsody'. When Freddie pitched up with it, recalled Brian, 'He seemed to have the whole thing worked out in his head.'

The song, an epic undertaking comprising an *a cappella* introduction, an instrumental sequence of piano, guitar, bass and drums, a mock-operatic interlude and a loaded rock conclusion, at first seemed insurmountable.

'We were all a bit mystified as to how he was going to link all these pieces,' said Brian.

The song brought to life a host of obscure classical characters: Scaramouche, a clown from the *commedia dell'arte*; astronomer Galileo; Figaro, the principal character in Beaumarchais' *The Barber of Seville*, and *The Marriage of Figaro*, from which operas by Paisiello, Rossini and Mozart had been composed; Beelzebub: identified in the Christian New Testament as Satan, Prince of Demons, but in Arabic as 'Lord of the Flies', or 'Lord of the heavenly dwelling'. Also in Arabic, the word *bismillah'*, which is a noun from a phrase in the Qur'an: '*bismi-llahi r-rahmani r-rahiim*', meaning 'in the name of God, most gracious, most merciful'.

I once put to Freddie, at a party in his hotel suite in Budapest in 1986, my own theory regarding these figures from 'Bohemian Rhapsody'. Scaramouche had to be Freddie himself, didn't he? His return to the tearful-clown theme in his songwriting (Pagliacci in 'It's a Hard Life') gave us a clue. Galileo Galilei the sixteenth-century astronomer, mathematician, physicist and father of modern science stood for scholarly Brian, surely. Beelzebub was clearly Roger, Queen's wildest party animal, with 'a devil put aside' for his pal. I was pushing it with an ironic reference to John, 'the shy one', whom I saw as Figaro – not the operatic character, but the tuxedo kitten from Disney's 1940 animated feature film *Pinocchio*. Well, Freddie did love his cats. Maybe not . . . but as Freddie said, all theories are allowed. He had never given away anything about the meaning of 'Bo Rap', telling even his DJ chum Kenny Everett that it was 'random rhyming nonsense'. So why would he come clean to me? I never expected him to. He stared at me for a moment before responding with a Mona Lisa smile.

That seemingly endless recording process took its toll on all concerned – not least, thanks to the layering and overlaying of endless vocals, on the actual tape.

'People think it's this legendary story,' said Brian, 'but you could hold the tape up to the light and see through it . . . every time Freddie added another "Galileo", we lost something'.

At Sarm East and Scorpio Studios in London, a feast of over-dubbing began. This was not without incident, as friend and former artist Robert Lee recalls.

'I had just started recording as part of Levinsky/Sinclair [a duo signed to Tony Stratton-Smith's Charisma, familiar from *The Kenny Everett Show*],' says Lee, who now edits The Who's official website.

'Freddie was friendly with a flatmate of mine, and we used to go antique shopping of a Friday morning in Portobello. I remember he always had impeccable taste: I still have two Chinese prints he insisted I buy when I was looking for a present for my mum . . . I nicked them back after she passed away.

'John Sinclair – now a rabbi living in Jerusalem – owned Sarm Studios at the end of Brick Lane. His sister Jill was there, bless her.' (She has since suffered a tragic accident.)

'Queen were in, mixing "Bohemian Rhapsody". Roy Thomas Baker at the helm. Freddie and co. at the desk. It was a twenty-four-track mega-mix, involving slave reels [bearing submixes of tracks from a master reel, to record overdubs against], pre-mixes, and rehearsals for the mix. So many faders had to be precisely cued, it was really tricky. They spent hours and hours trying to get it right, never quite succeeding. And then, miracle, this was the one. Everything was going perfectly. They were getting through it, nearly at the end. Everyone was tense with adrenalin, but very happy. And then, suddenly, the lights went out . . . and in walks Jill, proudly carrying a huge cake aglow with candles, and she was singing "Happy Birthday dear Freddie, Happy Birthday to you!" and they had to start all over again . . .'

'Is this the real life . . . is this just Battersea,' sings Allan James with a smile. '"Bohemian Rhapsody" was parodied from day one: the sincerest form of flattery. Queen changed everything with a six-minute single.'

'The recording was a sheer work of art,' says Searchers bass player Frank Allen, 'over and above what most other outfits were offering at the time. The way they layered their pieces at a time when we had only reached twenty-four analogue track machines, a lot back then but remarkably modest and limiting now, was so impressive, and of course culminated in their tour de force, "Bohemian Rhapsody". Even now it is mind-boggling how they achieved it. Every new layer of harmony meant a degeneration of sound quality, and the gap between brilliance and disaster was alarmingly narrow. They came away with brilliance in spades.'

It was not obvious at the time how much Freddie Mercury and Elton John had in common. Little did they know, in 1975, that Elton would be one of the last to hold Freddie's hand as he lay dying sixteen years later.

They had first met, briefly, in the late 1960s, when Freddie saw the then-little-known singing pianist perform at the famous Crawdaddy Club in Richmond, Surrey. The club was known around the world for hosting top American blues acts, and for its support of The Rolling Stones. Launched by filmmaker Giorgio Gomelsky at the end of 1962, it was originally located at the Station Hotel opposite Richmond railway station. It later moved to the local athletic ground to accommodate more fans. The Crawdaddy had staged early shows by Eric Clapton with The Yardbirds, Led

Zeppelin and Rod Stewart, and was precisely the kind of venue to which Freddie aspired. That was something to dream about when he started sitting as a naked life model in his college's Art evening class for a tenner a week.

To those on intimate terms with both Elton and Freddie, there were uncanny similarities. Both, in boyhood, had been devoted to their mothers. Both had been reclusive, sensitive children who had taken piano lessons from an early age. Both had changed their names – Elton from Reginald Kenneth Dwight to Elton Hercules John; like Freddie, he had picked the name of a mythological Roman god. Elton's road to stardom had also been long, winding and obstacle-strewn. Each had been at odds with his looks, and had developed an outlandish style – in Elton's case eccentric spectacles, platform boots, feathered and fringed outfits – to disguise his self-perceived ugliness. Each was confused to say the least about his sexuality.

James Saez, a musician, producer and engineer in Los Angeles who has worked with Madonna, Led Zeppelin, Radiohead and Red Hot Chili Peppers, believes that sexuality was the key to both Elton's and Freddie's artistry.

'Was there any bigger struggle than being a homosexual in the Seventies and trying to expose yourself without, well, exposing yourself?' wonders James.

'It seems pretty plausible that Elton created a whole persona for himself, which was full of costumes and theatrics, in order to handle this dilemma and still open himself up. I would assume that "Farrokh" was dealing with similar struggles. The thing that always cut me about him was that as strong and charismatically flamboyant as Freddie looked, he still somehow seemed really fragile and almost innocent.'

For Elton, as for Freddie, there had been girlfriends, and what looked to the outside world like conventional romance. German recording engineer Renate Blauel is said to remain heartbroken by the failure of her brief marriage to Elton in 1984. He has been openly gay since 1988, and entered a civil partnership with film-maker David Furnish in 2005; they have a son, Zachary Jackson Levon Furnish-John, born to a surrogate mother on Christmas Day 2010.

Freddie's and Elton's personalities developed in parallel, and they grew to depend on each other's friendship.

'Elton's a good old cookie, isn't he?' remarked Freddie. 'I love him to death and I think he's fabulous. To me, he's like one of those last Hollywood actresses of any worth. He has been a pioneer in rock 'n' roll. The first time I met him he was wonderful, one of those people you can instantly get on with. He said he liked "Killer Queen", and anyone who says that goes in my white book. My black book is bursting at the seams!'

But a more tragic dimension to their similarities would soon emerge. As one psychoanalyst would say of Elton in 'Tantrums & Tiaras', the TV documentary produced by David Furnish, 'He was born an addict. He is a totally obsessive-compulsive person. If it hadn't been alcohol, it would have been drugs. If it hadn't been drugs, it would have been food. If it hadn't been food, it would have been relationships. And if it hadn't been relationships, it would have been shopping. And you know what, I think he's got all five.' It was a verdict with which Elton himself did not disagree. As a result of his courage in allowing these views to be aired, the singer experienced an enormous upsurge in public support. It was a virtual mirror image of the person Freddie became in the mid-Eighties, when fame and all its diversions took their toll.

In 1975, the most significant thing the pair had in common was a feisty Scot named John Reid.

The twenty-six-year-old Paisley-born impresario, a power-hungry mogul controlling a business worth £40 million, had arrived via a circuitous route. Having worked in a men's outfitter's, his first job in the music business was as a record plugger. Socially-ambitious Reid had risen through the ranks, cultivated high-profile friendships, and was Elton's live-in lover for around five years, becoming his manager when Reid was still only twenty-one. Reid was another man who dithered over his sexuality: by 1976 he had switched sides, if only briefly, and was engaged to teenaged Sarah Forbes, a publicist from his own Rocket Records office. Sarah is the daughter of film director Bryan Forbes and actress Nanette Newman. She did survive the fall-out, and went on to marry actor John Standing (aka Sir John Ronald Leon Standing, fourth Baronet of Bletchley Park). Reid's business relationship with Elton survived for twenty-eight years, but ended acrimoniously. In 2000, Elton began a multimillion pound High Court battle against Reid, claiming mishandling of business affairs.

Also in 1975, Elton teamed up with a second Scot carving a name for himself: Rod Stewart. Both had worked with Long John Baldry, and had agreed to co-produce an album designed to revive Baldry's flagging career. It was during sessions for this LP that they hit upon the old theatrical custom of calling themselves by women's names. Elton was dubbed Sharon Cavendish, a name which he would use routinely on tour. Rod was Phyllis, after the actress Phyllis Diller. Baldry became Ada, and John Reid was Beryl, in homage to British actress Beryl Reid. When Freddie found out, he had to join in, and became Melina, after Greek actress Melina Mercouri. Cliff Richard, because of the vast number of framed records he'd been awarded down the decades, was Silvia Disc. Neil Sedaka, for similar reasons, was Golda Disc. Freddie would one day employ an entire entourage known by female names. His PA was Phoebe (Peter Freestone), his former lover turned chef was Liza (Joe Fanelli), and his personal manager Paul Prenter was Trixie. Nor were friends and band members immune: Brian was Maggie, as in Rod's hit 'Maggie May'. Roger was Liz, for Elizabeth Taylor. David Nutter, brother of famous tailor Tommy Nutter, was Dawn, and Mick Jagger's assistant and Freddie's long-standing friend, Tony King, became Joy. Mary Austin, taking things the other way, was Steve, as in TV's *The Six Million Dollar Man*, Steve Austin. Did she mind?

'Nobody was *allowed* to mind!' laughed Phoebe. 'You knew that someone was accepted if they got "a name". John Deacon never had one, curiously. Perhaps because he was so shy.'

With Elton in self-imposed semi-retirement after an arduous six-year global slog, John Reid, now running Elton's own label, Rocket Records, as well as managing the star, was keen to expand his empire. He jumped, inevitably, at the chance of managing Queen. Although the band had other possible managers in their sights – Led Zeppelin's Peter Grant, The Who's tour manager Peter Rudge and 10cc's Harvey Lisberg among them – a process of elimination led to Reid getting the gig. It was not what anyone would have called ideal, despite the fact that Reid's first, impressive move was to raise the £100,000 necessary for the band to pay off Trident. He did this simply by going to EMI for an advance against future publishing royalties.

Elton denounced it to their mutual manager as a sure-fire flop. EMI and the industry in general voiced misgivings. Radio stations wondered what the hell they were supposed to do with a six-minute single. Even bassist John Deacon expressed his fears, albeit in private, that to release 'Bohemian Rhapsody' would prove the greatest error of judgement of Queen's career. For a song that was to enter the annals of music history as *the* all-time rock classic, it had the shakiest of starts. Even those who recognised its magnificence immediately were reluctant to go on record, so dramatic was the departure of 'Bohemian Rhapsody' from any previous accepted convention of rock.

Who knew what really ignited Freddie's imagination and inspired him to create this song? Soaring and decadent, brimming with thinly-disguised personal agony and ecstasy, it is an impossible blend of baroque and ballad, of Music Hall and monster rock. Its incongruous elements are held together by a string of cacophonic guitar-grindings, classical piano sequences, sweeping orchestral arrangements and rich, multifaceted chorales, all dubbed, overdubbed and overdubbed again to the point that, depending on one's mood, it can be unbearable to listen to. There can be few rock fans on the planet who don't know it by heart.

'Even though it was the most amazing piece of work, revolutionary and incredible, I'm so bored with it now,' admits Radio 2 producer and record collector Phil Swern.

'It comes up with alarming regularity on playlists, and it is pretty well played to death. Still, no one could deny what an outstandingly clever piece of work it is. Nearly six minutes long, and it broke every rule. What comes close? Always The Beatles: "A Day in the Life" (the final track on their 1967 album *Sgt Pepper's Lonely Hearts Club Band*, 5.03 minutes). Led Zeppelin's "Stairway to Heaven" (8.02 minutes, and the most requested song on FM radio shows in the States, although it was never released as a single there). And "McArthur Park" (7.21 minutes) by Jimmy Webb and recorded by Richard Harris.'

'Get far enough away from it and perspective changes everything,' points out Paul Gambaccini.

'It's hard to get excited today about your three-and-a-half-minute rock song or pop record when lengthy masterpieces like "Bohemian Rhapsody", "McArthur Park", "Hey Jude", "Light My Fire" and "American Pie" have already been made. No one aspires to that level of musical achievement any more. We can now look back on these works as artistic achievements of the highest order. Don McLean didn't make "American Pie" to be a single, because he couldn't imagine it was possible for it to *be* a single. It was eight and a half minutes long. It was the record company who divided it in two. Don was a pure artist who couldn't even have conceived "American Pie" as a hit. It was clearly a masterpiece, but he recorded it as one long album track. The same goes for "Bohemian Rhapsody", which was the last track on Queen's 1975 album *A Night at the Opera*.

'OK, yes, Freddie wrote the song,' adds Paul, 'but Brian did that incredible guitar passage in the middle, Roger did the high notes, and John contributed, of course. To spread out the contributions in that way is fantastic, as they would later do with their own individual compositions, and I'm sure it's what helped keep them going as a group. It took the genius of Kenny Everett to hear and see "Bohemian Rhapsody" as a classic single.'

Everett, known as 'Ev', a close friend of Freddie's, was a Merseyside-born former Radio Luxembourg presenter and friend of The Beatles, who made his name as a Radio 1 DJ, and as presenter and comedian of his own *Kenny Everett Video* and *Kenny Everett Television* shows. He was diagnosed with HIV in 1989, and died of AIDS complications in 1995, aged fifty. In 1966, Ev married former pop singer 'Lady Lee' Middleton, singer Billy Fury's former girlfriend, who would eventually become the psychic and spiritual healer Lee Everett Alkin. The couple separated in 1979, when Everett came out. It is widely believed that he was infected by his promiscuous Russian lover Nikolai Grishanovitch, who was infamous in gay circles ('that careless twat Nikolai') for having done more to spread HIV around London during the early 1980s than any other individual. A former Red Army soldier who succumbed to the disease himself in 1990, Grishanovitch is sometimes named as the person who infected Freddie – although several people I spoke to believe it was the late Ronnie Fisher, a former CBS/Sony publicist.

'I don't think the dates fit on the "Nikolai-infected-Freddie" theory,' reasons Paul Gambaccini.

'I don't recall meeting Nikolai until the year [1987] the government made the original AIDS-awareness ads – because I remember meeting him with Freddie when the ads were about to come out. Freddie showed his first symptoms within one or two years of this. Bearing in mind that the average time between infection and onset of symptoms was ten years, this is just too short a time. Besides, I knew Freddie had been what our parents would have called "loose" since the late Seventies, which is a perfect match for the ten-year average. It's not impossible that it was Nikolai . . . but really unlikely.

'I don't know where Freddie and Nikolai met,' adds Paul, 'but I would not have been surprised if it had been at the Coleherne in Earl's Court. This was one of Freddie's favourite pubs [the other being the London Apprentice in Shoreditch], and had the distinction of being within walking distance of Freddie's home. This was the pub in which it is commonly assumed HIV was introduced to London by an American visitor. His entire circle fell to the disease.'

As 'Ev' and Freddie were movers and shakers on the same gay and music business scenes, it was inevitable that their paths would cross.

'I never thought that Freddie and Kenny were lovers,' says Paul. 'Had they been, I would have thought that everyone in our circle would have known. The reason I never entertained the thought they were is because their sexual personae were too similar. Of course, that means nothing in terms of one-nighters amongst two curious persons, but the idea just doesn't gain traction in my head. To be blunt, they were just silly together.'

Everett played a pivotal role in getting 'Bohemian Rhapsody' released as a single, and was famously first to air the track. A demo was sent to him with strict instructions not to broadcast it, but simply to get back to Freddie with his opinion. Everett adored the track, and played it fourteen times over one weekend, claiming to his boss on every play that 'his finger slipped'. While his cheek helped bring the most popular track of all time to the attention of the metropolis, it is disputed as to whether he made it a nationwide hit.

'In 1975 I had my own daily Radio 1 show,' says "Diddy" David Hamilton, of his hugely popular programme which attracted sixteen million listeners daily.

'The line-up was Noel Edmonds on the *Breakfast Show*, Tony Blackburn mid-morning, Johnnie Walker over lunch, me after lunch. We'd all have our Record of the Week. It would obviously have been very easy to pick Abba or the Bee Gees, as all their singles were automatically hits. But sometimes you'd think outside the box. That

October, along came the well-known record plugger Eric Hall to see me.

'I was living in a flat in Hallam Street behind BBC Broadcasting House, and I'd often get records dropped off to me at home,' remembers Diddy.

'Eric turned up this particular day with "Bohemian Rhapsody", going "Monster! Monster! This could be a big hit!" When I listened to it, I remember thinking that it was totally different from any pop record I'd ever heard before. It was innovative. Operatic. It soared and swooped and got under your skin. You couldn't stop humming bits of it. It got very mixed reviews in the office. Tony Blackburn said he didn't understand it. No one else seemed to like it very much. Compared to the disco sound going down at the time – K.C. and the Sunshine Band's "That's the Way I Like It" and all that – it was unique. Queen were so different. The Stones were the traditional rock band. This band could rock, but they were not essentially rockers. There is a difference.

'I told my producer Paul Williams that I wanted it as my "Hamilton Hotshot". He agreed. The record, of course, went on to be Number One for a record nine weeks, and by January 1976 had sold more than a million here, was a multimillion seller all over the world, and is arguably the greatest pop song of all time. I like to think that I played my part in that. I was always very proud of my Hotshot choices, and that one didn't let me down. Much has been made over the years of Kenny Everett having stolen a copy of the single ahead of release, playing it endlessly on Capital Radio, and then claiming that he introduced it to the world. He gave it enormous backing, and then took a lot of the credit for it having become a hit. But Capital was in those days exclusively a *London* station. Nobody else in the UK was hearing it at that time. Radio 1 never got the credit for bringing the single to the attention of the nation!'

The single would reach Number One again for five weeks in 1991, when it was re-released following Freddie's death. It became the UK's third best-selling single of all time, and topped charts around the world. In the US, the record made Number Nine in 1976, and then returned to the chart there in 1992 thanks to the massive popularity of the movie *Wayne's World*, which famously paid homage to 'Bohemian Rhapsody'.

The late Tommy Vance, one of the biggest names in rock broadcasting, with shows on London's Capital, Radio 1, Virgin Radio and VH-1 rock TV for MTV, described 'Bohemian Rhapsody' as 'the rock equivalent of the assassination of JFK'.

'We all remembered what we were doing when we first heard it,' he told me. 'I was doing the weekend rock show on Capital at the time. I heard it and thought it was a lunatic asylum of a pop song. It was so magnificently obscure, it had to make it. Technically, the song's a mess. It follows no known conventional nor commercial formula. It is just a string of dreams, flashbacks, flash-forwards, vignettes, completely disjointed ideas. It changes sequence, colour, tone, tempo, all for no apparent reason – which is exactly what opera does. But the intent was remarkable. It was the ultimate optimism. It had an indefinable quality, some remarkable magic. It is brilliant. And it is still revered as an icon today. What other song stands up against it? Absolutely fuck all. But try to dissect "Bohemian Rhapsody's" lyrics, and you'll find that it's meaningless.'

Oscar-winning lyricist Sir Tim Rice, co-creator of some of the greatest shows in stage-musical history, including *Joseph and the Amazing Technicolour Dreamcoat, Jesus Christ, Superstar* and *Evita* – and co-writer of songs with Freddie for the 1988 Montserrat Caballé extravaganza *Barcelona*, begs to differ.

'It's fairly obvious to me that this was Freddie's "coming-out song",' he tells me.

'I've even spoken to Roger about it. I heard the record very early on, and it struck me that there is a very clear message contained in it. This is Freddie saying "I'm coming out. I'm admitting that I'm gay."

'Yes, he was admitting his homosexuality to himself initially . . . but then, by default, to the rest of the world, because it was such a huge hit everywhere. "Mama, I just killed a man . . ." He's killed the old Freddie he was trying to be: the former image. "Put a gun against his head, pulled my trigger, now he's dead" – *he's* dead, the "straight" person he was originally. "Mama, life had just begun, but now I've gone and thrown it all away . . . " I mean, this is just my theory, but it *does* fit. He's shot and destroyed the man he was trying to be, and now this is him, trying to live with the new Freddie. It's very obscure, of course. But think about that middle bit: "I see a little silhouetto of a man . . . " that's him, still being haunted by what he's done and what he is. It works for me. Every time I hear the record on the radio, I think of him trying to shake off one Freddie and embracing another – even all these years after his death. Do I think he managed it? I think he was in the *process* of managing it, rather well. Freddie was an exceptional lyricist, and "Bohemian Rhapsody" is beyond any doubt one of the great pieces of music of the twentieth century.'

An echo, then, of the song's composer himself? Freddie resolutely avoided explanations.

'Does it mean this, does it mean that, is all anybody wants to know,' Freddie sighed. 'Fuck them, darling. I will say no more than what any decent poet would tell you if you dared ask him to analyse his work: if you see it, dear, then it's there.'

As far as Brian was concerned, it was vital that the song's meaning remain obscure.

'I don't think we'll ever know, and if I knew I probably wouldn't want to tell you anyway,' he said.

'I certainly don't tell people what my songs are about. I find that it destroys them in a way, because the great thing about a great song is that you relate it to your own personal experiences in your own life. I think that Freddie was certainly battling with problems in his personal life, which he might have decided to put into the song himself. He was certainly looking at recreating himself. But I don't think at that point in time it was the best thing to do, so he actually decided to do it later.'

I believe Brian meant that Freddie was resisting the inevitable: having to end his relationship with Mary to start a new life as a homosexual. But the thought of doing so terrified him, so he kept putting it off – not least because he dreaded the effect it would have on his parents. Coming out could have made his life so much easier in the long run, as it had for Kenny Everett, who alienated neither his fans nor his wife with his honesty. As Lee Everett told me, 'He was what he was. Didn't stop me loving him. We remained devoted to each other until the end.'

'Had Freddie come out to the world, it would have been as no one else coming out,' points out Simon Napier-Bell.

'It wouldn't have been like George Michael, who only came out when he was forced to, and anyway wasn't really a rock star, just high-class pop. Had Freddie come out, he would have rubbed homophobe noses in their own hypocrisy, and it would have been a smaller step than he thought – because to all his friends he was already out, and outrageous.

'When he said he was different in his private life from the performer he was on stage, what he really meant was that he was forced to retire into his shell because of the fear his Parsee family would have had of him coming out. Had he come out from the beginning, his long, slow death would have been something that the gay community could have thanked him for. They would have used it to their advantage, turned it into something wonderfully, tragically showbusiness, and made him the new Judy Garland. He might even have found himself enjoying it!'

'Bohemian Rhapsody' may well have been an allegory of the new, liberated Freddie killing the old persona and revelling in his true self, once hidden but at last revealed, according to The Searchers' bassist Frank Allen:

'But it might be something different entirely. I am not privy to the information, and I never asked him. When Don McLean was asked about the meaning of "American Pie", he replied, "It means I don't ever have to work again." Perhaps the reality of "Bohemian Rhapsody" contains a comparably innocent and more direct truth. I'm not clever enough to judge. I am content just to enjoy it as a beautifully-constructed major work in pop music. Magnificently assembled, it resulted in a three-piece suite of different time signatures and moods that approximated the great classics. In a pop sense, it worked in a way that no one had experienced ever before.'

As Tommy Vance pointed out, what really proved the worth of 'Bohemian Rhapsody' was neither its ground-breaking lyrics nor those brain-scrambling melodies. No amount of speculation as to its meaning, nor even unprecedented airplay, made it a hit. What did so was television.

12

Fame

'Bohemian Rhapsody' was one of the first videos to get the kind of attention that videos get now, and it only cost about five thousand pounds. We decided we should put "Rhapsody" on film, and let people see it. We didn't know how it was going to be looked upon, or how they were going to receive it. To us, it was just another form of theatre. But it went crazy. We recognised that a video could get to a lot of people in a lot of countries without you actually being there, and you could release a record and a video simultaneously. It became very fast and it helped record sales greatly.

Freddie Mercury

Every great artist gets his moment in history, but he's got to be ready for it. He's got to know that it could come at him at any time, and be ready for that ball, and catch it, and not drop it. If they get it right, they deliver a song which touches every man, woman and child. The sentiment is universal, it gets under your skin and it lives there for all time. The genius, the magic, is in creating something like that and then being able to get it across, and make it meaningful and exciting. It is no use having genius and keeping it to yourself.

Jonathan Morrish

'It was the first hit generated by a visual,' says former record plugger Allan James. 'Previously, The Beatles' visuals and so on were just fun little films to run alongside the singles. No one ever knew how to take Queen. It's why it took the video to really break them. After that, you could no longer dismiss them as just some quirkly camp rock band. They sent the entire industry in another direction.'

'The chart progress of "Bohemian Rhapsody" forced *Top of the Pops* to give it a chance,' remembered DJ Tommy Vance. 'Because they *had* to play it if a record got into the Top Thirty. The more they played it, the further up the charts it went. What was really incredible was that the video, directed by Bruce Gowers and produced by Lexi Godfrey for Jon Roseman Productions, was shot for just five thousand pounds.'

The video proved to be the making of Gowers, who went on to direct TV's *American Idol*. Gowers became the go-to producer-director for music and comedy specials, which he created for, among others, Michael Jackson, The Rolling Stones, Paul McCartney, and Britney Spears, Robin Williams, Billy Crystal and Eddie Murphy.

'Gowers was making a performance video with the band at Elstree,' recalled Vance, 'and shot the video for "Bohemian Rhapsody" on the same day in just four hours. It was truly creative stuff. He used prisms, for example, to create certain visual effects, long before electronics and computers. Where did he get his ideas from? He was inspired by the record. It was a collective of so many thrilling concepts that Bruce's ideas just flowed. But the fundamental concept was based on a previous album cover, which Bruce had to bring to life.'

That was the sleeve of *Queen II* (1974), featuring a stark black-and-white group shot, heads-only of each band member apart from Freddie, who appears in the centre with his hands folded like wings across his chest. The idea for that shot had been the brainwave of photographer Mick Rock.

'The band's brief for that album jacket *was* brief,' says Rock. 'It would be a gatefold, with a black-and-white theme. It would feature the band. Beyond that, it was my problem. I would art-direct and photograph it. As it happened, I had recently become friends with John Kobal, who was a keen collector of early Hollywood stills.'

Kobal, the late Austrian-born Canadian film historian and author had been an authority on Hollywood's Golden Age.

'In return for a photo session with himself, John gave me some prints from his collection,' explains Rock.

'Among them was one I'd never seen before, of Marlene Dietrich from the film *Shanghai Express*. Her arms were folded, and she was wearing black against a black background, and it was exquisitely lit. Her tilted head and hands seemed to be floating. I saw the connection immediately. It was one of those visceral, intuitive things. Very strong. Very clear. Glamorous, mysterious and classic. I would transpose it into a four-headed monster. They had to go for it. So I went to Freddie. He saw it too. He understood. He loved it immediately. And he sold the rest of the band on it. "I shall be Marlene," he laughed. "What a delicious thought!"'

Any misgivings on the part of the rest of the band as to pretension were soon dismissed by Freddie.

'He loved to quote Oscar Wilde,' laughs Rock: '"Often, that which today is considered pretentious is tomorrow considered state of the art. The important thing is to be considered."'

This cover was the inspiration for Gowers's 'Bohemian Rhapsody' video, which the band realised was a vital performance as well as promotional tool, as it would be impossible to play the song live in its entirety. Gowers took an image that they had previously created, then embellished and developed it, and brought it as far forward as he dared.

'It became the first record to be pushed into the forefront by virtue of a video,' commented Vance. 'Today, Queen are widely credited with also having been the first band to do a surreal-ist promotional video, but that was not actually the case. They were, I think, preceded by Devo' – an American post-punk art rock band formed in 1973, who were early pioneers of the music video.

'But Queen were certainly the first band to create a "concept" video. The video captured the musical imagery perfectly. And I have to say it had bugger all to do with Freddie. The song was the song. The visual interpretation made it what the song became. Because every time the song had an echo, the pictures reverberated in the listener's mind. The two quickly became indivisible. You cannot hear that music without seeing the visuals in your mind's eye. You could say that "Bohemian Rhapsody" was the first single to be "seen" everywhere. Because this was the first video ever to promote a song in such a way.'

Mike Appleton recalled the excitement generated at the *OGWT* studio by the arrival of the video.

'A truly wonderful concept,' he said. 'I was utterly mesmerised. All I had to do was put it on screen. I can remember feeling blown away by Freddie, by the sense that there had never before been anything like him. Nor has there been since. He matured with "Bohemian Rhapsody". He suddenly seemed like the only adult in a business dominated by a lot of spoilt, petulant kids. Queen knew exactly what they were doing, and they were gentlemen with it. I have never known a band work so hard.'

Tony Brainsby's first reaction to the single was 'bizarre'.

'Everybody thought so. I loved it without really knowing why. But it represented a turning point for me. I had taken them from virtual obscurity and seen them through to one of the greatest hits of all time. I felt like a father who'd just given birth.'

Brainsby's ecstasy was short-lived. Queen's new managerial arrangements with John Reid rendered Brainsby's position untenable.

'John Reid made it difficult for me to work with Queen any longer,' he affirmed. 'He preferred to use his own in-house PR people. It became a no-no.'

There would be a comeback for Brainsby. But for now, if not

forever, Queen were in orbit with the man who owned the then biggest act in the world, the guy who made the Rocket Man fly.

A Night at the Opera was released on 21 November 1975 and launched at a lavish party which, Paul Gambaccini remembers, '. . . was John Reid's way of saying, "Here you go, Queen are now in Elton's league." Reid was well aware of what he had in Queen, but didn't realise how lucky his timing was. If ever there was a time to get Queen onto your books, it was at the release of that fourth album.'

Beyond the professional relationship he would enjoy with the group, Gambaccini formed personal friendships which were, in Freddie's case at least, to last a lifetime.

'They were always the model of rock musicians understanding what this crazy game was about. They knew that it was a business. They didn't expect to be each other's best friends. All they had to do, they knew, was get along, and respect each other. This relaxed, even-handed attitude saw them through difficulties that would have split up other acts.

'Freddie was the one I was most intimate with. He was one of those guys who, when you did meet him, you'd always go directly to the heart of the matter. He was extremely personal and honest. Not one for small talk. Part of this, I believe, is that I happened, like him, to be one of the rock world's gay people.'

Perhaps Freddie envied Gambaccini's courage in having openly declared his homosexuality, because he longed with all his heart to do the same?

'Perhaps. He once said to me, "One day we'll do an interview, and we'll tell it all." We never did. But I will say that he made me feel like a tourist,' Paul says, referring to Freddie's promiscuity, which was far greater than his own.

'It was like he was the *real* homosexual. But while I was out there being up-front about it, he was keeping it quiet, but being gay with a capital "G". I was just this little pretender, compared to him.'

Five days after the album's release, 'Bohemian Rhapsody' gave Queen their first Number One single. The band celebrated in style on a brief, twenty-four-date, pre-Christmas tour, playing an electrifying Christmas Eve gig at Hammersmith Odeon which was broadcast by both *OGWT* and Radio 1.

Three days later, the album also reached Number One, going platinum with sales of more than 250,000: a figure that would double within weeks. It would also hang in the American chart for fifty-six weeks. The New Year brought even more accolades, including another 'Ivor' for 'Bohemian Rhapsody'. Parsimonious Reid uncharacteristically took out ad-space in *Sounds* magazine, to congratulate his 'boys' on their success.

It was time to plan a second American tour, this time as major rock stars. Their most gruelling to date, it would land in almost every state, under the guidance of new tour manager Gerry Stickells. His was a well-starred appointment: Stickells had been both roadie and tour manager for The Jimi Hendrix Experience, and was allegedly with the star the night he died – although the tragedy was shrouded in mystery, and not something he made a habit of speaking about. Stickells remained with Queen until the end of their touring career.

It was on this colossal hit US tour that the band perfected the art of the post-gig party. Queen after-shows acquired cult status from then on as the best in the game. Wherever the band played, local dignitaries, celebrities and party people would be invited to sample Bacchanalian delights. Journalist Rick Sky, whose personal tribute to Freddie, *The Show Must Go On*, was published shortly after the singer's death, recalls a 'quiet, discreet bash' to celebrate the success of a gig at New York's hallowed Madison Square Garden.

'I had been invited to New York for an exclusive interview with Freddie, and found myself backstage,' said Sky.

'There were a dozen topless waitresses with magnums of champagne, filling your glass constantly. Nobody was allowed to run dry. Freddie was dressed in a white vest, and was holding a plastic cup of champagne and a cigarette. He seemed laid-back and relaxed. He told me that the secret of happiness was living life to the hilt.

'"Excess is a part of my nature," he said. "To me, dullness is a disease. I need danger and excitement. I was not made for staying indoors and watching television. I am definitely a sexual person. I used to say that I would go with anyone, but I have become more choosy. I love to surround myself with strange and interesting people, because they make me feel more alive. Straight people bore me stiff. I love freaky people. By nature I'm restless and highly strung, so I wouldn't make a good family man. Deep down I am a very emotional person, a person of real extremes, and that's often destructive both to myself and to others.

'"I live life to the full," he later said, provocatively. '"My sex drive is enormous. I sleep with men, women, cats – you name it. I'll go to bed with anything! My bed is so huge, I can comfortably sleep six. I prefer my sex without any involvement."'

Fame and wealth had bought Freddie freedom to indulge as much as he wanted.

'He was really going for it,' said Sky. 'But it must have compromised the urge to settle down into a full one-to-one relationship, which is the thing we all crave. As he said, "When I have a relationship, it is never half-hearted. I don't believe in half-measures or compromise. I give everything I've got, because that's the way I am."'

America, and in particular New York, had turned Queen's heads, especially Freddie's. He had fallen for the city in all its density and intensity, and not least its underground gay scene. If by day he swanked it in luxurious uptown stores, hotels and salons, by night he prowled the cobbled streets of the old downtown meat-packing district, today a gentrified enclave, where the most notorious gay clubs and bars were then to be found. Although most of these would close during the mid-1980s, in the wake of the AIDS epidemic, at the time they were a magnet for gays and lesbians from all over the States. The Stonewall Riots of June 1969, which launched gay liberation, had kicked off at the most popular illegal gay bar in New York. The seedy Stonewall Inn on Christopher Street off Seventh Avenue in the heart of Greenwich Village was later famous throughout the world as the cradle of gay power. The new homosexual glasnost legalised a lucrative industry serving the gay community. Sex palaces, porn theatres, bath houses, leather, S&M and 'back-room' bars with names like The Mineshaft and The Anvil sprang up in abundance, promoting the anonymous sexual encounter. In those days, sexually-transmitted diseases were not yet regarded as a serious threat.

It was at The Anvil club one night, according to Mick Rock, who was with him at the time, that Freddie first set eyes on one of the Village People. The late Seventies 'YMCA' send-up group, which toyed with American cultural stereotypes – the cowboy, the cop, the construction worker, the biker, the Native American, the GI – were then a hugely popular disco act. Rock reported that Freddie was 'utterly mesmerised' by the sight of Glenn Hughes, the 'biker', dancing on the bar.

As Rock remarked, 'Freddie was never the same again.'

The Anvil experience was presumed to be the inspiration for both the 'leather' and 'gay clone' looks which Freddie would adopt. While the 'leather' phase was short-lived, the 'clone' image, so far-removed from his Seventies Bohemian pose, and which favoured closely-cropped hair, bristly moustache, a muscular upper body and tight denim jeans, would last. The look had actually originated in San Francisco, and was referred to as the 'Castro clone' look, after the Castro district, a once dilapidated Irish neighbourhood of San Francisco that had served the Haight-Ashbury hippies. Thanks to an influx of homosexual refugees, it became Gay Main Street. At first, the look had been a disguise, because straight people tended not to recognise it as an exclusively gay identity. But from that one image grew an entire code of homosexual behaviour. A gay man could even indicate his sexual preference by the colour of the handkerchief hanging from his back pocket.

'Hanky Code' or 'Bandana Code' was widely used among homosexuals in the late Seventies. Handkerchiefs were worn in the rear trouser pocket or threaded through belt loops: on the left side of the body for 'tops', the right for 'bottoms', as in whether your preference was over or under. While there is no universally-recognised colour code, some of the better-known include yellow for 'watersports', brown for 'scat', black for 'S&M', purple for 'into piercing', red for . . . let's not go there, light blue for 'oral', grey for 'bondage', and orange for 'anything goes'.

One of the most thrilling aspects of New York, to a newly world-famous Freddie in the late Seventies, was that homosexuality was a political triumph. Gays were out, united, and in charge of their lifestyle and destiny. Things could only get better. So they thought. The boundaries of sexual experiment could be pushed to limits not possible in any other city in the world at that time, except perhaps Munich.

'Freddie was quite well-behaved in London, compared with how he was in New York, or later, in Munich,' said Paul Gambaccini.

'Those two cities were the capitals of anonymous, one-time-only sex – which never interested me in the least. Freddie undoubtedly enjoyed those places. It's a whole world, as rich in its magnitude as popular music is. I got the impression from him that his times in New York were always really wild, but the gay scene there at that time was much harder than anywhere.'

In a discussion with pop columnist turned publisher John Blake, Freddie confessed to 'slutting himself' in New York.

'It's sin city,' Freddie cooed. 'But you have to come away at the right time. Stay a day too long, and it grips you. Very hypnotic. It's all tripping in at eight or nine every morning, and taking throat injections so I can still sing. It's a real place. I love it.'

While vaguely admitting here to his wild promiscuity, Freddie maintained discreet silence about his passion for cocaine. Apart from the fact that the drug was highly illegal in most countries, certainly in Britain and the States, Freddie had never fitted the 'druggie' mould, and never wished to.

He would have loathed to be regarded as an addict. Not that he became one: when he decided to stop using the substance, he relinquished his habit overnight. But for now, he was living the sex, drugs and rock 'n' roll cliché. What Freddie was hooked on was the instant high, the effect that excessive booze and cocaine had on his personality and his libido. Cocaine boosted his confidence. It gave him the nerve to be Freddie Mercury.

If Freddie metamorphosed into the ultimate 'shopping and fuck-ing' hedonist in New York, it was primarily because he could afford to. Growing bored of even his favourite hotels – the Waldorf Astoria Towers, the Berkshire Place and the Helmsley Palace – he would buy himself a lavish, top-security apartment with stunning views of the Chrysler building (Freddie's favourite Manhattan landmark) as well as the Twin Towers and the Empire State Building. On the forty-third floor of the Sovereign Building at 425 East 58th Street between First Avenue and Sutton Place, and a short walk from Central Park, Bloomingdale's department store and the Carnegie Hall, the apartment boasted a balcony with a view of seven bridges, including the 59th Street bridge made famous by Simon and Garfunkel in the song also known as 'Feelin' Groovy'.

'He was the classic refined person who loved to slum it,' observed Rick Sky. 'His ultimate fantasy would be to take a rent boy to the opera. Rudolph Nureyev was very similar to Freddie in that he had that rare ability to adore high culture and low culture at the same time.'

Although Freddie loved ballet dancers, and a hot affair with Nureyev was rumoured – the Russian having written about his 'relationship' with Freddie and visits to his Kensington home in personal correspondence published in 1995 – Freddie's PA Peter Freestone denied this. Nureyev never came to Garden Lodge, Freestone insisted. The alleged romantic interlude never took place.

Few understood the motivation for Freddie's promiscuity and decadence. The rest of the band simply shrugged, and let him get on with it. The world had moved on in terms of acceptance of sexuality, and anyway, who were they to judge? What Freddie chose to get up to in his private life was his business. Sexual orientation was only one facet of the whole. The fans tended to accept what they knew, turning a blind eye to the rest. It was only the media that got excited whenever there was a whiff of scandal. Later it was apparent that Freddie was one of the few rock superstars intelligent enough to perceive that ordinary folk adored him for daring. They loved him for trying and tasting life's dangers to excess, in a way they would never dream of doing. As well as entertaining his swelling audiences with brilliant music and an unforgettable show, he was providing them with the ultimate vicarious thrill.

'We went to a Queen gig, interviewed Freddie, got to see the size of all their excesses – and we got to eat the crumbs,' Rick Sky points out.

'That made us as privileged as they were, relatively speaking. Queen were never selfish. They were always anxious that everyone else was having just a great a time as they were. There was this incredible generosity of spirit as well as a sharing of material riches which defined Queen, of all the rock bands we hung out with, as the best in the world'.

13

Champions

The album A Day at the Races *... ends with a Japanese thing, a track from Brian called "Teo Torriatte" which means "let us cling together". It's a very emotional track, one of his best. Brian plays harmonium and some lovely guitar. It's a nice song to close the album.*

Freddie Mercury

There was a strength and an energy in Queen music which was breath-taking. The way technology has moved on, people have become very lazy. Blood, sweat and guts is what it takes. It was down to Freddie perform-ing those songs with every fibre and cell. Today, you'll get one artist with eighteen dancers behind them, you don't know if it's a recording, or whether he's miming, or what on earth you're getting. With Freddie you got the lot, and it was real.

Leee John, Imagination

Come February 1976, with all four albums in the UK Top Twenty, Queen were primed for further live dates in Japan and Australia, where their records and gigs were on fire. Their return to Britain saw them back in the studio to begin work on their fifth album, to be produced by the band themselves, having parted amicably from Roy Thomas Baker. This next album would be entitled *A Day at the Races* – another favourite Marx Brothers movie. In March, their feature film *Live at The Rainbow* was released. In May, Brian took time off to marry his girlfriend Chrissy Mullen. On 18 June, John Deacon's first Queen single was released. 'You're My Best Friend', a mellow song written for his wife Veronica (to whom he is still married – the only Queen member to last with his original partner) featured Deacon playing a Wurlitzer electric piano as well as his bass guitar. Though it differed significantly from previous Queen releases, it was quickly received onto the Top Ten. The track's video was shot in a vast ballroom in a heatwave, lit by a thousand candles.

During the Scottish Festival of Popular Music that summer, which was part-sponsored by John Reid, Queen played two gigs at the Edinburgh Playhouse. They followed this with an open-air concert in Cardiff. On 18 September, the sixth anniversary of Jimi Hendrix's death, in a typically touching Queen gesture, they staged a massive free concert in London's Hyde Park to thank the fans for their support. Close to 200,000 turned up to enjoy the show. The day was co-organised by Richard Branson, then the high-flying boss of Virgin Records. When Branson introduced his PA Dominique Beyrand to the band, he unwittingly gifted Roger Taylor a new girlfriend. The couple soon set up home in Fulham, and in a luxurious Surrey mansion set in several wooded acres with its own recording studio.

Brilliant weather held out on the day of the gig, which harked back to those given in the park in the late Sixties by Jethro Tull, Pink Floyd and The Stones. Support artist Kiki Dee, also managed by John Reid, had been due to perform her new chart-topping single, a duet with Elton John. Despite many popular releases, 'Don't Go Breaking My Heart' was Elton's first Number One. But he failed to make it, and Kiki had to settle for singing beside a giant cardboard cut-out.

'Welcome to our little picnic on the Serpentine,' said Freddie, resplendent in glittering white catsuit.

' "Tie Your Mother Down" is one of Brian's heavies,' he remarked later. 'I remember we played it at Hyde Park . . . before we had actually recorded it. I was able to come to grips with the song in front of a live audience before I had to record the vocal in the studio. Being a very raucous track, it worked well for me.'

Fledgling photograpaher Denis O'Regan blagged his way into the backstage enclosure and wedged himself under the stage during Queen's set. He had made it his business to befriend Rocket Records employees in an attempt to get close to Queen, so that he could photograph them officially. One of John Reid's friends and henchmen, Paul Prenter, had taken a shine to Denis, and soon began allowing him access during their shows.

'One of the earliest he let me into was in Paris,' remembers Denis.

'I was in the backstage area, and noticed that they had built another little stage behind the scenes. I immediately thought that Queen were going to do an impromptu session. They had all these chairs set out in front of it. The next moment, this girl came on and did a strip. Then another one, and then another one, until there were a dozen women on this stage. They then did this giant lesbian act in front of us all. Just for the amusement and entertainment of those working and lurking backstage. All a bit seedy for its time, but that kind of thing became Queen's party theme. They would always go for boobs and bottoms and decadent sex. Nothing really that sordid about it, just the thing they did for a laugh. Their preoccupation with sexy stuff was deliberately cultivated, and seemed to project a different side of Queen. I imagine it would have put paid to any rumours at the time about Freddie being gay.'

Although they would have denied so at the time, Freddie and Roger were undoubtedly the brains behind these outrageous bashes.

'I like strip clubs and strippers and wild parties with naked women,' Roger said breezily, as if to add, 'why shouldn't I?'

The most unusual thing to strike Denis was that they were one of the only big bands to stick around after their own shows.

'Which I used to hate, because I just wanted to go out and have fun after the work was done. But they always used to have their dinner together after the show. Bands didn't do that. They did a runner, limos waiting at the stage door as they came off, ready to roar away to the airport or back to the hotel. Much later, I can remember thinking that there was a real element of camaraderie about that. I think they genuinely liked each other's company. Later on there were stories about them not getting on and travelling in separate limos and so on. But everyone does that when they're big news and they can afford it. Freddie, in a tour bus? You must be joking.'

Besides, as Roger remarked in *Q* magazine in 2011 about the 'separate limos' scenario: 'That was the easiest way to do it. Limos are the stupidest cars. There's really only room for two passengers, and you'd usually have your girlfriend or wife or whatever, companion, or your assistant with you. We could afford four, you know? It was nothing to do with not wanting to speak to one another.'

On 10 December the album was released, with advance orders of half a million. To promote it in style, EMI Records took a marquee at Kempton Park and sponsored a special '*Day at the Races*' hurdle. Lavish food, booze and live entertainment by the Tremeloes and Marmalade, plus a telegram from Groucho Marx himself, made it another memorable day. The album was to some extent a disappointment, given what had gone before. But the first single, 'Somebody to Love', written by Freddie, wearing his heart on his sleeve again, went straight to Number Four on the UK chart, and all the way to Number One at Radio Luxembourg.

'That track was me going a bit mad,' said Freddie. 'I just wanted to write something in the Aretha Franklin kind of mode. I was inspired by the gospel approach she had on her earlier albums. Although it might sound like the same approach on the harmonies, it is very different in the studio, because it's a different range.'

Christmas 1976 saw the band celebrating a Number One album,

with countless requests to appear on television and radio. The BBC repeated the Hammersmith Odeon *Whistle Test* concert from the previous year. Freddie's Christmas present to himself was an unusual one: he finally plucked up courage to be honest with both himself and the love of his life, Mary Austin, and ended their long-standing romantic relationship.

'We were closer than anybody else, though we stopped living together after about seven years,' Freddie admitted. 'Our love affair ended in tears, but a deep bond grew out of it, and that's something nobody can take away from us. It's unreachable.'

It must have been difficult for him. While he had come to prefer his sexual encounters without any emotional involvement, he also loved the comfort and security that a steady relationship brings. Juggling his conflicting needs had taken its toll. Moving out of the cosy nest they had shared together, Freddie decamped to an apartment at 12 Stafford Terrace in London's Kensington, and bought Mary a place of her own. She would remain his devoted assistant and 'coordinator', at his side almost daily until his death fifteen years later.

1977 brought unexpected challenges, in the shape of punk rock. Punks were ugly and angry types, opposed to decadent bands like Queen, who stood for everything the Sex Pistols and their ilk had decided had gone wrong with the music scene. It was an argument neither faction could win. There was only one thing for it. Another New Year, another three-month world tour of North America, this time with Phil Lynott's Thin Lizzy as support. The latest American shows proved as successful as the last, except for a couple of West Coast cancellations due to Freddie's throat.

'My nodules are still with me,' he said. 'I have these uncouth callouses growing in my interior. From time to time, they harm my vocal dexterity. At the moment, however, I am winning. I'm going easy on the red wine, and the tour will be planned around my nodules.'

It was during this tour that Freddie became involved with

twenty-seven-year-old chef Joe Fanelli. Once their affair was done with, Joe tended to come and go, working at a string of restaurants including the popular September's on London's Fulham Road, before becoming a full-time member of Freddie's household at Garden Lodge. Like the master himself, Fanelli too would succumb eventually to AIDS.

The European tour began in Stockholm and moved on to Britain, where it kicked off at the Bristol Hippodrome that May. At the London Earl's Court shows in June, proceeds from the second night of which were donated to Queen Elizabeth II's Jubilee Fund, the band introduced their special 'Crown' lighting rig, a huge construction that rose from the stage in a swirl of smoke and dry ice. No sooner had the tour concluded than they were back in the studio yet again, to record another new album. By now, Freddie, Brian, Roger and John were also venturing into the solo arena, as well as guesting on albums and singles by other artists.

If fame and fortune had begun to feel like a slog, at least music still got them out of bed in the mornings. There was always plenty of healthy tension, competition and one-upmanship in the studio to spur them on, while performances seemed to go better when they'd just had a good spat.

'Although he needed the emotional stability to record, it seemed that Freddie needed conflict and confrontation as a vital catalyst to performing,' his future personal assistant Peter Freestone would later remark.

This was undoubtedly driven by his perfectionism.

'Freddie knew in his mind exactly what he wanted, and was prepared to throw a tantrum to make sure everything went the way he desired . . . Freddie knew the value of the tantrum. To throw one to greatest effect, it had to be done to either the band or business associates . . . He knew that the other people involved knew that *he* knew that *he* was indispensable.'

Their next major single, 'We Are the Champions', would prove to be one of their best-loved and most enduring anthems. While poorly received by a British press locked for the moment in the maelstrom of punk rock, it made Number Two on both the UK and American Billboard charts, and gave Queen their first US Number One on trade paper *Record World*'s chart. Released as a double A-side with 'We Will Rock You' in the States, the 'Rock You' chant was adopted by legions of American football supporters, while 'Champions' was borrowed by both the New York Yankees and the Philadelphia 76-ers. Revenge was sweet. The song remains hugely popular in countless territories, thirty-five years on, and is played regularly at major sporting events throughout the world.

July to September was spent recording their sixth studio album, *News of the World*, at Notting Hill's Basing Street Studios, founded by Chris Blackwell of Island Records fame (the studios later became Sarm West, world-famous as the venue where Band Aid's 'Do They Know It's Christmas?' was recorded), and at the now-defunct Wessex in Highbury New Park, where Johnny Rotten once threw up in the piano. Bizarrely, at the same time as Queen were in, the Sex Pistols were recording *Never Mind the Bollocks* in an adjacent studio. On one occasion, Sid Vicious fell through the door and confronted Freddie with an insult about his 'mission' to bring ballet to the masses, in reference to an interview Freddie had given to Tony Stewart of the *NME*, headlined 'Is This Man a Prat?' Freddie responded, to his eternal credit, with, 'Ah, Mr Ferocious! Well, we're trying our best, dear!'

October brought Queen a Britannia Award from the British Phonographic Industry for 'Bohemian Rhapsody', voted best British single recorded over the past twenty-five years. That month also saw Queen publicising *News of the World*, an exuberant album not to every fan's (nor critic's) taste, the sleeve of which featured a giant robot created by Frank Kelly Freas.

It had become obvious that John Reid lacked time to manage them properly. Queen, who now matched Elton in terms of star quality and status, were in desperate need of management who could focus exclusively on their needs. Lawyer Jim Beach was again summoned, this time to negotiate their exit from the contract with

John Reid Enterprises – a relatively painless if costly procedure. As the agreement was severed ahead of expiry, Reid departed with a handsome pay-off plus 15 per cent of royalties on sales of all Queen's previous albums, in perpetuity. Pete Brown, who had taken care of Queen's day-to-day affairs, left with the band and was made personal manager. Another Reid sidekick, Paul Prenter, also joined the team. Beach would henceforth handle all legal and contractual business full-time, and Gerry Stickells would manage Queen on the road. Queen Productions Ltd was created, followed by Queen Music Ltd and Queen Films Ltd. At last, they owned as many rights to their own work, and to themselves as artists, as it was possible to secure.

This was a turning point in several ways. While their business dealings were sorted, creatively Queen remained at a crossroads. They knew they needed to find new challenges if they were to maintain inspiration and enthusiasm. Treating themselves to their first private jet, they committed to two ambitious American tours that year. On the first, starting in Portland, Oregon on 11 November, Freddie performed 'Love of My Life' live for the first time, inviting audience participation in what was to become a staple of the Queen live show. In December, they were back in New York, where Freddie attended Liza Minnelli's stage production 'The Act'. After having cited Minnelli and Hendrix as his favourite artists and his inspiration for so long, admiration between Liza and Freddie was finally mutual. Years later, the *Cabaret* star would be one of the first to agree to perform at 1992's Freddie Mercury tribute gig.

At Madison Square Garden, Freddie wowed his audience by reappearing for the encore dressed in a New York Yankees hat and jacket. The Yankees had just claimed baseball's World Series, and fans were delighted by his nod to their sacred game. The personal touch was something he would introduce time and again throughout Queen's touring career: a sentence in another language here, a folk song there, a British Union Jack for a cloak lined with the national flag of wherever they were playing ... sometimes Freddie would ponder for hours, trying to think up precisely what gesture. It was his way of giving back, and the fans adored him for it.

At January 1978's MIDEM music industry fair in Cannes, and thanks to 'We Will Rock You' at Number One on the French chart for more than twelve weeks, Queen collected a radio award as rock band with the most potential. Even France – '*vous appelez cela de la musique rock!*' – had finally woken up to Queen.

So had the tax man. 1978 would be a year of to-ing and fro-ing as tax exiles, spending most of their time abroad to avoid being penalised for earning too much. Queen toured Europe again, and played five more shows in England during May, after which they began work on the next album at Mountain Studios in Montreux. The facility had been chosen because it was technically the finest in Europe at the time, and Queen were always looking for the best. The fact that it was set in one of the most breathtaking havens on earth was an added extra. Beautiful Lake Geneva and the majestic snow-capped Alps took their breath away. Brian and Freddie remained at home, at first: Brian for the birth of his first child, Jimmy, and Freddie to work on an album for his own newly-formed Goose Productions, which would be recorded by his close friend Peter Straker.

A Jamaican-born actor, Straker met Freddie in 1975 in the London restaurant Provan's. The former was with his manager David Evans, while the latter was dining with John Reid. By quirk of fate, Evans also worked for Reid.

'I remember the ratty fur and the black-painted fingernails, the white clogs and the hair,' recalled Straker to their mutual friend Evans. 'There was also the characteristic hunching of his posture, a slight stoop. However, the real impression with which I was left was his extraordinary shyness. He kept his eyes to the ground, something he always did throughout his life when he was first introduced to strangers.'

After bumping into each other around town, Straker invited

Freddie to his birthday party at his small Hurlingham Road flat that November, 1975. The theme was 'Come As Your Favourite Person'. Freddie, who was at the time having a covert fling with young theatre hand David Minns, told his host that if he came (he did), he would not be in fancy dress because he was his *own* favourite person.

'Freddie arrived with David Minns earlyish, bearing a jereboam of champagne: Moet et Chandon, of course! I think it was that night, in a haze, I first asked him to produce an album for me.'

The pair arranged to meet for lunch.

'Thereafter, it seems, we became mates. It's hard to remember definite dates and events, as our lives from that point onwards became inextricably tangled. In other words, we hit it off.'

Freddie and Straker, whose mother had been an opera singer, were soon enjoying nights at the ballet and the opera together, as well as ducking and diving around the seedy pubs and clubs. They even took to playing tennis together at London's smart Hurlingham Club. Straker, well-bred in demeanour and possessed of a marvellous voice and arresting vocal range, which should have earned him more success than he ever achieved, asked Freddie to produce his album of post-glam rock and Vaudevillian cameos. Freddie not only agreed to do this, but generously invested £20,000 of his own money in the record, entitled *This One's On Me*. The LP spawned two singles: 'Jackie' and 'Ragtime Piano Joe'. Mutual friends remember them as 'two naughty schoolgirls' or as 'brothers', never lovers, and brotherly conflict was the foundation of their relationship.

'Straker helped relieved the pressure for Freddie,' said Peter Freestone. 'He was always there with a ready laugh.'

'The deep friendship between Freddie and Peter was founded on a love of opera and the classics,' remembers Leee John, dazzling frontman with Eighties soul and dance trio Imagination, and a loyal friend to both.

'I came from soul, R and B and jazz, and I was making an effort to understand Blues and all the music of Africa. But Freddie told me I really must take some time to learn about opera, that it would be beneficial to my career. *Scheherazade* [by Rimsky-Korsakov and based on the book, *One Thousand and One Nights*] was the only thing I knew. "Darling," he said, "it's a good start." So one whole summer, on Freddie's advice, I went to a new opera every week. Everything from *Don Giovanni* to *The Ring*. I fell asleep! I emoted, I laughed, I learned so much. I mean, I was into Motown, check out *this*! A lot of classical music has African origins, and Freddie knew that. There is a unique rhythmic sense. He also talked to me a good deal about vocal technique. It all makes sense, as you reflect back over the years. With Straker, though, I always had the impression that he and Freddie were teaching each other equally. As friends, they'd met their match.'

Brian and Freddie joined Roger and John in Montreux, where work proceeded apace. That summer, EMI Records received the Queen's Award to Industry for export achievement, one of the UK's most coveted distinctions for manufacturers. To mark the occasion, EMI pressed a commemorative blue vinyl edition of 'Bohemian Rhapsody': 200 hand-numbered, limited-edition copies pressed on seven-inch blue vinyl. The edition had been intended as a purple and gold presentation, to reflect the band's original colours as seen on *Queen I*. But according to then general manager of EMI's International Division, Paul Watts, things didn't quite go according to plan.

'We decided upon a maroon and gold sleeve, and a single in purple vinyl,' recounted Watts. 'But when the record came back from the factory, it wasn't purple at all, but blue! . . . The blue vinyl was a cock-up. As we only had two hundred [1,000 or 1,500 being the usual minimum run], it wasn't worth changing it.'

The Award was presented to EMI directors and management in July 1978, in the Cotswold Suite of London's Selfridge Hotel. It was attended by neither Queen nor Her Majesty. The ironically tax-exiled band were having one of their riotous parties for Roger in Montreux on the day, which happened to be his twenty-ninth birthday.

The first four of those framed, limited-edition blue vinyls were despatched to the band members in Switzerland. Select EMI executives received the next batch. Press kit copies came packaged with the luncheon's two invitations. The remainder were presented as gifts to some of the lunch guests, while others received a pair of commemoratively-etched champagne glasses or a special EMI silk scarf. Only the lucky few walked away with all three items.

This disc remains one of Queen's most collectible, not to mention one of the most highly sought-after items of rock memorabilia in the world.

Recording progressed to another studio, SuperBear in Nice. This was also for tax reasons, the Queen machine now being obliged to get about. They could not risk recording an entire album in one country for fear of incurring tax liability in yet another territory.

Freddie's thirty-second birthday party was held in exquisite St Paul de Vence in the South of France, where Rolling Stone Bill Wyman kept a home. The riotous bash culminated in Freddie and Straker harmonising drunkenly on Gilbert and Sullivan arias. Two days later the band were raising a glass to the memory of Who drummer Keith Moon, who had overdosed on Clomethiazole in Harry Nilsson's apartment in Curzon Place, Mayfair – the same flat in which Mamas and Papas star Cass Elliot had died of a heart attack four years earlier.

Queen's next single release was 'Fat-Bottomed Girls', a double A-side with 'Bicycle Race', inspired by the Tour de France passing through Nice while they were recording there. To promote the single they hired Wimbledon Stadium in London and paid sixty-five naked girls to stage a bike race. Hilarious footage ensued. The bikes were on loan from cycle retailer Halfords, who insisted that Queen pay for the replacement of the sixty-five used leather saddles. The single rose to Number Eleven on the chart, but not without controversy: the bare race-wining bottom on the record sleeve was deemed offensive. Further copies featured scanty black knickers scribbled in.

By October they were touring again in the U.S. On Hallowe'en night in New Orleans, Queen hosted what could only be described as an orgy with which to herald the release of their next album, *Jazz*. The 400-strong guest list featured press representatives from all over America, South America, Britain and Japan. A hotel ballroom was converted into a steamy, overgrown swamp, teeming with dwarfs and drag queens, fire-eaters and female mud-wrestlers, strippers and snakes, steel bands, voodoo dancers, Zulu dancers, hookers, groupies and grotesques, some performing unimaginable and possibly illegal acts on themselves and on each other in full view of revellers. One model arrived on a salver of raw liver. Others writhed in cages suspended from the ceiling. The madness made headlines around the world, and further confirmed Queen's status as the most debauched party-givers in rock.

All this, and Tony Brainsby was back. Their old PR was handling the band's publicity again, and was in his element. Brainsby wasted no time in assembling a posse of bloodthirsty hacks, whom he chaperoned from London to Louisiana for the night.

'Wild,' was his in-a-nutshell assessment. 'We went from the airport to the party and the party to the airport, without having been anywhere near a bed, as it were. I'd seen parties in my time. But never like that. Some of the journalists' eyes were hanging out by the time it came to leave. Freddie was signing his name on a stripper's buttock – and that was the very mildest thing I witnessed. Took me the best part of a month to get over it.'

But the American backlash had started. Disapproval was rife at the inclusion of a poster in the *Jazz* album sleeve of the nude bicycle race. The poster was denounced, and in some states banned, as 'pornography'. From then on, copies of the album came complete with an application form, enabling fans to send off for the offending item. Queen had thought it harmless fun, and were genuinely taken aback by so much objection. However, it didn't stop them bringing a bevy of bike-riding, bell-ringing girls onto the Madison Square Garden stage during 'Bicycle Race'.

Back home, the *Jazz* album went in at Number Two, and remained on the chart for twenty-seven weeks. Now, they needed to top that. What could they come up with for the next album? Then the next one? Then what after that? The band, it seemed, had forgotten how to relax.

14

Munich

I like Munich. I was there so long that after a while the people didn't even consider that I was around. I have a lot of friends over there and they know who I am, but they just treat me as another human being, and they've accepted me that way. And that to me is a very good way of relaxing. I don't want to have to shut myself up and hide. That's not what I want. I'd go spare. I'd go mad . . . even quicker.

Freddie Mercury

He was unashamedly sexual, which was a breath of fresh air. Few people were, back then.

Carolyn Cowan, Freddie's make-up artist

Roger, Brian and John had settled down and were now toeing the line as committed family men and fathers – when they were not on the road, at least. Brian had already managed to fall in love with a girl called Peaches down in New Orleans. John, generally mindful of his domestic commitments, had taken up with the bottle. Roger was always the life and soul of anyone's party, rarely knowingly alone between midnight and breakfast. Freddie, mind you, was out there eclipsing the lot of them, hurling caution into the hurricane as never before. If the band were no angels on tour, Freddie was devil incarnate. As their circus thundered across

Europe for a mammoth twenty-eight dates early in 1979, including two first-time performances in what was then still Yugoslavia, their front man indulged himself like it was going out of vogue. Queen's twelfth single, 'Don't Stop Me Now', emerged in January, with a zestful music press onside. Then it was back to Montreux to toil on tapes recorded throughout the tour for the double album *Live Killers*. Always at home on the shores of Lake Geneva, and content to be working in Mountain Studios, the band jumped at the chance when their accountants suggested acquiring the studios outright, which would alleviate their complicated tax situation. David Richards, Mountain's resident engineer who would become Queen's producer, joined their team. An invitation from producer Dino De Laurentiis (*Barbarella, Death Wish, King Kong, Hannibal, Red Dragon*) to compose and record a soundtrack for sci-fi movie *Flash Gordon*, based on the comic character, settled another long-standing collective Queen ambition.

Back in Japan for further live dates, more mayhem and adulation ensued, after which the band spent the summer months of 1979 at the now-defunct Musicland Studios in Munich, famous as the hub of producer Giorgio Moroder's disco-era success. Still recording abroad for tax reasons, Queen would work with a fresh producer, the acclaimed German maestro Reinhold Mack, who had co-created Musicland with Moroder. Marc Bolan, Deep Purple and The Rolling Stones had all recorded there. For Mack, Queen were not the easiest bunch of musicians he had ever taken on.

'They were set in their ways, like pensioners,' Mack recalled. 'Their credo was "this is how we are used to doing things" . . . I had the advantage of being a fast decision-maker compared to the band. I would always try things while people were pondering delicate details.'

Mack's relationship with Queen throughout was 'quite relaxed', he said.

'The band came off a tour of Japan, and had some time to spend before going back to England . . . right time, right place. The project did not start out as an album [although it would later become *The Game*]. It was a bunch of one- and two-week sessions. The first track we attempted was "Crazy Little Thing Called Love". Freddie picked up an acoustic guitar and said, "Quick! Let's do this before Brian comes". About six hours later, the track was done. The guitar solo was an overdub later on. Brian still hates me for making him use a Telecaster for the part. It was released as a pre-album single, and went to Number One. That obviously helped a great deal to inspire confidence and the working relationship tremendously.'

As far as actual songwriting went, Mack remembered it as complicated.

'There were two camps of songwriting: Freddie and Brian. Fred was easy. We thought along similar lines, and it took him fifteen to twenty minutes to come up with something absolutely brilliant. Brian, on the other hand, would come up with a great idea, but get completely lost in insignificant details after the first rush of creativity.'

Munich's motto when Queen came to stay was still '*Weltstadt mit Herz*' – 'cosmopolitan city with a heart'. (Since 2006 it has been '*München mag Dich*' – 'Munich likes you' – but that's another story.) Their sojourn was to have a profound and even destructive effect on all four members of the band, particularly Freddie, who quickly became addicted to its more dubious delights. Anyone else on an extended stay in a major European cultural centre would have immersed themselves in its rich history and diverse architecture, enjoying the many attractions it has to offer. The city had flourished culturally since the eighteenth century, and was a colourful place during Germany's between-the-wars Weimar period. Mozart, Wagner, Mahler and Strauss, writer Thomas Mann and expressionist painter Kandisnky were all attracted to this hypnotic rainy town.

But Munich's main attraction, for Freddie, was its effervescent gay scene. This was concentrated in a small, central area known as 'The Bermuda Triangle'. The enclave had become a haven for homosexuals from every country in Europe, just as New York's

Village and San Francisco's Castro district had attracted gay refugees from all over America. The Munich scene was laid-back and relaxed. Freddie felt able to experiment openly without hungry hacks doorstepping him and headlining his every move. Another thrill, for the whole band, was that Munich's disco club scene was then in its heyday. Gay bars were abundant, all heaving with bodies seven nights a week. Nightlife could be a sordid trip taken at breakneck pace, within the dark, deafening confines of clubs like the Ochsen Gardens, the Sugar Shack, New York and Frisco. Few took much notice of openly outrageous gay behaviour in The Triangle, because people were enjoying themselves too much – straight men and women as well as gays. As Mack would later recall, 'Freddie loved to be around a real mix of people. He never liked the purely gay world. He was a private person, and never behaved outrageously out of context. He didn't thrust homosexuality in your face. He would never cause a scene, and always behaved impeccably in mixed company. His attitude was very much "everything in its place".'

As Brian later explained in official Queen biography *As It Began,* 'Munich had a huge effect on all our lives. Because we spent so much time there, it became almost another home, and a place in which we lived different lives. It was different from being on tour, when there would be an intense contact with a city for a couple of days, and then we would move on. In Munich, we all became embroiled in the lives of the local people. We found ourselves inhabiting the same clubs for most of the night, most nights. The Sugar Shack in particular held a fascination for us. It was a rock disco with an amazing sound system, and the fact that some of our records didn't sound very good in there made us change our whole perspective on our mixes and our music. In retrospect it's probably true to say that our efficiency in Munich was not very good. Our social habits made us generally start work late in the day, feeling tired, and (for me especially, and perhaps for Freddie) the emotional distractions became destructive.'

Despite Freddie's blatant promiscuity in the Bavarian capital, Mack believed that the attraction of this type of gay lifestyle was beginning to pall.

'Freddie told me a number of times, "Perhaps I'll give up the whole gay thing one of these days." He more or less decided when he was twenty-four or twenty-five that he was gay, and before that he was considered straight. With him, nothing was impossible. I do think he could have given up being gay, because he loved women. I saw what he was like in their presence, and he wasn't the kind of gay man who didn't like them in his life. He was the opposite.'

Freddie became a frequent visitor to Mack's home, and grew close to Mack's wife Ingrid. The couple chose him as godfather to one of their children. Mack described how Freddie was not immune to the comforts of family life, and even suggested that Freddie had implied a desire to radically alter his lifestyle. The star, Mack said, would have loved to marry and have children himself, despite the fact that there was no significant other in his life at that point.

'Freddie's biggest thing was to have a family and a normal life,' Mack insisted.

'I was once badly screwed and found myself having to pay a load of back tax. I was very depressed, and I talked to Freddie about it. He told me: "Fuck, it's only money! Why worry about something like that? You've got it made, you've got everything you need – a wonderful family and children. You have everything I can never have." That's when I became aware that when he was at our house, he was watching everything and taking it all in. Seeing what a family life was like, and how it could have made him happy.'

But in New York the following year, Freddie would tell Rick Sky: 'By nature I'm very restless and highly strung, so I wouldn't make a good family man. I'm a very emotional person, a person of real extremes. And often that's destructive, both to myself and others.'

His sister Kashmira agreed with the view that Freddie would not have made a good father: 'No, I don't think so at all. He was very good at spoiling you, but not so good at laying down the law.'

Mack also discovered, during the time they spent together in Munich, that Freddie had been painfully lonely as a child.

'One day I overheard a conversation between Freddie and my second son, Felix,' he said. 'Freddie was telling him, "I never had any of this. When I was young, I spent a lot of time away from my parents because I was at boarding school. Sometimes I would hardly ever see them." He talked to my kids about his childhood quite a lot. Freddie adored children. As soon as they could walk and talk and respond, he got on with them.'

As for the music Queen made in Munich, Brian was the first to admit that the change in direction was inspired by Freddie.

'We approached it from a different angle,' he said, 'with the idea of ruthlessly pruning it down to a coherent album rather than letting our flights of fancy lead us off into different areas. The impetus came very largely from Freddie, who said that he thought we'd been diversifying so much that people didn't know what we were about any more. If there's a theme to the album, it's rhythm and sparseness – never two notes played if one would do, which is a hard discipline for us, because we tend to be quite over the top in the way we work . . . that was breaking new ground for us, because for the first time we went into a recording studio without a deadline, purely with the intention of putting some tracks down as they came out . . . This was to put ourselves in a totally different situation,' he explained.

'It's a way of getting out of that rut of doing an album, touring Britain, touring America, etc. We thought we'd try a change, and see what came out. You have to make your own excitement after a while.'

Mack continued to rave about Freddie's studio technique, his spontaneous inventiveness, his commitment, his enthusiasm, the speed and dexterity with which he worked. Only Freddie's limited attention span got the better of him, as it tended to do in his personal life. If something appeared too laborious and long-winded, Freddie would suddenly lose interest. As Mack remembered, he could never focus on any one thing for more than about ninety minutes at a time.

'With "Killer Queen", you can tell that he just sat down at the piano and did it. The end is a little bit unresolved. I think that was a typically Freddie quality. He just loved to get on with something new and different. I got on exceptionally well with Freddie. I liked the fact that he was a genius. He really was, in terms of perception of music and seeing the focal point of where the song should be.'

Together, they added a new dimension to the Queen sound, which matched the mood of the era and inspired the band towards new creative heights.

After performing at open-air German festivals that August, Freddie returned to London to join rehearsals for a charity performance to be given by the Royal Ballet on behalf of the City of Westminster Society for Mentally Handicapped Children. Freddie had been persuaded to take part by his close friend Wayne Eagling, then a Royal Ballet principal. 'Bohemian Rhapsody' and 'Crazy Little Thing Called Love' were both choreographed, and Freddie added live vocals. On performance night, at the London Coliseum, he danced so well that he received a standing ovation.

'I only really knew about ballet from watching it on television,' Freddie confided to John Blake, then a pop writer on the *London Evening News*. 'But I always enjoyed what I saw.'

'Then I became very good friends with Sir Joseph Lockwood at EMI, also chairman of the Royal Ballet board of governors, and I began to meet all these people who were involved in ballet. I became more and more fascinated by them. I finally saw Baryshnikov dance, and he was just mind-blowing. More than Nureyev, more than anyone. I mean, he can really fly. When I saw him on stage I was so in awe that I felt like a groupie.'

Referring to his own performance with the Royal Ballet, he commented: 'They had me practising at the barre and all that, stretching my legs . . . trying to do things in a week that they'd been doing for years. It was murder. After two days I was in agony. It was hurting me in places I didn't know I had, dear. Then, when the night of the gala came, I was just amazed at the backstage scenes. When I had my entrances to do, I had to fight my way through Merle Parke and Anthony Dowell and all these people, and say, "Excuse me, I'm going on now!" It was outrageous.'

Freddie danced his scene while singing 'Bohemian Rhapsody'.

'Yes, dear, I did this leap. A wonderful leap, which brought the house down, and then they all caught me and I just carried on singing!'

Asked if he would have liked to have been a professional dancer, Freddie replied, 'Yes, but I'm very happy doing what I do. You can't suddenly say at thirty-two, I want to be a ballet dancer.'

The dance led to rumours that he might be something of a 'man's man', at which Freddie roared his head off. 'Oh *God*, dear! Let them think what they want. You see, if I actually said no or yes, that would be boring. Nobody would ask me any more. I'd rather they just kept on asking. Oh, it's all just so boring. My dear, the private life is up to the individual. I mean, with someone like Elton, I think: what can I say? He's more press-oriented, isn't he? I'm not that mad about it.'

Freddie later joked further about his Royal Ballet performance to his journalist friend David Wigg.

'Singing upside down is wonderful. I was shivering in the wings with nerves. It's always much harder when you are put outside your sphere, but I always like a challenge. I'd like to see Mick Jagger or Rod Stewart try something like that.'

He also dropped into the conversation, with customary mischief, that his most vivid memory of the entire evening was having his bottom pinched by famous Rhodesian-born ballerina Merle Park: 'She's outrageous, that woman!'

Freddie's excursion into the world of *pointes* and *pliés* was soon to provide him with a friend for life.

15

Phoebe

I generate a lot of friction, so I'm not the easiest person to have a relation-ship with. I'm the nicest person you could ever meet, my dears, but I'm very hard to live with. I don't think anyone could put up with me, and I think sometimes I try too hard. In one way I am greedy, I just want it all my own way, but doesn't everybody? I'm a very loving person, you know, and I'm a very giving person. I demand a lot, but I do give a lot in return.
Freddie Mercury

I was Freddie's chief cook and bottle-washer, waiter, butler, secretary, cleaner ... and agony aunt. I travelled the world with him, I was with him at the highs and came through the lows. I acted as his bodyguard when needed, and in the end, of course, I was one of his nurses.
Peter 'Phoebe' Freestone

Backstage at the Royal Opera House during preparations for his ballet debut, Freddie met young wardrobe assistant and dresser Peter Freestone. Indispensable at first sight: promptly re-christened 'Phoebe', Peter was to become the singer's personal assistant. He remained his devoted companion until the end of Freddie's life.

'Freddie came up to the Opera House to try on the outfits that he was going to wear for the Royal Ballet Gala at the Coliseum,' Peter told me. An amiable, larger-than-life character for whom nothing was too much trouble, it was easy to see why Freddie had taken an instant shine to him.

'Freddie was extremely nice and polite that day I first met him,' remembered Peter.

'I'd later discover that he was always polite, unless people really annoyed him, in which case he would let rip. He was pretty in awe of the Opera House. He was out of his normal sphere of experience. This was a bastion of the Establishment, and Freddie was the total opposite. The Gala was brilliant. The way Freddie was manipulated around the stage by those dancers was superb.

'He sang "Crazy Little Thing Called Love" and "Bohemian Rhapsody". He came out in all his leather gear for the first one, then went behind a wall of dancers and reappeared dressed in sequins. It was the first insight I had into the showman in Freddie. Up until then I'd vaguely heard of Queen, and I'd once seen Freddie with Mary having tea in the Rainbow Room at Biba in 1973. He had the hair down to here, and a fox fur jacket. It was unmistakably him.

'I remember his very being there was a performance,' he later added.

At the after-show party at Legends, Peter bumped into Freddie with manager Paul Prenter, and stood chatting with them both.

'Three weeks later, Paul telephoned my boss and asked if he knew anybody who would be interested in a six-week contract to do wardrobe for the Queen tour. After watching that performance on stage, I just wanted that excitement. I'd watched *Sleeping Beauty* and *Swan Lake* a thousand times . . . Now, I wanted to see more of this exciting person. See more of rock. I had no way of knowing what I was letting myself in for. All I thought was that wardrobe for four people couldn't be nearly as bad as running wardrobe for the Royal Ballet Company.'

Having quit his permanent job 'with prospects' to take up the short-term contract with Queen, Peter found himself out of work. He was forced to accept temporary employment as a telephone operator for British Telecom, 'Until Queen went on tour again, and I was invited back. After that, I was kept on a retainer when they weren't on the road. When they were home, I'd do bits and pieces in the office. After the American tour, Paul and Freddie decided that I should look after Freddie exclusively. I'd still do wardrobe for everybody on tour, but otherwise I was only concerned with him.'

The pair soon discovered that they had both attended boarding schools in India, thousands of miles from home and separated from their parents. A bond was struck, and Freddie's barriers began to come down. One of the first things that struck Freestone was Freddie's aversion to confrontation.

'He was never a rude man,' Peter said. 'If something started happening, he'd appear to withdraw and let others get involved while he sat back and observed. He'd just throw a line in here and there. It's true that he and Mary squabbled a great deal. But that was mainly because he had expectations of people, and if people didn't live up to them, he'd get annoyed. You would tend to learn your lesson. If something happened once, he told you about it, and you'd make sure you didn't do it again. But that didn't stop Mary doing things again and again. Once she'd got something into her head, she would just do it, the best way she saw fit. But if that didn't fit in with Freddie's plans, there would be the big row.'

Peter knew instinctively how to keep a low profile and his opinions to himself. He also sensed when it was appropriate to cross professional boundaries with Freddie, and when it was not. Queen's wild world was an alien realm, and Peter trod carefully. There were times when he felt overwhelmed by the privilege and excess that the band took for granted.

'With each new tour, they had to have that many more lights, that much bigger a sound, a more and more fantastic set,' Peter recalled. 'Everything they did had to be never-been-done-before. It was the ultimate show. For that alone they were just so exciting. A few years ago at Wembley I saw Michael Jackson in concert two days in a row.

Everything was exactly the same the second day as it had been on the first. Queen were totally different. You never knew quite what you were going to get. They also had to have the most expensive band meetings ever: actually in the recording studio, where they were being charged a fortune by the hour. Nobody would do that now.'

So harmonious was their relationship, so discreet and easy was this new assistant to have around, that he was quickly given responsibility for all Freddie's personal needs.

'I'd even pack for him,' Peter says. 'I'd arrange the car to pick him up. I made sure he had money, cards, passport, tickets – in fact, I would be the one holding on to the money, the cards and the tickets. I'd be the one to actually get him on the plane. It was like caring for a child, a lot of the time. I was always with him, literally at his side, in the very next seat on every aircraft. Considering the amount of time we spent in each other's pockets, we got on incredibly well. While we were in Los Angeles, where we lived for a while when Queen were recording, other people were always around, which took the pressure off me a bit. But when we were in New York, it was just Freddie and me. The easiest way for me to describe the relationship was that there was a line: there's employer, and there's friend. The dividing part was never static. After a short period of time, I could judge instantly where it was, depending on what was happening. On whether he needed his employee there doing this or that for him, or whether he needed his friend around to lean on. It had to be like that. That way, he knew he could shout at me – which he frequently did, mainly to work his frustrations out. We both knew why, and that was fine. It would never be mentioned again, and Freddie never held grudges against anybody. He'd have his go, and that would be it.'

Being constantly at the beck and call of a demanding master must have taken its toll at times. Surely Freestone felt like a servant? He denies he ever did.

'Mainly, I think – and this is a dreadful thing to admit – because Freddie never treated me in the "do this, do that" way I used to treat the servants we had in India. He was incredibly nice to me, most of the time. While admittedly he was paying me a salary, none of us who worked for him ever had to pay for anything. He never expected anybody to pay for a meal or buy him a drink. If we did buy him a drink, he'd be very happy, but it wasn't expected. If he went out to a bar and there were ten people in the entourage, it would all be on his bill. But he never carried his own money – we'd carry it. He was just like royalty in that respect. But no, it never made me feel awkward.'

With hindsight, Peter felt that he'd had 'one of the luckiest lives going' during his years with Freddie and Queen.

'I effectively lived Freddie's life without the responsibility of having had to earn it. I never had to create music or face the press. But I got to travel by Concorde endless times, stayed in the best suites in the best hotels around the world, shopped for him at the finest auction houses with his own signed blank cheques. I lived and spent at his level. How on earth could I have felt like a servant?'

The intense personal friendship that the pair enjoyed until the end of Freddie's life was based on mutual respect and trust.

'Freddie didn't trust people that easily,' said Peter.

'He would either trust someone within a relatively short period, or he would never trust them at all. For him to have accepted me in that role was the basis of our friendship, and that happened within the first year. We had only one huge falling out, in about 1989' – when Peter became aware that Freddie thought he had been gossiping about Freddie's illness outside Garden Lodge, which he had not.

'But it was pretty short-lived. I told him that I'd had enough, and that I wanted to go. "Please don't," he said. "I want you here. I *need* you." That was all I needed to hear. Everything was instantly forgotten, and I was there for the duration.

'Those of us in his personal group were actually his family. We did everything for him. I would have done anything for him – and not just because he was paying me. I did what I did out of respect. Freddie was up there on a pedestal to me. But I didn't do it because I was in awe of him. I did it because I was lucky enough to be a friend. I couldn't have done it for anybody else.'

Freddie was already indulging in a private life of such lunatic excess by the time Peter came on board that many have since wondered how he managed it behind the media's back. Relatively easily, thinks Peter. It was simply a matter of keeping himself to himself.

'There are certain members of the rock fraternity who will go to the opening of an envelope,' he points out. 'If something isn't happening, they will create something, simply to keep themselves in the public eye. Freddie mostly went out of his way *not* to appear in the press. He'd do the odd bits of publicity required of him, but he wouldn't go to any of the big showbiz parties or premieres. He rarely went to other artists' gigs. He was a private person. Music was his work. The studio was his office. When he was not in the office he didn't want to be working.'

Despite the recklessness, Peter insisted that he never felt afraid for Freddie, given the lifestyle he had chosen.

'It was part of the times,' he shrugged. 'This was the early Eighties. Anything went.'

Freddie was in high spirits for another reason in October 1979. Queen's fourteenth single, Freddie's 'Crazy Little Thing Called Love' backed by Brian's 'We Will Rock You', was a smash with the music press, and reached Number Two on the UK chart. Freddie's bohemian image long dispensed with, he was now into his 'leather' look. Black or red leather pants with macho caps were his stage attire, part of a harder and more aggressive, if short-lived, image. This too would soften and evolve, into his final stage-wear preference of plain vest and jeans. Freddie was in control and taking a defiant stance. The focused image was right for a new decade.

'From now on, dressing up crazily on stage is out,' Freddie declared. 'I'm going to put our music across dressed more casually. The world has changed. People want something more direct.'

Queen's long career was taking its toll. The band were feeling restless and jaded. Their relationships with each other flagged as their enthusiasm and energy waned. I have witnessed this often over the years with bands of Queen's stature; there comes a point when it's no longer the be-all and end-all, when they are simply not into it as much. Brian, Freddie, Roger and John were getting older. Adults now, with partners, children, houses, staff, a global public profile, solo commitments, charity work, each one of them was now a mini-industry in his own right, with endless and exhausting responsibilities. Queen could no longer be what they had started out as: a band of supremely talented, driven yet carefree young dudes wenching and wassailing their way around the world, doing as they pleased. Their personalities and predilections gave them different priorities, too. Roger had long felt comfortable with playing the rock superstar, commanding as many column inches as their front man – especially for his colourful private life. Brian was a reluctant celebrity at first, but grew more comfortable with stardom after falling in love with future second wife, Anita Dobson, an actress, who understood showbusiness. John was deeply immersed in the sort of 'ordinary' domestic set-up that Freddie had turned his back on, and possibly felt alienated by.

I think this stance was born of guilt. John seemed content as precisely the kind of family man Freddie's parents would have given anything for their son to have been. He was a reminder of all that Freddie didn't have.

Of all four band members, it was Freddie, surprisingly, who was the least heat-seeking. The way he saw it, he was a musician and performer first, a rock star second. What mattered to him was honing the recordings until they were perfect; belting out a dazzler of a performance night after night and always being the best – for the fans, as well as for himself.

'He was very much the perfectionist,' agreed Peter Freestone. 'He would spend hours making sure that there was no better way of constructing the song, no better tune to express the feeling that he wanted to put over. His music, first and foremost, was for himself . . . It was his own perfection he was seeking, not other people's.'

Freddie wasn't interested in the 'right' parties or the 'important' premieres. He couldn't be bothered to schmooze. He did not court celebrity friends, he let them come to him. If there was common ground to be enjoyed, he let them in. He could not have cared less about being 'seen'. While the flimsier stars of today obsess endlessly over preserving 'public profile' and landing the splash headline, to Freddie that was at best boring, at worst the most distasteful and pointless pursuit.

'You've got to have nerves of steel to survive the pace,' he remarked. 'When you have success it becomes really difficult, because then you really learn the things behind the business. You find out the real baddies. Before, you don't know anything about it. You have to be very strong and sift them out. It's like playing rock 'n' roll dodgems. You've got to make sure you don't get hit too often. Anyone who is successful will always be burned once or twice. There's no such thing,' he added, obscurely, 'as a clean escalator to the top.'

A rock band's massive global success invariably causes a separation from the fans who took them there. Mindful of this, and nervous of the inevitable knock-on effect, Queen opted to shun vast stadia on their forthcoming tour in favour of more intimate venues, some of which fell ridiculously short of the requirements of a supergroup and its set-up. Dubbed 'The Crazy Tour' for the unsuitability of some of the concert halls, and promoted by Harvey Goldsmith, the band played Dublin – their first Irish gig, Birmingham, Manchester, Glasgow and Liverpool, where Freddie sported one red and one blue knee-pad, to charm both Everton and Liverpool soccer fans. They also played Brighton, and modest venues in London, including the Lyceum Ballroom and The Rainbow. Approaching this tour with deliberate enthusiasm, Queen were able to report, for the first time in a long time, that they'd actually enjoyed themselves. This had been a tangible reminder of how great performing had felt in the good old days, when fortune and fame were still little more than a dream.

After the Brighton show, Freddie confided to a friend that he was partial to 'the odd orgy'.

'The night before last, we were in Brighton, and the road crew had one of their parties,' he said. 'One of Queen's things: we're very good at giving parties. It was full of naughty women, and every-body jumped in. I'm not going to tell you names, but it was very well-cast, and there were props and goodness knows what flying all over the place. It was wonderful.'

What Freddie did not confess to was the passionate night he had spent in the arms of young DHL courier Tony Bastin. Tony would become Freddie's first long-term homosexual relationship, if no antidote to his promiscuity. Their on-off affair lasted for two years, neither of them under any illusion that he had met his match.

'Freddie was not Tony's type at all,' Peter later lamented, refer-ring to the fact that blond, smiling Bastin's average looks and build were not what Freddie normally went for.

'Freddie liked chunky and hunky and a relatively blank slate, someone upon whom he could leave his mark,' explained Peter. 'Freddie simply liked the stability of a permanent partner as a secure base from which he could continue to play the field,' he added.

All Freddie's lovers had very unsophisticated roots. 'Although a country boy himself, which he was loath to admit, he had an acquired sophistication which always rubbed off on his lovers and raised their expectations.'

Bastin more or less moved into the Stafford Terrace flat, even bringing his cat, Oscar, and took to joining Freddie at a string of destinations when the band were away on tour. He quickly got a taste for the high life, which he could hardly be blamed for when Freddie was showering him with first-class plane tickets and expensive presents. Not that Bastin appeared to appreciate any of it. It dawned on Freddie eventually that Tony was using him. Worse, word had reached him that Tony had been seen around town with a slim young blond. It was the first of many similar betrayals.

'He was often let down badly in relationships, and became extremely cautious about who he got involved with emotionally,' reveals David Wigg.

'Once they'd got the Cartier bracelet or the car . . . you know. They weren't very clever, these "friends" of his. It happens a lot with these people. The entourage have inflated egos, sometimes bigger than the ego of the star they serve. They start to believe that they can do it too, forgetting the fact that they haven't an ounce of talent themselves, and are only where they are because of who's paying them.'

This could explain why Freddie developed such a passion for no-strings sex with ever-changing partners, withholding emotional commitment for the friends he could truly trust.

In the end, Freddie summoned Bastin all the way to the States, ended the relationship and put him straight back on the plane, with instructions to clear out his things from the flat, but to leave the cat.

Queen welcomed the New Year and a new decade with their fifteenth single, 'Save Me', Number Eleven on the UK chart. The Elvis-esque 'Crazy Little Thing Called Love' was seducing the rest of the world, giving them their first mainstream Number One in the States and topping charts in Australia, New Zealand, Mexico, Canada and Holland. The band retreated to Munich to work on new album material, and on the *Flash Gordon* soundtrack.

★ ★ ★

In London, early in 1980, Mary Austin had at last found Freddie the home of his dreams. When she sent him the spec of Garden Lodge in Logan Place, W8, a short, quiet residential street in the Royal Borough of Kensington and Chelsea, just off his beloved Kensington High Street, Freddie fell in love with it on the spot.

Enclosed within lofty old brick walls topped with railings forti-fied by trellising, affording almost total privacy, only the pitched roof of the two-storey, eight-bedroom gabled Edwardian property could be seen from the street. Unusually for that neighbourhood, the house was set in an acre of mature landscaped gardens. The entrance was a nondescript dark green wooden door, which in years to come would be engraved with ever-changing graffiti by fans from all over the world.

The house had belonged to a member of the Hoare banking family, a gag not lost on Freddie, who re-christened it 'the Whore House'. The asking price was more than half a million pounds. Freddie, unabashed, offered cash. As it was divided at the time into two separate residences, extensive renovation and conversion was required to restore it to one grand house. It would be years before Freddie could call the mansion 'home'. It didn't stop him boasting about it.

'I saw the house, fell in love with it, and within half an hour it was mine,' he told former pop writer Nina Myskow.

'It's in a terrible state at the moment, with all the changes I'm having made. I won't be able to move in for about a year. I call it my country house in town. It's very secluded, with huge grounds, right in the middle of London. Once a month, I get inspired, and go there with the architect. "Why don't we have this wall removed?", I ask. Everybody groans, and the architect dies. I went in there sloshed the other day, after a good lunch. There's a wonderful bedroom area at the top – I'm having three knocked into one palatial suite. In this sort of haze, I said, inspired, "What would be nice is a glass dome over the top of all this bedroom area." The architect flinched, but went rushing back to his pen and drawing pad. I haven't seen the sketches yet, but they're on the way.'

Rick Sky heard about it in an interview for the *Daily Star*.

'I like to spend, spend, spend,' Freddie gushed. 'Recently I bought a new house. I love buying antiques at Sotheby's and Christie's. Sometimes I could go to Cartier's the jewellers, and buy up the whole shop. Often, my sprees begin just like a woman buying herself a new hat to cheer herself up. Some days, when I'm really fed up, I just want to lose myself in my money. I work up a storm and just spend and spend. Then I get back home and think, "Oh, God, what have I bought?" But it's never a waste. I get an awful lot of pleasure out of giving presents.'

Freddie confided to Ray Coleman of the *Daily Mirror*, 'I don't like life too easy. If I keep spending a lot, then I'll have to keep earning it. That's how I push myself. I drink a lot, smoke a lot, enjoy my wines and good food. And I will never again eat hamburgers.'

His obsession with his house, like most of his interests, was just another way to offset boredom.

'It is the biggest disease in the whole world,' Freddie admitted.

'Sometimes I think there must be more to life than rushing around the world like a mad thing, getting bored. But I can't sit still for long. I've got all this nervous energy.

'You become accustomed to different things. Your standards and your expectations become higher. If you know you need constant entertainment, you make sure you have it. When I tell people what I've been up to, they're amazed. But that's all I know. It's my way of having fun. That's why I can't sit down and read a book. I can read all the books in the world when it's all over and my legs are in bandages. I may be just being greedy, but I'm an entertainer. It's in the blood . . . I am just a trouper, dear. Give me a stage. But in a way you've created a monster, haven't you. And you're the one who has to live with it.'

Queen's sixteenth single 'Play the Game' emerged on 30 May 1980. Female fans were outraged by the toughened image flaunted by nailbrush-moustached Freddie in the video. Many bombarded the Queen offices with bottles of nail varnish. Despite the protests, the single still reached Number Fourteen.

Summer 1980 brought another US tour, this time a forty-six-date epic with every performance sold out. Queen's ninth album, *The Game*, was released in the UK. Slated by the music press, it conquered the chart at Number One. In Vancouver, the fans who usually lobbed panties and blooms at their idol hurled disposable razors and blades. The moustache stayed on. John Deacon's 'Another One Bites the Dust', for which the bassist played most of the instruments – bass, piano, rhythm and lead guitars, NB, no synth, with Roger later adding some drums and Brian some guitar and harmoniser – was released that August. Cruising to Number One on the US Billboard Hot 100, it lingered there for five more weeks. It also secured the top slot in Argentina, Guatemala, Mexico and Spain, and reached Number Seven in the UK. The track is still credited as Queen's best-selling single, with sales of over seven million copies. John credited the inspiration for its bass line to disco group Chic's 'Good Times'.

'Freddie sang until his throat bled,' commented Brian in *Mojo* magazine. 'He was so into it. He wanted to make that song something special.'

The Game became Queen's first Number One album in America, exceeding all expectations. They ended their longest-ever tour with four sell-out nights at New York's Madison Square Garden, reeling from the death of Led Zeppelin drummer John Bonham. Just thirty-two years old, Bonham choked to death on vomit, having downed forty shots of vodka in one day. His death that September killed another of Queen's favourite bands.

It was during the 1980 tour that Freddie met his own personal Viking. Thor Arnold, a strapping blond nurse by day and darling of Manhattan's downtown gay haunts by night, lived near Greenwich Village and picked Freddie up in one of the local clubs. While the affair was short-lived, they were to remain close friends until the end. The primary reason their friendship lasted was that Thor wanted nothing from his famous pal. If he decided on the spur of the moment to fly into another city and surprise Freddie at work, Thor would purchase his own ticket and put himself on the plane. This, to Freddie, was adorable, and he loved him for it. It was through Thor that Freddie met three other close Manhattan friends, Joe Scardilli, John Murphy and Lee Nolan. These four soon became known as Freddie's 'New York Daughters', and much hilarity was had whenever Freddie was in town.

A brief October holiday afforded not enough time to relax. If they could remember *how* to relax. With their tenth album, the *Flash Gordon* soundtrack, still to complete, their eighteenth single 'Flash' was ready to go. There was a further European tour to prepare for, taking in three nights at Wembley Arena.

The death of John Lennon distracted them from all that. When he was gunned down outside his New York home in December, the celebrity fraternity was forced to confront its vulnerability. There were other Mark Chapmans out there: John Hinckley Jnr, for example, who was obsessed with actress Jodie Foster, and who would attempt to assassinate US President Ronald Reagan in 1981. Queen had never paid much attention to security. This needed to change.

In a tribute to Lennon at their Wembley Arena show, Queen performed his 1971 hit 'Imagine'. Never mind that Freddie forgot the lyrics and Brian lost track of the chords. The chorus was taken up by a sobbing throng of shocked and heartbroken fans.

Awards flooded in. Two Grammy nominations, for Best-Produced Album (*The Game*), and 'Best Rock Performance by a Duo or Group With Vocal' for 'Another One Bites the Dust' (they lost to Bob Seger). 'Crazy Little Thing Called Love' and 'Another One Bites the Dust' both featured in the top five best-selling American singles list of 1980, the latter having shifted more than three and a half million copies. As the year concluded, and as Queen sat planning their New Year dates in Japan, they took stock. To date, they had sold more than 45 million albums and 25 million singles world-wide. They had made their debut as highest-paid company direc-tors and as their own primary asset in *The Guinness Book of Records*. Bigger, better, never-been-done-before, was the brief. Where could a bunch of rock stars go from here?

16

South America

We went to South America originally because we had been invited down. They wanted four wholesome lads to play some nice music. By the end of it I wanted to buy up the entire continent and install myself as president. The idea to do a big South American tour had been in our minds for a long time. But Queen on the road is not just the band, it involves a vast number of people and costs a lot of money for us to tour. In the end we said, 'Fuck the cost, darlings, let's live a little!'

Freddie Mercury

People in our industry all desperately want to be loved. We're all insecure little show-offs. We make it look fab, we entertain people to the best of our abilities. We make it look like we know what we're doing. But we're paddling about like ducks on crack underneath.

Francis Rossi

Having conquered five of six possible continents (there being a negligible rock following in Antarctica), only South America remained uncharted territory. False rumours that the best-selling, most hysterically worshipped band in Argentina and Brazil were planning to tour there had been doing the rounds for years. A handful of artists had ventured that far south before, including Earth, Wind & Fire and Peter Frampton, but never on the colossal scale that Queen had in mind. If it could be done to their exacting standards, in the finest football stadia those countries had to offer, then game on. Thanks to soccer's all but religious status in South America, there was no shortage of suitable venues. If the World Cup was the most widely-viewed sporting event on earth, Queen were the planet's top rock act. This was 1981, and Freddie was in his thirty-fifth year.

Many well-placed Argentinians stood to make fortunes from the Queen tour. José Rota was appointed chief promoter. Influential businessman Alfredo Capalbo agreed fixtures at the Vélez Sarsfield, Buenos Aires, Mar del Plata's municipal stadium, and at the athletic stadium in Rosario. The band were delighted with these World Cup venues, and considered them more than appropriate.

After all, as Brian told me, 'A Queen audience is a football crowd which doesn't take sides.'

In the run-up to their so-called 'South America Bites the Dust' excursion, Freddie flew to New York with Peter Freestone to finalise the purchase of his apartment. It was a welcome relief on his wallet: $1,000-a-night hotel suites were an extravagance, even to Freddie, when he would stay for up to three months at a time. His magnificent forty-third floor residence boasted panoramic north–south views.

'I remember how excited Freddie got during the New York celebrations for the 100th anniversary of the Brooklyn Bridge,' recalled Peter Freestone.

'We watched simultaneously from his balcony and on television. The apartment had belonged to a senator or a congressman called Gray. Freddie had bought it from his widow. The whole place was decorated in grey: four bedrooms, five bathrooms and the den, all covered in grey material of the kind used to make men's business suits. The dining room walls were lined with silvery satin. Although one of Freddie's great passions was redesigning and redecorating his properties, he left that place exactly as it was.'

While Freddie was sorting his East Coast residence, forty tons of rigging, lighting and sound equipment was making its way by ship from the United States to Rio de Janeiro, to be installed ahead of Queen's historic concerts. Twenty tons more were transported on a specially-chartered DC8 on the world's longest city-to-city flight, from Tokyo to Buenos Aires.

When the band landed in Buenos Aires in searing 80-degree heat on 24 February 1981, they understood for the first time what a 'heroes' welcome' was about. They had known adulation in their time – not least in Tokyo. But not even the Japanese could match this. Since the day their government-endorsed tour was announced, the media had been Queen-crazy. In the days preceding their arrival, fans began flooding into the capital in their tens of thousands. On the day itself, it seemed as though all of them had converged on the airport at once. Also there to greet them was a presidential delegation and a police escort. The day's proceedings received non-stop live coverage on national television. Even Freddie was speechless.

'As we walked into the airport building, we couldn't believe our ears,' he said. 'They stopped all the flight announcements and were playing our music instead.'

Argentinian journalist Marcela Delorenzi, then a fifteen-year-old fan, described it as 'the first big rock event in our country.'

'It caused an unbelievable revolution across the land,' she said. 'In the press, and on radio and TV, twenty-four hours a day for the month before they arrived, people talked about nothing but Queen. In the wake of their tour, our own rock artists were forced to change their image and adopt a completely new approach. All their equipment, sound, lighting, every aspect of the live performance had to be improved and upgraded. Suddenly, everything that had previously passed as acceptable seemed pathetic when compared to Queen. This, in Argentina, was like the rock version of BC. From then on it was all Before Queen, and After Queen. Their effect on South America was profound. Hordes of people from Chile, Uruguay,

Paraguay and Bolivia crossed the borders to see the Argentina shows. The Buenos Aires dates are engraved on my memory: 28 February, 1 March and 9 March.'

When Marcela met her idol Freddie Mercury for the first time, she said tearfully, it changed her life.

'He was staying at the Sheraton Hotel in Buenos Aires. I was there with a lot of other Queen fans, waiting for the band. They had to go to a press conference at the stadium. There was a huge crowd waiting outside to see Freddie, screaming and chanting like it was the end of the world.

'I was dressed entirely in pale blue,' recalls Marcela.

'And it was a great surprise, when the lift door opened in the hotel lobby, to see that Freddie was dressed from head to toe in exactly the same colour. He was surrounded by bodyguards, but I felt this incredible urge to break through and hug him. I smashed through the circle and I did hug him, and I gave him a letter, saying that I would like to meet "Frederick Bulsara" – not Mercury – and put my address and telephone number, never expecting him to call, of course. I referred to him by his original name because I always regarded Freddie as having two sides: the good and the bad, the white and the black. Freddie Bulsara was the good, the white side. It would not be until years later that I discovered that I wasn't so wrong.

'Then one of the bodyguards hit me, and they pushed me away. I could not blame them for being anxious, in case somebody intended to wound Freddie, but obviously I meant him no harm. I just had to touch him. I imagine there must be millions around the world who felt exactly like me. The band then left the hotel, got straight in their car and were driven away. Only Brian hung behind to sign autographs. They had to throw him in the back of the car [an armoured vehicle, complete with machine guns] in the end. As they drove away, I watched Freddie open and start reading my letter, and I was so elated.'

This was the same Argentinian girl who brought me a copy of Freddie's birth certificate in London, five years after his death.

At the Vélez Sarsfield stadium in Buenos Aires, fans queued from eight a.m. for the three sell-out shows – even though, due to the unbearable heat, performances would not kick off until ten p.m. Marcela attended two of the Buenos Aires gigs, watching her idols take to the stage flanked by armed guards.

'Argentina had never seen anything like it,' she said. 'At the beginning, they had something like a UFO descend onto the stage, amazing lights, smoke – it was like magic. Everyone had goose pimples. People were literally sobbing, all around. The pitch was protected with Astroturf, and security was extremely tight, police everywhere, because we had such a strict, extreme-right military government at that time, led by General Viola. The General said that he wanted to meet Queen, and sent an invitation for them to visit him. The whole band went except Roger, who objected, saying that he was in Argentina to play for the people, not for the government.'

It was an inflammatory statement. The country was then in the grip of a military Junta led by Roberto Eduardo Viola Redondo. He would be ousted in a coup that December by the Army's commander-in-chief, General Leopoldo Galtieri and was later imprisoned for alleged human rights violations. Galtieri would preside over the build-up and pursuit of the Falklands War, which would rage between the UK and Argentina in 1982. When the troubles erupted, all Queen music was banned from the airwaves.

'Within two years of Queen's first visit, we achieved democracy for the first time in nearly fifteen years,' Marcela pointed out. 'A similar thing happened in Brazil. Queen also went down to Sun City in South Africa in 1984, on a highly controversial visit. Within a couple of years, apartheid had fallen and the people had democracy. And shortly after they played gigs in Hungary in 1986, the old regime was abandoned and Hungarians had a new democratic future to look forward to. All probably coincidence, but a really amazing thing: wherever Queen went, it was as if they were bringing freedom and peace to the people. It was as if they were the band of liberty.'

Freddie was at the peak of his game, and looked muscular, tanned and fit. For their live performances, he went with his new stage look of tight jeans and white vest, with a scarf threaded through his belt loops. His neatly trimmed moustache was kept thick, to hide his protruding teeth. It was the identity he would maintain for the rest of his performing career which, although he did not know it at the time, was to be just five more years.

Pumping with energy, Freddie rushed at the stage each night. The roar of the crowd was deafening, but Freddie met it head-on.

'Not only did he cast a spell on his audience,' recalled David Wigg. 'He cast a spell on himself.'

Freddie conducted the audience while belting out enthusiastic 'Yeahs!' 'All rights!' and 'OKs!' '¡Cantan muy bien!' he praised the fans: 'You sing very well!' One special song stole the show: 'Love of My Life', which Freddie had written for Mary Austin. A live recording of that sweet ballad, released as a single throughout South America in 1979, had reigned at Number One in Argentina and Brazil for a year. The fans knew the song by heart. Their English was word-perfect. The throng was suddenly transformed into a sea of swaying flames as thousands pulled their lighters out. Freddie raised further thunder when he arranged himself at the piano to introduce another familiar number.

'This is sometimes known as "Bo Rap".'

The band launched into their signature, leaving the stage during the backing track of the choral sequences. Not even for the faithful of South America could that section of the song be performed live.

One of several interviews which Freddie gave in Buenos Aires was to *Pelo* (Hair), the massive-selling Argentinian equivalent of *Rolling Stone* magazine. Asked why he appeared always to be apart from the rest of the group, Freddie responded: 'As Queen play and record together, people see us as having a super-unit image. But

Queen is a musical group, not a family. Each one of us does whatever we like.'

In fact, a hallmark of that tour, and the shape of things to come, was a distinct divide between Freddie, his companions and the band management – Peter Freestone, Joe Fanelli, Jim Beach, Paul Prenter and Freddie's visiting current squeeze Peter Morgan – (all 'poofters' apart from Beach) in one camp, and the rest of the band and crew (the 'heteros') in another. Off-stage, the two factions lived separate lives, with the tour held together by Gerry Stickells, who took charge of the road and stage crew.

Freddie was, as usual, struggling with conflict in his private life. Morgan, a high-profile former Mr UK body-builder, infamous for having starred in one of the earliest homoerotic videos, had been having a sizzling on-off relationship with Freddie for some time, and flew out to join his lover for the Buenos Aires experience. But during his stay, Morgan betrayed Freddie with a much younger man, which Freddie discovered by chance when he spotted the couple strolling along the street one day. Two-timed by a lover yet again, Freddie could not be blamed for losing confidence in love. He dumped Morgan and focused his attention on the job in hand for the time being.

Not that the experience taught him a lesson. Freddie's next disastrous lover would be an American, Bill Reid, a stocky homosexual from New Jersey whom he met one night in a bar back in Manhattan. That relationship was to prove perhaps the stormiest of all. Freddie's entourage remember physical fights, smashed glass and shameful behaviour from the 'Bill Reid era'. According to Peter Freestone, Reid would be the reason Freddie eventually went off New York, withdrawing from the scene there, and even perhaps why he settled for the 'safer option' of a 'different guy after every show'.

'There were many intense emotional moments,' reflected Freestone. 'It was almost as though Freddie needed these surges of passion to start his creative juices flowing. That either because of the high pressure of work, he finished relationships, or conversely engineered dramatic rows when he needed the extra boost.'

Emotional conflict certainly seemed to enhance his creativity.

In Buenos Aires, fuelled by the anger and heartache Peter Morgan had caused him, Freddie threw himself at the job in hand as rarely before.

What were his expectations of the tour?

'I knew a lot about Argentina,' he said, 'but I never imagined that we were so well-known here. I am amazed by the nation's reaction to our being here ... we had long wanted to do a big South American tour. The idea had been in our minds for a long time. But for the past six months we have been working hard. Non-stop, really. Queen is not just the band. It involves a vast number of people. And therefore it costs a lot of money for us to tour.'

As for the price of fame, and of problems with the press, Freddie was dismissive. 'It bothered me for a long time,' he shrugged. 'But, as you can see, not any more.'

In another interview with since-defunct *Radiolanda 2000* magazine, he declared his love for the Argentinian people.

'I was accustomed to another kind of reaction and behaviour from audiences,' he said.

'But Argentinians are amazing, and I want to come back. I must admit I love it that people think I'm an idol. I do want to be a legend, but you must understand that our work is a joint effort. Queen is not just Freddie Mercury. It's the band. You just have to remember 'Seven Seas of Rhye', 'Killer Queen', 'You're My Best Friend', 'Somebody to Love' (Freddie's and his mother's personal favourite), 'Bohemian Rhapsody' – which actually was the most satisfying moment of my career. This was all Queen, not Freddie. I think the best proof of our respect for the audience is our work.'

To avoid kidnapping or acts of terrorism, security on that tour was the tightest yet. Each band member was assigned a local bodyguard and translator, in addition to the English security staff who now travelled with the group. Freddie would amuse himself by getting his own bodyguard to write autographs on his behalf, when fans left mountains of items for him to sign. He would also infuriate his caretakers by pushing all the buttons in the lift at once, causing the doors to open on every floor. Described as 'like a small boy having mischief', Freddie would do press-ups on the hall carpet or challenge his minders to running races along the hotel corridors whenever he found himself waiting around, which was often.

He also started insisting to all and sundry that cigarettes were bad for the health. To that end, he banned his chauffeurs from smoking. The drivers naturally assumed that Freddie was talking about his *own* health. Imagine their surprise when he slid into the limousine and lit up a menthol cigarette. 'It's for the good of *their* health, not mine!' he howled, tickled by his own joke.

One suffocating night, Freddie demanded dinner at exclusive Buenos Aires restaurant Los Años Locos (The Mad Years). With such a high-profile charge in such a visible place, his bodyguards were on tenterhooks – especially when he begged to go to the men's room alone instead of uttering his usual 'pi-pi!' and waiting to be taken. As his party's table was on the second floor, with the Gents nearby, his guards relaxed. They didn't see why he shouldn't relieve himself alone for once. They would notice, surely, if anyone tried to sneak into the toilet while Freddie was inside. But after almost twenty minutes, Freddie had not reappeared. The guards realised something must have happened, and rushed to the men's room.

'We found two men and two women banging on one of the cubicle doors, which appeared to be locked from the inside,' a guard reported. 'We could only assume Freddie was in there. These people were terrorising him, shouting at Freddie to open the door, they *had* to see him, they *must* have autographs. Freddie was not responding, and I could now see that he had locked himself in. I feared something must have happened to him. We yelled at the people to get out. When things calmed down a little, and Freddie realised it was us, he opened the door. He seemed terrified. "You were right," he said with a white face. "I can't even go to the bathroom alone, can I?"'

The night before Queen's final date at Vélez Sarsfield, the band were invited to a celebratory '*asado*' (barbecue/roasting) at the *quinta* (weekend retreat) of stadium President Señor Petraca. The huge estate was beautiful, and the band fell in love with it. All went well until the press appeared. Freddie's mood changed. Not that he objected to journalists per se. I was a journalist myself when I met him, and he was always the perfectly relaxed host. It was simply the unimaginative questions that foreign journalists tended to ask which exasperated him.

'They've been asking me the same stupid questions for the past ten years,' he said.

Freddie was in a mischievous mood when two local journalists approached him, one of whom worked for *Pelo* magazine, neither of whom spoke English. Unbeknown to the hack, Freddie and his interpreter had cooked up a deal. The latter would translate questions for Freddie, so that he knew what was being asked. While Freddie spouted nonsense, the interpreter would tell the journalist whatever came into his head. When the interpreter obtained a copy of the magazine, they were amused to see that all the answers were accurately fictitious – except one, relating to Diego Maradona.

Argentina had been world football champions since claiming the trophy for the first time, on home turf, in 1978. Soccer was sacred. Maradona was a national god, and Queen had long admired him. As Brian once wrote of him in a letter to me, 'The spirit of the pursuit of excellence lives in the man.'

Freddie met Maradona at a party in Castelar outside Buenos Aires, and invited him to appear on stage during Queen's final Buenos Aires show. Maradona accepted readily.

'Freddie hadn't really known who he was, as he was not what you could call a football fan,' laughed Peter Freestone. 'Footballers' thighs, maybe. Rugby players' thighs, even better!'

Still, Freddie could not help but be amused by the young soccer star. To some extent, he could identify with him: they shared modest stature and an unquenchable thirst for success. Maradona duly appeared to ecstatic applause, whereupon the footballer peeled off his Number 10 team shirt, and swapped it for the rock star's 'Flash' T-shirt. He then introduced 'Another One Bites the Dust', and retreated, as Queen tore in to one of Argentina's all-time favourite rock numbers.

Perhaps the *Pelo* journalist was not so stupid when he quizzed Freddie at the *asado*. He put it to Freddie that the shirt-exchange moment with the nation's greatest sporting idol had been a 'demagogic act'. Freddie, incensed by the implication, denounced the suggestion as 'ridiculous'. He declared it to have been a friendly gesture, nothing more.

'If the audience thinks it's OK to do such a thing, and appreciates it for what it is, I don't give a damn what the press might think,' he retorted. 'I'm going to do what I like, regardless of whether the press label it "demagogic" or wrong.'

The South America experience was not thrills all the way. Followed and harassed by both media and fans, who would congregate around him in a flash, Freddie spent more time legging it from madding crowds than he would have liked. Recognised wherever he went, he found peace and quiet only behind the locked doors of his hotel suite. He slept more than usual, rarely leaving his room before two p.m. He would occasionally ask to go for a drive around the city, but his favourite off-duty pastimes were eating and shopping. His entourage were run ragged trying to arrange a different restaurant every evening, even though Freddie ate next to nothing when he got there. At least his shopping trips were fruitful. On one excursion alone he purchased 25 pairs of socks, 10 identical T-shirts, and 20 pairs of matching trousers. His bodyguards wondered why he bought so many of each. They were surprised when he explained that, as a teenager, he never had the opportunity to just be a kid, and to wear exactly what he wanted. This, he told them, was his way of making it up to himself.

'Now and then he would have a childish turn, such as the day we visited the Japanese Garden in Buenos Aires,' reported one bodyguard.

'It had a nursery, pathways and little bridges. Freddie found it enchanting. He said that he wanted to create a similar garden in London. At one point, he climbed to the top of a waterfall to take a picture. The Japanese guard saw him, and ordered Freddie down. I had to explain who Freddie was, and persuade the guard to let him stay up there to take photos. Freddie would only come down when he was ready, when he fed the Koi carp and left two autographs in the visitors' book.'

Queen's elation at their historic tour of Argentina was deflated by news that their ambition to perform at Rio's most famous stadium had been dashed by red tape. The fabled Maracanã had a capacity of 180,000, making it the biggest in the world at the time. The technical, legal and political difficulties encountered by Queen's promoters in Brazil could hardly be underestimated. The governor of Rio de Janeiro refused them permission to play at the stadium, declaring that it could only be used for sports, religious and culturally significant events. The Pope had appeared there the year before. So had Frank Sinatra, but it was a puzzling 'no' to Queen.

The show must go on. They settled for the Morumbi stadium in São Paulo further south, where they performed for 131,000 people. It was the largest paying audience for a single act anywhere in the world. The following night, another 120,000 turned up to witness the magic, hemmed in by mounted riot police and with armed plain-clothes officers moving among the crowd. Again, in a city where few spoke English, the sight of more than a hundred thousand fans singing along to 'Love of My Life', Queen's anthem to South America, was spectacularly moving. Over two nights,

251,000 people watched Queen play live. It was a greater audience than most artists can expect over an entire career.

The unrivalled success of Queen in South America was the brightest feather in the cap of lawyer-turned-business manager Jim Beach, now known to the band as 'Miami'. Having spent five months convincing authorities in both countries that all would benefit from Queen's pioneering rock adventure, he was vindicated.

'In seven concerts, Queen have been seen by over half a million people who were totally unfamiliar with rock concerts,' said Beach in Brazil. 'The actual costs of appearing down here are so enormous that the profit margin for the band is quite small. But the promotion is marvellous. During our last week in Argentina, every one of Queen's ten albums filled the top ten positions in the charts. Before we came, everyone said that no group could play successfully in South America, but we have proved that they can.'

'We had no idea how they were going to react to us,' added Brian.

'In Europe and America, we know what to expect. But for these fans down here, it was a completely new phenomenon. In Argentina, where they are relatively more sophisticated, they did have some idea of what to expect, but for the Brazilian fans every-thing was totally new. One of the most exciting moments in my life was when I looked out and saw a hundred and thirty thousand people waiting for us.'

The critics got provocative. Did Queen not have a moral obli-gation to shun performances in oppressed countries with volatile political climates such as Argentina? Were they not, by default, supporting the very regimes of which the world disapproved? Jim Beach was unrepentant: 'If we took that attitude,' he said, 'then there would be very few countries in the world outside Western Europe and North America where we would ever be able to play at all.'

Freddie kept schtum, having learned the hard way that a digni-fied silence in the face of criticism was advisable.

'He doesn't talk any more because he's a little tired of Queen and himself being misrepresented,' commented Brian. 'I think anybody who meets Freddie would be in for a bit of a surprise. He's not quite the prima donna you'd imagine. Obviously, he's a positive character, but so are we all. When all is said and done, he works damned hard and puts on a good show.'

Where would the restless Queen spirit take them next?

17

Barbara

Barbara Valentin fascinated me because she's got such great tits!
Barbara and I have formed a bond which is stronger than anything I've
had with a lover for the last six years. I can really talk to her and be myself
in a way that's very rare.

Freddie Mercury

It was all a crazy time, far better and worse than anyone could ever
imagine.

Barbara Valentin

With Queen's scheduled *Greatest Hits* album put back until the end of the year, April 1981 became Roger's month. *Fun in Space*, his first solo album, had been recorded in Montreux the year before, and was all set. He had found the process exhausting, he admitted, being used to the presence and support of the three musicians he had worked with non-stop for ten years. But break-out was inevitable, after such an intense and all-consuming decade together.

'There were certain things I wanted to do which weren't within the Queen format,' he said. 'It's like flushing out your system. Until you've done it you just don't feel fulfilled.'

The other members of Queen, in their own time, would follow suit.

After Brian's daughter Louisa was born in May, he joined Freddie, Roger, John and Mack in Montreux to work on *Hot Space*. In July, tranquil Montreux prepared itself for the masses, who descended for Claude Nobs's annual jazz festival.

'I was living above Montreux at around the time Queen bought Mountain Studios,' says Rick Wakeman, who had gone there in 1976 to record Yes album *Going for the One*, having rejoined the band. There, he met Mountain Studios assistant Danielle Corminboeuf, for whom he left his wife Ros.

'Switzerland is a very staid country,' says Rick, 'but there was always an element of acceptance for what you were. The locals were thrilled that Queen owned the studios. Nobody gave a monkey's toss what you did behind closed doors. The press in Switzerland didn't give a toss either. So, a great place for rock musicians to live and work.

'There was one pub on the main street called the White Horse, which we called the Blanc Gigi (still at Grand Rue 28). It was the place where everybody working at Mountain Studios would congregate. If a couple of bands overlapped, or if Queen were in, the Blanc Gigi was where we'd end up. I'd hang out there mainly with Roger and Brian, but Freddie would often turn up, invariably with a young French boy, but so what. He wasn't openly out, of course, but nobody said anything. Those were different times. Queen loved Montreux. To have their own studios made good business sense. Plus, they got to go and stay there whenever they wanted.

'Bands back then were essentially bone-idle. You'd rock up at the studio costing thousands a day. One would be off skiing, one would be in bed pissed from the night before. Jon (Anderson) and I might turn up, write a bit of a song, toddle off down the pub, and then finally get down to it at about seven p.m. It was rare for anyone ever to do a full day's work. What should have taken five or six weeks was taking five or six months. The studios were making a fortune. You couldn't record like that now. With today's technology, you can just about make an album in your bedroom.

'My neighbour there for years was David Bowie. It was on one particular night when David wandered into the pub, had dinner with the Queen lads and then went back with them to the studio, that things kind of turned into history.'

Mountain Studios' engineer David Richards, who was working on the Yes album, had earlier assisted producer Tony Visconti on David Bowie's 1977 *Heroes* album in Berlin. Bowie was booked in with Richards at Mountain Studios to record the track 'Cat People (Putting Out the Fire)'. He wandered into the studios after the pub, and found Queen mid-session.

'An extremely long night,' said Brian.

'We were playing other people's songs for fun, just jamming,' said Roger.

'In the end, David said "this is stupid, why don't we just write one?"'

The result was their co-production 'Under Pressure' – initially entitled 'People On Streets'.

'It came about by pure chance, my dears,' explained Freddie later.

'We began to dabble on something together, and it happened very spontaneously and very quickly indeed. We were both over-joyed by the result.

'It may have been a totally unexpected thing, but as a group we are all strong believers in doing things which are unusual, not expected of us, and out of the ordinary. We never want to get into a rut or become stale as a band, and there is a danger of doing that when you have been together as long as we have. There is a danger of resting on your laurels and just getting lax.'

David was 'a real pleasure to work with', said Freddie. 'He is a remarkable talent. When I saw him play in the stage version of *The Elephant Man* on Broadway, his performance fuelled me with thoughts about acting. It is something I may do in the future, but right now I'm looking at other projects to do with Queen. We never want to stay still. There are so many vistas still to explore.'

Brian remembered the recording differently.

'It was very hard,' he said, 'because you already had four precocious boys and David, who was precocious enough for all of us. Passions ran very high . . . I got so little of my own way. But David had a real vision, and he took over the song lyrically.'

A fortnight later, Freddie, Roger, Bowie and Mack reconvened at New York's famous Power Station studios to remix the track, Brian having backed out of the project.

Power Station, known for artists as diverse as Tony Bennett, Aerosmith and later Duran Duran, had been a working power plant on West 53rd Street, and was remodelled as a recording studio by producer Tony Bongiovi. The place had a fantastic acoustic. When Bongiovi gave his second cousin a leg-up into the music business by offering him a run-around job at the studio, also covering the cost of his demos and singing lessons, he unwittingly provided Freddie and Bowie with a teaboy who would one day be as famous as they were. Bongiovi's young cousin, Jon, later changed his surname to Bon Jovi, launching a band of that name. The cousins would fall out, and Power Station would become Avatar, but the legend endured.

'Under Pressure' turned out to be one of the most challenging recordings any of them had ever worked on. The mixing desk collapsed, Bowie wanted to remake the track from scratch, and things came to a head. At one point Bowie refused to allow its release, but later backed down.

'"Under Pressure' is a significant song for us," Brian would say, nearly thirty years later, 'and that is because of David and its lyrical content. I would have found that hard to admit in the old days, but I can admit it now. One day, I would love to sit down quietly on my own and remix it.'

The October 1981 single was Bowie's first released recording with another artist.

Reaching Number Twenty-Nine in the US, it was to be Queen's second UK Number One single. It would also be their last until 'Innuendo', almost a decade later, a few months before Freddie died. 'Under Pressure' also appeared on Queen's tenth studio album *Hot Space*, released in May 1982. Later it would be sampled by rapper Vanilla Ice on his 1990 single 'Ice Ice Baby' – without Queen's permission – and would become the debut single of Jedward, the identical twins from ITV's *The X Factor*. Their version reached Number Two in the UK and Number One in Ireland.

Come September, Freddie was ready to party. He celebrated his thirty-fifth birthday in style, at a cost of £200,000, by flying a posse of pals including Peter Straker and Peter Freestone to New York on Concorde. Freddie had taken a lavish suite at the Berkshire Place Hotel on East 52nd Street, on the corner diagonally opposite the Cartier store. Over five misspent days, a staggering £30,000-worth of vintage champagne was downed.

'I remember the absolute mess our suite got into,' groaned Peter Freestone. 'And I remember Freddie sprawled out on a huge heap of gladioli. Those were what you could call "parties".'

That birthday marked a turning point for Freddie. He gave a rare press interview, explaining how he had changed, and how he now viewed fame and fortune rather differently than he had in his younger day.

'I hate mixing with lots of showbusiness personalities,' he confessed. 'I could do a Rod Stewart and join that crowd, but I want to stay out of all that. When I am not in Queen I want to be the ordinary man in the street.

'I've changed. In the early days, I used to enjoy being recognised. Not now. I spend a lot of time in New York, where a lot of people don't know me. I may be very rich, but the days of posing and pretending to have money have long gone. I'm a jeans-and-T-shirt man around the house and everywhere else. I don't put on a show any more when I leave the stage, because I'm secure in my own knowledge of who I am and what I have. Gone are the days when I wanted to walk into a room and stop everyone's conversation. I can't predict whether we will go on, but as long as we keep breaking new ground, the fire will remain in Queen. If I lost everything I had tomorrow, I'd claw my way back to the top somehow.'

Could these have been his most honest public words to date? Was this statement confirmation from Freddie that a deliberate metamorphosis was underway, or was he going all out to convince himself? Some saw this as a thinly-disguised attempt to show the world that he was finally comfortable in his own skin. Was he really, though? Whether or not he felt genuinely at one with his true personality, or whether this was mostly wishful thinking, we could only speculate.

Freddie joined the rest of the band in New Orleans after his birthday party, to begin rehearsals for another Latin jaunt. This second foray, dubbed 'the Gluttons for Punishment' tour, for all the obvious reasons, was the antithesis of their first. First, they travelled to Venezuela to perform three gigs at the Poliedro de Caracas. But their schedule was interrupted by the death of former president and national hero Rómulo Betancourt, resulting in several Venezuelan shows being cancelled. With ten days to wait before the next wave of gigs in Mexico, Queen withdrew to Miami.

There was no accounting for the ensuing wave of Mexican mishaps: serious crew illness, shocking corruption, threats to personal safety, their promoter's arrest, and, not least, the collapse of a bridge outside Monterrey's huge Estadio Olímpico Universitario – 'Volcano' stadium – after one show, which resulted in a number of injuries to fans. The second gig was cancelled and Queen moved on to Pueblo, where they were booked to play two nights at the Estadio Ignacio Zaragoza. The experience was a fiasco.

'We thought we could repeat what we'd done in South America,' said Brian. 'But we escaped by the skin of our teeth.'

Earlier that year, the *New York Times* had reported the phenomenon of a rare form of skin cancer affecting forty-one previously healthy homosexuals. At least nine of them suffered unexplained immune system deficiency. Kaposi's sarcoma had until then occurred almost exclusively in elderly males of Mediterranean descent. Other cases were reported in San Francisco and Los Angeles. By the end of August, the number had risen to 120, most of them in New York. It was soon confirmed by the Atlanta Center for Disease Control that Kaposi's sarcoma and a rare, parasitical form of pneumonia called pneumocystis carinii pneumonia (PCP) were inexplicably on the rise across America. Of all reported diagnoses, more than 90 per cent of victims were gay men. Thus began speculation that a new 'gay plague' could be linked to a promiscuous homosexual lifestyle, and/or to drug abuse. Conclusive evidence showed that the disease originally referred to as GRID (Gay-Related Immune Deficiency) also affected millions of heterosexual men, women and children, and that it occurred notably in haemophiliacs and intravenous drug-users. It was eventually established that the disease now renamed AIDS (Acquired Immune Deficiency Syndrome) was spread via blood, blood products, the sharing of hypodermic needles, and through unprotected sex.

Freddie didn't pay too much attention. Queen were preoccupied with other things. Tenth anniversary products included their *Greatest Hits* album, the *Greatest Flix* collection of all their promo videos, and a set of portraits by Princess Margaret's former husband, Lord Snowdon. They also starred in their first feature film of a live concert, filmed in Montreal. The final weeks of 1981 sent them scuttling back to Munich. Officially still tax exiles, they were due to begin another album there, and the Arabella-Haus apartment hotel welcomed Freddie back.

'Only for a night or two, because he hated it so much,' recalled Peter Freestone. 'It was above the Musicland Studios, and was yet another dreadful concrete block, its corridors filled with the pungent smells of Arab cooking. At first, Freddie lived with Winnie Kirchberger (a local boyfriend) at his place. Later it was the Stollbergplaza apartment hotel in a more elegant part of central Munich, where he met Barbara Valentin, a well-known actress who lived opposite.'

With Peter to see to his needs and accompany him on nightly jaunts, Freddie's lifestyle in Munich seemed quite charmed. Worryingly for the rest of the band, however, he seemed to have lost the taste for work.

'He got to the point where he could hardly stand being in a studio. He'd want to do his bit and get out,' remembered Brian.

Queen's return to the Bavarian capital marked the beginning of a frantic and confusing period in Freddie's personal life, when he would become embroiled in a distressing tangle of love affairs.

The first was with Winfried Kirchberger, rechristened 'Winnie', naturally: an aggressive, uneducated Tyrol-born restaurateur with thick black hair and a bristly moustache. He was so bluff and ready that none of Freddie's entourage could fathom the attraction. They had not taken on board that 'unwashed truck driver' was now Freddie's preferred male type.

The second was with an Irish hairdresser called Jim Hutton, whom Freddie had picked up in a London club. He would fly Jim to Munich and parade him to make Winnie jealous. Ironically, a much deeper bond was to develop between Freddie and Jim, who would remain at Freddie's side for the rest of his life.

The third lover in the equation was perhaps the most unexpected. Freddie's new drinking partner, Barbara Valentin, was a famous Austrian-born former soft-porn actress and model dubbed 'the German Jayne Mansfield' or 'Brigitte Bardot'. She had made her name in edgy, stylised films about love, hate and prejudice with cult movie director Rainer Werner Fassbinder of the New German Cinema movement. Fassbinder, who would die the following year aged just thirty-seven from a sleeping pill and cocaine overdose, was a complicated man with a scandalous lifestyle. He was described by one of his wives as being 'a homosexual who also needed a woman', thus appearing to have plenty in common with Freddie. But it was Barbara, not Fassbinder, who would become Freddie's live-in lover and almost constant companion – bizarrely sharing him with both Winnie Kirchberger and Jim Hutton, who were also his lovers. As Barbara herself remarked, it was all a 'crazy time'.

I visited Barbara Valentin in Munich in 1996, at the chintzy third-floor apartment she and Freddie purchased together on HansSachs Strasse in the by then seedy Bermuda Triangle district. The flat was cosy: all rugs, drapes and velvet sofas. There were valuable-looking paintings, rustic Bavarian furniture and a fine antique chandelier. Her sideboard was crammed with framed photographs of her children, her grandchildren, and of Freddie, and heaving with Queen and Freddie Mercury videos and CDs, which she said she could never bring herself to watch or listen to. Tarzan, the sixteen-year-old 'child' (cat) which she shared with Freddie, lay snoozing on a plump armchair.

Barbara had endured a lengthy and bitter legal battle with Queen's management to retain the apartment after Freddie's death. She was consequently nervous about revealing too much, and it took several months to persuade her to talk to me.

'Other people have to live on,' said thrice-married Barbara, who would die of a stroke in 2002, aged sixty-one. 'I don't want to hurt anybody by talking about Freddie. Let Mary Austin be the widow, I've always said. I have refused to talk about Freddie until now.'

Well into her fifties when we met, she retained the allure that Freddie must have fallen for. A heavy-boned, big-breasted former baroness by marriage, she filled the room. The one-carat diamond stud in her right earlobe was the first present Freddie gave her, she said. On the street, the well-known actress still turned heads.

What Freddie saw in Barbara was a woman who could not have been less like Mary Austin if she tried: a strong, determined female in charge of her destiny. Like him, Barbara was a mass of contradictions. Her imposing image concealed an intense sensitivity and fragility. Perhaps for the first time in his life, Freddie connected with another human being with whom he felt able to be himself, warts and all. They had no secrets. He did not feel any need to protect her from aspects of his personality and behaviour, the way he did with Mary.

Barbara understood. She was the same way herself, never caring what others thought. Her attitude towards people, life and the world in general was a breath of fresh air to Freddie. She looked pneumatically all-woman but she acted like a man, thinking nothing of knocking people out of her way, and causing even bodyguards to retreat. Freddie was intoxicated by Barbara's ferocity and majesty. They responded to the longings of each other's souls.

That Barbara was willing to relinquish a potentially lucrative theatre career to be with Freddie, and the fact that he allowed her to do so, was, by her reckoning, the ultimate proof of undying love. She would accompany Freddie on Queen and private business, to Rio, Montreux, Ibiza and Spain. She stayed with him in London 'forty or fifty times', and was given her own bedroom at Garden Lodge.

'I used to see him out with his cronies in the Munich clubs, mostly the "New York" disco, night after night,' Barbara recalled. 'I vaguely knew who Freddie Mercury was, but to be a famous rock star was no great shakes in Munich. I was probably more famous here than him. He always had an entourage, he was an industry all by himself. Freddie even had his own little corner in the club: "the Family Corner". He was with Winnie then. They were living together at Winnie's place. They had quite a long relationship, with several breaks. They couldn't keep away from each other. They made an unusual couple, and would have terrible fights. Each would pick up unsuitable guys to make the other jealous.'

At the time Winnie owned a simple rustic restaurant, 'Sebastian Stub'n', where customers were always complaining about the food. After the place burned down, its renovation was partly funded by Freddie, who seemed always to be investing in the dreams of friends.

'Winnie was a tragedy to Freddie,' said Barbara. 'They were undoubtedly in love, but they were always fighting each other, hurting each other. It made me think, why do lovers have to hurt each other? To me, it is one of the greatest tragedies. He was very simple in his mind, Winnie, you know. Not much education, no decent school, whatever, and I think he had a chip on his shoulder about that. There were times when he obviously felt that he really wanted to show Freddie: "Who cares that you're a stupid rock 'n' roll star? I'm Winnie Kirchberger, the macho shit." He would show him up dreadfully in public, treat him badly, do stupid things, terrible things, just to hurt Freddie and put him down. It occurred to me that Freddie adored Winnie *because* he was so awful to him most of the time. Freddie couldn't just have Winnie's approval and adoration the way he seemed to get it so easily from the rest of the world, and that made Freddie work all the harder to get him. Perhaps Winnie, in his simple way, understood this: that the only way he could keep hold of Freddie Mercury was to treat him like shit, and pretend he didn't want him at all. Whatever it was, it worked. Freddie went back to him time and time again for more.'

The relationship had its compensations.

'It was the only time in his adult life that Freddie knew what it was like to live a relatively ordinary life with another man,' Peter Freestone said.

Much later, their relationship over, Freddie had gone for good and Winnie descended into madness, the HIV virus having claimed his mind as well as his body.

'At the end I found him starving in his apartment,' sighed Barbara, 'the cat eating its own fur to survive. I got him into hospital and paid his medical bills, but it was far too late to help him.'

In their heyday, however, Winnie, Freddie and Barbara had been a trio around town to be reckoned with.

'One night Freddie and I wound up having a drink together in a rowdy club, adjourned to the Ladies' toilets where it was quiet enough to talk, and it went from there. He told me all about Zanzibar, the boarding school, the father, the mother, how he didn't believe they'd ever accept him as gay – although I later got the impression that they had come to terms with it. At the end of his life, certainly, they were close. But they liked Mary. Freddie said they always expected that she'd have his baby. He told me about his sister Kash, and the kids Natalie and Sam who she and her husband Roger had adopted. He said he didn't usually talk about such things, not even with friends, but that with me it was easy.'

In fact, Freddie had always maintained a 'remotely close' relationship with his sister, her husband Roger and their children, just as he had with his parents. He never denied their existence, nor turned his back on them. He saw them infrequently, but always lovingly. He simply saw it as his duty to protect them from his own wild lifestyle, as well as from the public gaze.

'We never really went to "those parties"!' Freddie's brother-in-law told the *Mail on Sunday* in November 2000, nine years after Freddie's death. 'Only to family gatherings. Freddie kept his life strictly in compartments, and they rarely overlapped. We used to celebrate our kids' birthdays at Freddie's. He'd always have a massive cake or Easter egg for them. He never had any kids of his own, so I guess he liked the novelty, but I think he would have liked to have seen our children grow up.'

That Munich night, Freddie and Barbara couldn't bear to tear themselves away from each other.

'He laughed so much at me, usually putting his hand up to his face to hide his teeth. But when he got drunk, he'd laugh openly and loudly.'

While brave enough to acknowledge that they were now on a

dangerous treadmill, Barbara insisted that she and Freddie did derive enjoyment from the mad Munich lifestyle they lived to excess, and which they went for so shamelessly and deliberately.

'It was the best defence. From what? I can't tell you. A number of things. Every day, something new. Freddie and I were always up against it for one reason or another, but at least we had each other. We would never let anyone else see when we were wounded, but we'd show each other. We both had things to hide from our families, for example. Freddie was protecting his parents and sister, and I certainly did not want my children to know everything about my lifestyle. Now and again it might happen that I'd run into my son at a disco and I'd go, "Oh my God, wrong disco!" Freddie and I became each other's second family. We always left our private family sides private.'

On 26 November, Winnie's birthday, Barbara, Freddie and Winnie found themselves in bed together.

'We are all stark naked and the doorbell goes, seven o'clock in the morning: tax police! "Come back later!" yells Freddie. "If you don't let us in, we're breaking the door down now!" they yell back. Freddie was frantic. He came screaming back into the bedroom crying, "Get up! Get up!" The next minute, the police were inside and stationed in every room. There was Freddie, naked except for a little towel around his waist. We three were told to stay exactly where we were. They tore the place apart. Finally Freddie says, "I really need to take a piss, guys." So they let him go. And suddenly, the policeman beside the bathroom recognises him: "It's Freddie Mercury!" Freddie got cheeky then. Being Freddie, he couldn't resist. He said to the policeman, "If you're nice to my girlfriend, I'll sing a song for you. Come on mate, let's have a glass of champagne together." It was still not even eight o'clock, and the policeman sheepishly said, "Sorry, we're on duty." "OK then, go fuck yourself!" Freddie retorted. "You're all too ugly to be sung to anyway!"'

Barbara claimed there was no question that she and Freddie were passionately in love.

'Quite possibly, yes,' agreed Peter Freestone. 'They were very close. I liked her enormously. They had a lot in common: status, fame. Barbara didn't care. She had that wonderful take-it-or-leave-it attitude which Freddie found so refreshing. They had similar tastes, and were both very classy. Barbara was very, very important to Freddie.'

Freddie talked to Barbara constantly about Mary Austin.

'Apparently he had once promised to marry her. Because of that, he felt guilty. He was dutiful and had a deep sense of obligation. It had been expected of him, and he'd gone back on his word. The guilt never went away ... although I wondered how much of that guilt she herself made him feel. It wasn't Freddie's fault that he turned out to be mostly gay. That's life. Still, he couldn't get over the way he had let her down. He said that he hadn't been gay, not in the beginning, but then he just turned around, flipped out completely, and started to live a gay life. It was a choice, not a biological thing, with him.'

'That is absolutely true,' agreed Peter Freestone. 'Freddie was very emotional at that time.'

Although Mary often came to stay in Munich, the two women never grew close. 'She was cool, and quite wary of me,' said Barbara.

'Not that she wasn't nice. She *was*, extremely. But it was reserved and polite, not warm. We did at least exchange Christmas presents. One thing I must say for her is that she always had Freddie's best interests at heart.

'Once, she phoned me from London to say that one of Freddie's cats had died. "You break it to him, Barbara," she said, "but go gently, find the right moment." I agonised, and finally told him. He broke down uncontrollably, and said, "We're flying to London right now." "Freddie," I said, "the cat is dead." But he wouldn't hear otherwise. Back to London it was.'

Homosexuality was a role he chose to play, Barbara believed.

'He *was* the Great Pretender. It excited him, because it was forbidden fruit. While all this was going on, he and I were lovers in the truest sense. We did have sex together regularly. Yes. Yes. It took a while. When it happened, it was beautiful and innocent. I was completely in love with him by this time, and he had told me that he loved me. We even talked of getting married. Of course, he'd still pick up dozens of gay guys and bring them back night after night, but I didn't mind. Sounds insane, doesn't it, but that's the life we were living, and I couldn't stop him even if I wanted to. I continued to take lovers myself. To a certain point I was allowed. Then Freddie started to show off and would kick them out.'

In the end, said Barbara, Freddie didn't care about sex.

'He'd get together with people just for tenderness, affection. His longings had nothing to do with the body any more. He was like a little child. He'd cry like a baby. He'd say to me, "Barbara, the only thing they can't take from me is you."'

Whether by 'they', Freddie meant the Queen machine, the wider music business, the fans, or even the all-pervasive Jim Beach, Barbara never knew.

'It all sounds so far-fetched when I talk about it now. You had to be there to make sense of it.

'Sometimes I'd say to him, "Darling, there's more to you than your prick, you know." He would say to me often that he didn't enjoy sleeping with all those guys. But Freddie wouldn't be told by anyone what he could or couldn't do.'

The single most lethal threat to Freddie's sanity was his dependence on other people, Barbara perceived.

'He didn't know the difference between one Deutschmark and a thousand dollars. Money meant nothing to him. He was terrified of planes, and of getting stuck in elevators, and more afraid than anything of being alone. He couldn't go anywhere by himself – not even to the toilet. I always had to go with him. Wherever Freddie was, there was a mess. But he was perfect at delegating people to clean up.'

'We were both trying far too hard to be happy,' she admitted.

'Because we were *not* happy. You get drunk, you take blow, you play the monkey, you lay as many people as you can, all as if you are daring your body to stay alive. It is a sort of death wish. In the end it just makes you *more* lonely, *more* empty. Freddie and I were both as bad as each other. We identified with each other. In the end, we were the only one that each of us could turn to. If he hadn't had me, and I hadn't had him, I think that we would both have been dead much sooner.'

18

Jim

I'm very happy with my relationship at the moment, and I honestly couldn't ask for better. It's a kind of ... solace. Yes, that's a good word. We won't call it menopause! I don't have to try so hard. I don't have to prove myself now. I've got a very understanding relationship. It sounds so boring, but it's wonderful.

Freddie Mercury

Freddie was the love of my life. There was no one like him. He always said that you must get on with life. I know that when I die, Freddie will be on the other side, waiting for me.

Jim Hutton

John Travolta had a hand in it, when he made an unlikely hero of blue-collar Tony Manero in *Saturday Night Fever*. The 1977 film, based on a New York magazine feature conjured by Britain's original rock journalist, Nik Cohn, told the tale of a teenage Italian American who found refuge from grim reality in a neighbourhood disco. The Bee Gees' album became the biggest-selling soundtrack of all time. Disco-fever was born, and New York City was at the vanguard. Studio 54, Le Jardin and Regine's were *the* hotspots, to which every imaginable freak pitched up nightly. It was the heyday of playboys, supermodels, stretch limos, champagne and cocaine, with Halston, Gucci and Fiorucci thrown in. City clubland became an outlet for sexual emancipation and reflected the decadent gay scene better than a mirror.

Midtown's Le Jardin, on West 43rd Street, attracted the coolest crowd: Andy Warhol, Bianca Jagger, Liza Minnelli, Lou Reed. The bars boasted mirror tiles for chopping 'blow', black lights flared down on white sofas fringed with palm trees, and its rooftop featured waterbeds where clients reclined, inhaling outlawed substances while gazing across Times Square.

By comparison, London's gay scene was still waiting to go on. It offered little beyond 'a few grubby pubs and some tiny basement coffee bars' when Jeremy Norman came down from Cambridge in the late 1970s to work on *Burke's Peerage*, the definitive guide to British royalty and aristocracy. Norman heard about the new wave of discos flooding New York's gay and club scenes, and paid a visit. At Le Jardin he met club promoter Stephen Hayter and they returned to London together to launch the Embassy Club on Old Bond Street. There, Hayter reigned supreme as 'Queen of the Night', boasting that he kept his press cuttings in a bank vault in Switzerland, and disapproving vociferously of 'screaming queens' who had 'a regrettable tendency to call each other by girls' names'. He would become the first high-profile club owner to die of AIDS.

The Embassy was a revelation: a sexually ambiguous fantasy realm which attracted all-comers and which served as both antidote to and distraction from the high inflation and government corruption of the era. Suddenly, folk were dressing up to go dancing again. But not just any old folk. Transsexuals, rock stars, divas, drag queens, European crown princes, millionaire counts and Page Three popsies. Waiters wore jaunty red and white satin shorts modelled on those worn by the boys in Studio 54. Poseurs simulated sex on the counters while the hard-nosed did it for real behind bathroom doors. Cocaine and amyl nitrate were ingested in brain-blasting quantities. Strobe lighting, dry ice and a silver disco ball gilded the effect. The club could draw the in-crowd like no place else. Pete Townshend, Mick Jagger, Marie Helvin and David Bowie were regulars. Even cool New Romantics would divert from the Blitz Club to take a twirl on the Embassy floor.

'When Hayter had a party, you did your best to get in,' recalls Dave Hogan. 'Freddie, Kenny Everett, the cream of London's gay mafia would be there. You'd witness wonderful scenes, and go along with all of it, but you were only there to enjoy it. You knew you'd never take a picture and get out alive.'

The Embassy was the prototype for Jeremy Norman's even more ambitious project: a nightspot catering almost exclusively to the needs of gay men. Situated off Trafalgar Square beneath Charing Cross station, Heaven occupied 21,000 square feet under the arches. As one of the world's first openly gay clubs when it launched in 1979, it made headlines and the gay clubbing scene acceptable.

Freddie adored the place, and he and his entourage were frequent visitors.

'For gay men, the dance floor was truly a place of liberation,' remembered Jeremy Norman, who later revealed all in his memoir *No Make-Up: Straight Tales From a Queer Life*. [It was] a place where we could feel free to express our sexuality and the unity of our tribe. The dance club was, in a sense, our cathedral.'

It was also, in many cases, their Waterloo. While Norman, who would found two AIDS charities, by no mean stands accused of having brought the disease to Britain, there is no question that his club had a fatal attraction.

Paul Gambaccini remembers with chilling clarity the night in 1984 when he realised that Freddie was going to die.

'I was standing in a particular spot in Heaven with him, and I asked him if he had altered his behaviour in the light of recent developments,' Paul says. 'And with that characteristic flash of the arms, he said, "Darling, my attitude is, fuck it. I'm doing everything with everybody."

'I had that literal sinking feeling. I'd seen enough in New York to know that Freddie was going to die. There are too many ghosts for me to pretend that Heaven can ever be a carefree environment'.

Whether or not Freddie was taking precautions now that he was aware of AIDS, to ensure that other people didn't die, even if he was prepared to, Paul was not prepared to speculate.

'With infection to disease taking an average of ten years, Freddie would have been infected before the disease was known,' Paul explains.

'Which puts him in the category of having been horribly and unfairly exposed. This was a brief period in history between syphilis and AIDS, when people could not die from having sex. All forms of sex were being tried out, whether through enjoyment or experimentation. There *was* no stigma then. In the music business, especially, everything went. No one was judgemental. Then suddenly, you could kill someone by having sex with them. So everyone became morally responsible. And there were consequences.

'With Freddie, I'm assuming he knew, and must have reconciled himself to it . . . I also think he thought that somehow he would beat it. He was still healthy enough in 1983 (by which time, in New York, the disease had become an epidemic) to carry on. But when the time for Live Aid came [July 1985], his doctor actually recommended that he should not perform, because he had a bad throat infection. I thought, at the time, is this the beginning?'

The fact that Freddie was at that point picking up and having sex with dozens of men each week, while openly flaunting his relationship with Barbara Valentin, suggests that he had come to regard himself as bisexual rather than gay. But, counters Paul, 'Remember that the concept of homosexuality only came about in the 1860s, when a German psychologist invented the word "homosexual". The sexual spectrum is broad. Between the two extremes, there are a lot of people who make love to both sexes. For those going outside their majority activity, as it appears that Freddie did with Barbara, there is usually a great emotional contact. I don't see any contradiction between the statements that, in the course of his life, Freddie would have had sex with more men than women – which I believe is probably true – but that in the end he would recall his love for Mary. These are not contradictory positions. It just means that she was one of his exceptions to the rule. It means that emotion came into play as well as lust. I'm not saying that Freddie did not love some of the men he loved, but she could easily have held a special position in his heart.'

Freddie betrayed both Barbara and Winnie, if that were possible, when he hit on Jim Hutton in Heaven one night in 1985. He couldn't resist. The pair had met two years earlier, at the Copacabana, a gay bar near Freddie's home. Jim was in a relationship at the time, so the encounter had not gone further. This time, the humble barber was single, and raring to go. Freddie was immediately attracted by Jim's lustrous dark hair and thick moustache. The likeness between him and Freddie's German lover Winnie Kirchberger was striking. Taken aback by Freddie's chat-up line – 'how big's your dick?' – Jim was persuaded to join Freddie's gang, which included Peter Straker and Joe Fanelli. He spent the rest of the night dancing with Freddie before returning with him at dawn to the singer's Kensington flat. After which, Jim heard nothing from Freddie for the next three months – Freddie was still living as a tax exile in Munich and had been on the road with Queen, performing in Australia, New Zealand and Japan.

When the encounter was all but forgotten, Freddie phoned Jim out of the blue to invite him to a dinner party at his place. When he arrived, Jim was astonished to see Peter Freestone. The pair had once worked together at Selfridge's store on London's Oxford Street. Neither had imagined they would meet again thanks to Freddie Mercury.

Jim, who died of lung cancer on New Year's Day 2010, three days short of his sixty-first birthday, was the least likely of Freddie's partners. Prior to their meeting, Jim, one of ten children born to an Irish Catholic baker and raised in a tiny two-bedroom council house, worked as a £70-a-week barber at the Savoy Hotel. Freddie, according to Jim, was 'sensitive, shy, had terrible mood swings, and always wanted his own way. Whereas I'm quiet and don't have much of a character – unless you want to pour a few gallons of beer down my throat.'

For Jim, it was smitten at first sight: 'I fell in love with so much about him,' he told me, 'regardless of what he did for a living. He had big brown eyes and an almost child-like personality. He was not like the men I usually fell for. I normally fancied big guys with stocky legs. Freddie had this waspish figure, and the thinnest legs I'd ever seen on a man. He also seemed totally sincere. He was lovely. I was hooked. For all his achievements, he seemed remarkably insecure to me,' said Jim, contradicting Barbara's impression of Freddie, and proving what his closest friends had long suspected: that Freddie revealed different aspects of himself to different people, but never his whole self. His modus operandi in personal relationships indicated a lack of confidence in the ability of any individual to fulfil all his needs. By the same token, Freddie himself could never give a single partner everything. It could explain why his closest and longest-lasting partnerships were with people not his equal in terms of breeding, status or wealth. With those who were 'less' than him, Freddie could call the shots. He would always come first.

The couple embarked on a love affair which, thanks to Freddie's imposed absences, demanded a regular routine. Freddie would fly back to London one weekend, Jim out to Munich the next. On Jim's first visit, he found Freddie, Joe Fanelli and Barbara Valentin waiting at the airport to greet him. He hardly knew what to make of it. When he realised that Freddie was only using him to make Winnie Kirchberger jealous, which was blatantly the case at first, he was desperately upset.

'Jim was a puppet on a string,' declared Barbara. 'Freddie treated him quite badly during that time. He'd bring him over from London, then send him home again, sometimes all in one day. I heard many sad stories during that time. Jim would cry very often. I'd say to him, "Just resist. Say no for once. Don't let yourself be used." "Yes," Jim would say, "Yes, but I love him." For that, he was shoved around like a monkey. He'd do anything Freddie said. It was always on Freddie's terms, and Jim came running, every time. It was quite pathetic. Freddie was often mean.'

The relationship was deeper and more meaningful than it appeared to almost everybody else – even though it was Mary, not Jim, who accompanied Freddie to celebrity events and public gatherings, and who would be paraded as 'the widow' in the end. Peter Freestone, who had observed all Freddie's affairs at close range, did accept the affair as the real thing.

'I believe Jim and Freddie did love each other – in their own way,' he told me. 'The book that Jim wrote about their relationship is to some extent idealised. Jim wanted a one-to-one happy relationship with someone. But I don't think he could ever appreciate how much more there was than a relationship to Freddie's life, and later on to his home life, at Garden Lodge. Freddie had his life, and it was a big, extravagant, multifaceted life. Everybody knew that you had to adapt to Freddie's life. He was never going to adapt to yours. Part of their problem was that Jim was too stubborn to accept that. Consequently, their relationship was very 'Upstairs Downstairs'. Jim wanted Freddie to come downstairs, but Freddie wanted Jim to come upstairs. Having said that, Freddie would certainly not have had such good years at the end without Jim. Overall, Jim was right for Freddie at that time in his life. He meant a great deal more to Freddie than a lot of people have suggested.'

With Garden Lodge finally ready to move into, and his period as a tax exile almost up, it was Jim, not Barbara, whom Freddie chose to bring home as his live-in lover when it was time to return. Although Jim talked about their 'eight-year relationship', they were a couple for six years. Even so, this suggests that Jim meant more to Freddie than devastated Barbara wanted to believe.

'Jim had nothing to say,' she scoffed. 'When they went back to Garden Lodge, he was good for Freddie's cats and the fish and for the garden, that was it. Freddie would sometimes really lose his temper with frustration over the whole thing. Once, when I was staying at the house, Freddie went completely crazy and rushed into the garden. He tore up all the tulips Jim had planted and threw them around on the ground. I said to him, "What are you *doing*? Poor plants!" Freddie said, "I *hate* him, this asshole." He said that Jim was good for nothing, more than once.'

Yet there was clearly something between Freddie and Jim that other lovers could not provide – not even Mary. Even Barbara conceded this.

'We often thought of Jim as no more than a servant, really. But in one way, I know that Freddie loved him. He kicked Jim around, but then some people need a kick in the ass. They thank you for it. In the end, it was good that he was there. Six years together – that's quite a time. Freddie moved back to London, and Jim stayed with him until the end. Thank God, in a way.'

America, meanwhile, was in the grip of an AIDS epidemic of catastrophic proportions; it would soon be the scourge of the world. Most of the victims were young, sexually-active gay males, suffering from HIV-defined illnesses: weight loss, lesions, swollen lymph glands, herpes, cryptococcal meningitis and toxoplasmosis, characterised by jaundice, enlarged liver and spleen, and convulsions. Cellular immunodeficiencies were on the increase. New manifestations of immune disorders, including exhaustion, shingles and night sweats, were appearing all the time. Candidiasis (thrush) in the throat was on the increase, in some cases the yeast infection so advanced that the victim could hardly breathe. Paranoia, forgetfulness and disorientation were complained of. Of all cases of AIDS reported throughout the States, the New York City area accounted for half. A quarter of a century later, the disease is pandemic. There is no known vaccine or cure.

It was Barbara who first noticed in Munich that Freddie's health was failing.

'It started with little things,' she told me. 'You couldn't really say that Freddie was losing his appetite, as he never had much of one to begin with. "I eat like a bird and shit like a bird," he'd say. His favourite food was caviar with mashed potato, and these little cheese crackers his mother used to send him. He liked Italian, Indian and Chinese food, but never ate much of it. He'd always wash everything down with Stolichnaya vodka.

'Freddie started getting sick for no apparent reason,' she said. 'Once, when he was taken ill in my apartment and I didn't know what to do, I called my gynaecologist, whom I trusted as a friend. He came right over, and found Freddie quite delirious. Suddenly he woke up in a terrible state. I said, "It's OK, this is my gynaecologist." "Oh my God, I can't believe it," said Freddie. "Am I pregnant?"'

It was around this time, she remembers, that Freddie began to bitch about the other members of the band, which she had never previously heard him do. Later came Freddie's famous falling-out with his dear friend Peter Straker. Their relationship, which had lasted many years, was over in a flash and would never be restored.

'Straker was funny, he was a clown, he was good for Freddie because he kept his spirits up and made him laugh,' Barbara said. 'But Straker was not settled. He drifted. He was always "living with friends". Eventually he got a flat in one of Jim Beach's buildings in London. But the bathroom badly needed doing: new tiles, bath, sink, everything. Five times Freddie gave Peter the money to do up the bathroom. The work never got done. Eventually Freddie just lost his rag and banished Straker from his life for good. Straker never understood what he'd done. That kind of behaviour became typical of Feddie. He would give and give, never counting the cost, but eventually one straw breaks the camel's back.'

Perhaps the stress of knowing that he was seriously ill – despite the fact that he did not confess it, Barbara believed he was already aware, confirming Paul Gambaccini's suspicions that Freddie knew what was coming back in 1983 – was causing him to act in such an extreme manner. The day eventually came, said Barbara, when she could no longer ignore 'the growth in Freddie's gullet'.

'It would well up suddenly, in the back of his throat. We called it "the mushroom". It came and went, but after a while it never went away again. He said he felt as if he was rotting from the inside out. One night I was lying in bed with Freddie and one of his boyfriends, and Freddie got a terrible coughing attack, which was what this thing used to do to him. He sat up to cough into some tissues, then leant over this guy to put the tissues in the bin. The guy woke up: "Oh my God," he said. "I never thought I'd have a naked rock star dying on top of me in a bed!"'

Aware of the information coming out of New York, Barbara suspected that Freddie had been HIV positive when they became lovers.

'When we first met, he was either denying it to himself or he simply didn't know,' she said. 'After he made his first test eventually [in 1985, she believed, contrary to other reports, though she could not confirm what prompted him to get tested], it changed his life.'

Was she afraid for her own health? Was she angry that he had put her own life at risk? 'No. I loved him. Simple as that. I took one test myself – negative – and that was it. Since there would be no more sex, and no further risk, I didn't need any more tests. I discovered that he had AIDS by chance, after we'd been out one night. Freddie went to the toilet and cut his finger accidentally. There was a lot of blood. I was trying to help him and got blood all over my hands, and he was screaming 'NO! Don't touch me! Don't touch me!' It was then that I realised. He never told me, but after that I knew. I had suspected for some time, of course. He had marks on his face, like dark blue bruises. I'd cover them up for him with my make-up whenever he did a TV show or a video shoot, before the make-up girl arrived.'

Barbara and Freddie never discussed the fact that he had AIDS.

'He knew that I knew, and I knew he knew that. He'd make casual remarks about maybe not living much longer, but that was it. I was aware, from things he said, that he never found out which of his lovers gave him AIDS. But when one of his very early American gay lovers died of AIDS, he said "Oh my God this is it," and got very worried. He knew from that moment that his days were numbered.'

Barbara and Freddie ceased sexual relations. With Winnie gone, the only person with whom Freddie would have sexual contact from then on was Jim.

Freddie's departure from Munich towards the end of 1985 was abrupt, inexplicable, and unbearable for the woman he left behind.

'One minute we were inseparable, doing literally everything together. The next, he was gone,' she wept. 'He just disappeared out of my life. I couldn't understand it. I sent the birthday card, I wrote, I called. He was never there. It didn't make sense. What he was doing was a lie. But OK, I thought, if he wants it over, then it's over. It really was a break without a reason'.

Some months after Freddie left Munich 'for good', Barbara Valentin was at home late one afternoon, getting ready to go to the launch of a friend's boutique, when she heard someone ringing on her doorbell.

'I was cursing, who the hell is that now,' she said, 'then I realised it must be my taxi. I yelled into the intercom, "I'm coming! I'm coming!" but there was no answer. I thought the street door was open, so I had to run down. There was a man standing there in front of me, and I was going, "Oh my God, someone's brought me a dummy of Freddie Mercury."'

She could barely believe her eyes.

'I was moaning to myself, oh no, oh yes . . . I thought I was hallucinating. The man had some little white flowers . . . and he said, "No, it's *me!*" "I know! I *know!*" I said, but I didn't want it to be. I went to shove him away, had to get to the boutique opening, I

thought my mind was playing tricks, and then I touched him . . .
I couldn't stand it. I marched off to the boutique, made pictures
with the owner and a few actors for the press . . . and walked back
home. Freddie was still there, sitting quietly on the couch, playing
with the TV remote control. It was then that it hit me. I fell into his
arms and cried. He did too. We cried and cried, and cried and cried,
and cried.'

It took Freddie weeks to find words to explain himself. He had
wanted to cut off completely when he left Germany, he told her.
He had wanted to start a new life. Munich wasn't allowed to be
mentioned by anyone. Neither was Barbara's name.

'About a hundred of our friends had died of AIDS by this time,'
said Barbara, 'and not even that could be discussed. He said that
trying to forget about his life in Munich and giving me up was like
trying to break a drug habit. If you are addicted to something and
one day you decide that enough is enough, you say no, draw a line,
and then you break the habit completely. 'Barbara, I almost died,'
he told me. 'How many times I had the phone in my hand, dialling
your number, and then hung up.'

'Phoebe told me later, everything about me had disappeared. My
photographs had gone from the house, my name was never spoken.
Everything that would have reminded Freddie of me and Munich
was thrown away. He'd wanted to break free from those crazy times.
To live a calmer, different life, and to die, eventually, in beauty. But
he couldn't stay away from me. He said that one of the things that
frightened him most was that he couldn't be alone. He'd want to
be, and he'd try to be, but whenever it happened he just couldn't
bear it.'

Barbara and Freddie renewed their relationship, though not
their love life. She became a frequent visitor to Garden Lodge, and
started travelling with Freddie again.

'Jim had replaced Winnie [after an on-off relationship spanning
around four years], but it was complicated with Barbara,' remembered Peter Freestone.

'I think Freddie had simply had enough at the time. Stories about Freddie and Barbara were appearing in the German press with alarming regularity, and Freddie got it into his head that Barbara was the one leaking the information. I don't believe she would do that, but Freddie was convinced. Could it be that the idea was put into his head, and rumours fuelled by those who wanted rid of Barbara for good?

'Who knows?' sighed Peter. 'All I know is that, from then on, his only partner was Jim. Soon after Freddie moved into Garden Lodge, Jim was evicted from his flat, so Freddie invited him in.'

'Freddie and I never talked about how long we'd be together,' said Jim. 'We accepted that we were, and would be. Now and then he'd ask me what I wanted from life. "Contentment and love," I'd say. I found both in Freddie.'

Not until 1987 would Freddie be officially diagnosed – a fact which neither he, the band nor his entourage would admit publicly until the eve of his death in November 1991. He had confessed his diagnosis to Jim, offering him the opportunity to leave. Jim refused to desert Freddie. They resolved to stay together as 'man and wife', and the word AIDS was never mentioned in the house again. Jim tested HIV positive in 1990, but did not reveal this to Freddie until a year later, just before his partner died. Contrary to reports which would circulate at the time of Jim's own death, he did not die from AIDS-related complications. Brian May confirmed this on his personal website, writing that Jim had been killed by a smoking-related illness.

As for the rest of the band, Freddie made no official confession. In May 1989, Jim thought he was going to: Freddie personally arranged a special meal for the band and their partners at Freddie Girardet's at Crissier near Lausanne, Switzerland, which at the time was described as 'the world's greatest restaurant'. The finest wines and dishes on the menu were served, and the bill ran to thousands, which Freddie paid. About his illness, nothing was said: perhaps

Pike's Hotel, Ibiza, 1987. Back row, from left: Peter Straker, a bodyguard, Freddie, chauffeur and friend Terry Giddings, 'Alex', Mike Moran, Jim Hutton. Front row, from left: Tony Pike and Barbara Valentin.

'Viking' male nurse Thor Arnold relaxes with Freddie in Los Angeles.

Team photo on the steps of a gay bar in Ibiza. Front row, from left: Barbara Valentin, Winnie Kirchberger, Freddie. Back row, third from left: Peter 'Phoebe' Freestone.

At Roger Taylor's home, Ibiza. From left: chauffeur and friend Graham Hamilton, Freddie, Barbara Valentin, Jim Hutton, Peter Freestone.

Freddie with Mary Austin and Dave Clark at Freddie's 41st birthday party, Ibiza, September 1987.

Who's got the balls? . . . Freddie at Pike's Hotel, Ibiza, Spain, September 1987.

Barbara Valentin with Freddie
at Roger Taylor's house, Ibiza.

Freddie, Barbara Valentin and Peter
Straker celebrate their final Christmas
together at Garden Lodge.

Singer Elaine Paige with Freddie at the Royal
Opera House Terrace Bar, London, 1987.

Freddie with new West End sensation
Catherine Zeta Jones and TV actress
Jill Gascoigne, April 1987.

Freddie with Annie Lennox at the
Ivor Novello Awards, 21 April 1987.

Freddie's 'proudest moment', with opera
star Montserrat Caballé at the *Barcelona*
album launch, 1988.

Freddie at home with one of his many beloved cats, 1988.

Freddie poses for a portrait with one of his favourite cats,
in the grounds of Garden Lodge.

Roger Taylor, Freddie, Rod Stewart and four hundred friends celebrate Queen's 20th Anniversary at London's Groucho Club, 1990. The cake was in the shape of a Monopoly board with Queen hits pasted into all the squares.

Freddie with Liza Minnelli at the Groucho Club party for Queen's 20th Anniversary, 1990.

Freddie's 44th birthday party, Garden Lodge, September 1990.
From left: Piers Cameron (Mary Austin's then partner and father of their sons);
Mary, Peter Freestone, Freddie, Joe Fanelli, Barbara Valentin, Dave Clark.

Flanked by Mary Austin and Barbara Valentin, Freddie celebrates his 44th birthday.
Behind them, Joe Fanelli and Dave Clark look on. The cake is a replica of India's Taj
Mahal, one of Freddie's favourite monuments. He liked the notion of 'a queen buried in
the Taj Mahal'. The track 'The Miracle' features the lyric 'All God's creations, great and
small/the Golden Gate and the Taj Mahal, that's a miracle'.

Freddie's final journey: to West London Crematorium,
Kensal Green, Wednesday 27 November 1991.

the majesty of the setting and its glorious views made him lose his nerve. A few days later, however, the same gang reconvened for a low-key supper in the Bavaria restaurant, near Mountain Studios, and Freddie took the plunge.

'Someone at the table was suffering from a cold, and conversation turned to the curse of illness,' remembered Jim. 'Freddie still looked quite well at that point, but then suddenly he rolled up his right trouser leg and lifted his leg onto his chair. Everyone could see the open, weeping wound on his calf. It was shocking. "You think you've got problems!" Freddie retorted, in his typical blasé fashion. No one said a word, and I think they were all shocked. But then he dismissed it, and we talked about something else.'

Brian confirmed the same moment in a recent television documentary.

'Looking back, I'm sure the band were all aware that Freddie was very ill, but didn't want to know, because what could they say?' said Jim.

'When we got back to London, he did an interview on Radio One with DJ Mike Read. In it, Freddie said that he didn't want to go out on tour again. He said he'd done his bit, and that anyway he was getting too old to strut his stuff any longer. In fact, he was far too weak by then to ever go on the road again. The press, of course, got the wrong end of the stick, and made up stuff about Freddie refusing to tour and upsetting the rest of the band and so on. The usual nonsense.'

None of this made a scrap of difference to Jim's feelings for Freddie. If anything, the tenderness between them grew.

'Freddie was the love of my life,' Jim told me, his words an eerie echo of Barbara's. 'There was no one like him.'

Although they lived together as a couple until Freddie's death, Peter Freestone is certain that Freddie's idea of the relationship was *not* 'standard man and wife'.

'We were *all* so important to him,' he said. 'But there was a different part of Freddie's heart for Jim. Even to say that is strange, when I think about it: Freddie had had a relationship with Mary, and with Joe, but never with me. His capacity for guilt was enormous, which was why Joe and Mary were still around. He felt responsible for them. He felt he'd disrupted their lives by having relationships with them, and that it was down to him to take care of them – as if to compensate. When you think about it, that's ridiculous. But that's how Freddie was.'

Freddie's permanent household now consisted of Peter, 'Phoebe', his personal assistant and valet; Jim, who gave up his hairdressing job at the Savoy to become Freddie's gardener; and Joe Fanelli, aka 'Liza', Freddie's former lover who came back to cook. Having met years earlier in the States, their extremely volatile relationship had been short-lived. Joe had stayed for a while with Freddie at the Stafford Terrace flat, acting as head cook and bottle-washer, and had assisted Peter Freestone in Munich from time to time. His relationship with Freddie boiled and froze at random, and the pair fell out of touch for long periods. Joe had worked in any number of restaurants before returning to the fold, taking up the position of cook at Garden Lodge. The payroll also included two members of staff who did not live in: Terry Giddings, the chauffeur, and Mary Austin, the gofer, who had her own flat nearby.

Of all Freddie's close friends and staff, Mary was the only one Jim had a problem with.

'Mary seemed to never really let go of Freddie,' said Jim.

This belief was echoed by Peter:

'I felt she never accepted that it was over between them. In many ways, she was a driving force for Freddie. She didn't let him get away with anything. She was very strong, and in that sense absolutely what Freddie needed. In a way, she was like a mother to him. He trusted her for that, and he relied on her. She ran his life. That's how their relationship lasted. Freddie used to say that even when they were a couple, they were more like brother and sister. It was a long time before he met me that he went public with his promise that he would be leaving most of his wealth and worldly goods to Mary. Freddie was one that, once he'd made a promise, he would stick to it. He didn't go back on his word.'

19

Break Free

Will my music stand the test of time? I don't give a fuck! I won't be around to worry about it. In twenty years' time . . . I'll be dead, darlings. Are you mad?

Freddie Mercury

Many people who make it in 'n' and roll are totally unprepared for the consequences. What usually happens is that you get rich, you separate yourself from normal people, and you then start using your money to buy people. You divorce yourself from reality, or you get into drink, drugs or both. Queen happened to be very intelligent about it all. Even so, they made some big mistakes.

Dr Cosmo Hallstrom

Had Freddie's personal life at long last taken precedence? Had he lost his way with the band? If his obsession with work was waning, the same could not be said for Brian, Roger or John. The trio soldiered on, bringing in Freddie when necessary, and laughed off rumours that they were on the verge of separating. The press had a field day regardless, running 'Queen Split' stories throughout 1983. The reality was that, wrung out by life on the road, they had agreed to a break from the circuit and each other, and were spending time on solo pursuits.

'I think each of us thinks of leaving quite a lot,' admitted Brian. 'But we all know that, even though we might get our own way if we left, we'd still lose something. We'd lose more than we'd gain at the moment. It's a stimulating environment, and because we don't always agree, it's good for us. If you split up, you lose your vehicle. It has a certain balance of talents, a name people identify with. Getting your own way doesn't always make you happy in the end'.

'I used to think we'd go on for five years, but it's got to the point where we're all actually too old to break up,' said Freddie.

'Can you imagine forming a new band at forty? Be a bit silly, wouldn't it?

'There will come a point where there will be a unanimous vote, or whatever, when we feel instinctively that Queen have gone as far as they can go and there's nothing left, constructively or creatively,' he also said.

'And the last thing I want to do is actually force things within Queen. I'd rather leave it at a nice level, and then do something completely different. I'm sure that all of us have that kind of way of thinking.

'The reason I personally needed a rest was because I just got too tired of the whole business. It got to be too much. I decided I really needed a long break. I don't think we'll ever split. It would seem like cowardice. I suppose if people stopped buying our records, we'd call it a day. And I'd go off and be a striptease artist or something.'

The decision came after one of their most demanding years ever. A contract with EMI for a further six albums had been signed in April 1982, just before Queen embarked on another European tour, taking in several dates around the UK in May and June. It concluded, predictably, with erotic revelry: a 'Shorts & Suspenders' blow-out at London's hottest club, the Embassy. *Hot Space*, their tenth studio album, was released in May. Brian later alluded to his disappointment in the disco-oriented album, which was panned in the USA.

'I think *Hot Space* was a mistake, if only timing-wise. We got heavily into funk, and it was quite similar to what Michael Jackson did on *Thriller*. The timing was wrong. Disco was a dirty word.'

Ignoring for now their rapidly waning reputation in America, Queen pushed on with their summer tour, playing two nights at Madison Square Garden, one of their favourite venues. In Boston, the band were handed the keys of the city by the mayor on 23 July, and the date was officially declared 'Queen Day'. They also made guest appearances on US TV's *Saturday Night Live* and *Entertainment Tonight* in September. On to Japan, bracing themselves for Queenmania, after which Freddie withdrew to New York. By November, Elektra Records in the States were smarting from an almighty flop with 'Staying Power', the final Queen single of their existing contract. To have renegotiated the deal would have been complicated and expensive. Freddie especially was unhappy with Elektra, primarily for their poor handling of *Hot Space*, and told the others he was not prepared to make another album for the label. That Elektra contract also covered Australia and New Zealand, where Queen felt they could be doing far better than they were. After heated discussion, they declined to re-sign there too. With Queen's unsatisfactory deal with Elektra Japan also terminated, they were at a crossroads. While the band did succeed in extricating themselves from their American contract, freedom cost them a million dollars. Jim Beach negotiated a one-off solo deal for Freddie with CBS Records in the UK, and Columbia in the States. By October 1983, the band were signed to EMI's American affiliate label, Capitol.

While working on ideas for his solo album in Munich, Freddie would decamp frequently to New York. On one such trip he detoured to Los Angeles, where he would join the band to begin work on another Queen album, and also find time to visit Michael Jackson at his bizarre mock-Tudor, pre-Neverland mansion on Hayvenhurst Avenue in Encino. The house had a tower for an entrance, manned by guards, and there were fairy lights in every visible window.

'He has been a friend of ours for a long while,' explained Freddie. 'He used to come and see our shows all the time, and that is how the friendship grew . . . just think, I could have been on *Thriller*. Think of the royalties I've missed out on!'

Michael and Freddie had long toyed with the idea of collaborating on some tracks. This was the first time they found themselves in the same city at the same time, with a little time to kill.

'I'm always quite interested in working with other musicians, like Michael Jackson,' Freddie later said.

'Although she's a worry: all that money and no taste, my dears! What a waste! We had three tracks in the can ['There Must Be More To Life Than This', which later appeared on Freddie's first solo album; and 'Victory' and 'State of Shock', which went on to feature on the Jackson 5's 1984 comeback album *Victory*, the latter a duet with Mick Jagger].

'But unfortunately they were never finished. They were great songs, but the problem was time – as we were both very busy at that period. We never seemed to be in the same country long enough to actually finish anything completely.

'Michael even called me to ask if I could complete ['State of Shock'], but I couldn't because I had commitments with Queen. Mick Jagger took over instead. It was a shame, but ultimately a song is a song. As long as the friendship is there, that's what matters.'

'Freddie did do a couple of demo tracks with Michael in the studio at his house in Encino,' confirmed Peter Freestone.

'I was there. I even played video games with Michael. On one of the tracks, I can be heard slamming the bathroom door, as it made a good bass drum sound. Their schedules never really allowed them to pursue their friendship. But they did like each other, and recognised each other as geniuses in their own right.'

Although it seems likely that Freddie was thrown by the control-freakery of the Jackson clan, which few outsiders could handle, there was another, more sinister reason which would soon be exposed in print.

In London, May 1983, Freddie indulged his passion for opera, attending a Covent Garden Opera House production of Giuseppe Verdi's *Un Ballo in Maschera* (A Masked Ball). The stars were the late Italian tenor Luciano Pavarotti, and the spellbinding Spanish soprano Montserrat Caballé, then in her fiftieth year.

'Until that point, Freddie had always adored the tenor voice,' said Peter Freestone.

'Placido Domingo and Luciano Pavarotti were his favourites. I had a huge collection of opera records, and Freddie was tremendously keen to learn as much as he could about opera. One day I said to him, "OK, if you claim to like Pavarotti so much, he's singing at the Opera House soon. Why don't we go?" He thought this was a splendid idea, and got me to book tickets straight away.

'Pavarotti came on and sang an aria in the first act, and Freddie thought it was brilliant. In the second act the prima donna came on, and it was Montserrat. Because we had been so taken with the idea of seeing Pavarotti, we hadn't taken much notice of who else was in it. She started to sing, and that was it. Freddie's jaw dropped. He just about forgot that Pavarotti was on the stage. He only wanted her from then on.'

Freddie was mesmerised, particularly by the famous love duet between ardent Riccardo and exquisite Amelia, a woman tormented by guilt but unable to resist. The sentiment was one with which Freddie identified. He could tear neither eyes nor ears from the powerful yet delicate Caballé. After the performance, Freddie could not stop drooling over her 'limpid tone', 'vocal versatility' and 'impeccable technique'. 'Now *that's* a real singer,' he said, over and over.

'If I were asked to come up with ten images of people being happy in my life, one of them is Freddie about to see Monserrat perform at Covent Garden,' says Paul Gambaccini.

'I'm sitting in the orchestra stalls. To my left, sitting in the front row of the box seats, is Freddie. There is a look of such wonder and delight in his eyes. His left hand makes a gesture towards the stage, and there is such happiness in his face, like a child's. It's a great moment . . . and proof that, no matter what success he may have had, he never lost his respect and admiration for his great favourites. Even the stars have their stars.'

Little did Freddie know that night that he and Monserrat would soon be performing and recording together as one of the music world's least likely duos.

Rest and relaxation was more than the bored band members could handle. All were itching to be working again. An attempt to score director Tony Richardson's screen adaptation of John Irving's novel *The Hotel New Hampshire*, starring Rob Lowe and Jodie Foster, was aborted when it emerged that the film's budget couldn't run to a rock superstar soundtrack. At least it inspired them to get back in the studio. Regrouping in Los Angeles at the Record Plant, they would plot their next album, *The Works*.

Record Plant, famed for having recorded Jimi Hendrix and the Velvet Underground, was founded in New York in 1968. After opening a branch in Los Angeles, the LA studio rose to become hugely successful throughout the 1970s, when pop and rock migrated west. In 1985, the LA studio would move from Third Street to a new Hollywood location in the former Radio Recorders 'Annex', fabled for work with Louis Armstrong and Elvis Presley, and would eventually belong to Chrysalis Records, under Beatle producer Sir George Martin.

Eddie DeLena was the assistant engineer on *The Works* album at Record Plant, alongside engineer and co-producer Mack.

'Mack was a mild-mannered man of few words,' Eddie remembers. 'I later discovered it was one of his advantageous traits. He never took sides, and kept out of any potential conflicts between band members, managers and record company executives. Mack was Switzerland, which was why no one ever had any contention with him.'

Mack's mildness notwithstanding, Eddie found that making *The Works* with Queen was 'like working on four different solo records'.

'As opposed to collaborating from the beginning, every member of the band brought their own song ideas to the table, worked them out, and the other members overdubbed their parts later.' Not that he regarded this as a problem.

'The members of Queen were among the nicest and most talented people you can imagine working with. All well-educated gentlemen, and each with their own distinctive personalities. Roger Taylor was charming, fashion-conscious and more of a socialite than Brian or John. Brian was bright, extremely polite, and totally dedicated to his craft, in which he excelled. He possessed great knowledge of music composition and theory, and spent long, concentrated hours developing his parts in the studio. John was introverted, and kept out of the scene. He also spent less time at the studio than the others. When he was needed, however, he was always spot-on.

'Freddie Mercury, of course, was larger than life. He had a tremendous presence; it filled the room when he entered. His speech patterns were often very dramatic and colourful, with intonations of a stage actor. Queen's rock opera style was actually an extension of Freddie's personality. He was an extremely gifted vocalist, and a great composer. There were times when we were recording his vocals, and he would be singing his next part in a complex harmony arrangement as fast as you could change tracks on the multitrack recorder. He would have the entire arrangement in his head, and sing every part perfectly in one take. It was a demanding task just to keep up with him.'

Eddie was not surprised to note that Freddie travelled with his own entourage from the gay community.

'In this case, friends and acquaintances from the West Hollywood "Boystown" area. He often boasted about his escapades from the previous night . . .' – by which we can take it he means the number of men Freddie could get through in a session, although Eddie is too discreet to divulge detail – '. . . none of which the other members cared to hear about.'

Freddie's favourite Boystown clubs were The Motherlode, The Spike, and The Eagle on Santa Monica Boulevard. One such excursion had wafted Freddie into the arms of 'Vince the barman' from The Eagle: a tall, dark, chunky and bearded specimen who could take or leave the fact that Freddie was a world-famous rock star. Vince owned a serious motorcycle, and Freddie could never resist a guy with a bike. The pair were soon inseparable. But when Freddie asked his lover to join him on the road, Vince turned him down. To describe that refusal as a first would be an understatement.

'Everyone except Freddie kept a very closed guest list of friends who they allowed to visit them at the studio,' said Eddie. 'They were there to make a record without distractions. One could only assume they'd been in studio party situations in the past (again, Eddie would not elaborate, we must use our imaginations), ". . . and were over it."'

One particular night, however, turned into a rock-star extravaganza in Queen's Studio C.

'Rod Stewart was down the hall, recording in Studio A,' recalls Eddie. 'Jeff Beck was also there, working in Studio B. Everyone ended up in Studio C, jamming together. There was a priceless moment when Rod Stewart and Freddie were together at the Bosendorfer grand piano, making up lyrics on the spot and mocking each other's physical attributes in typically British comedic fashion. Freddie would describe Rod's hair and nose, Rod would hit back about Freddie's protruding teeth. It was hysterical. I was beside myself, trying desperately to get everyone situated with appropriate amps and microphones, because no one was going to allow this moment to go undocumented. Jeff Beck and Brian May exchanging guitar licks, Rod and Freddie exchanging vocals, Carmine Appice and Roger Taylor sharing drum duties. It was chaotic, for sure, but the multitrack tapes do exist somewhere. Queen's management made sure that no one would have the opportunity to play back the tapes, for fear of leaked cassette copies getting into the wrong hands. They removed the tapes from the studio that same night. I never once heard the playback.'

Another memorable moment during the recording of *The Works* was Freddie's thirty-seventh birthday party at his rented Stone Canyon Road house, a gorgeous mansion in the Hollywood Hills that had once belonged to Elizabeth Taylor. Freddie had the palatial house filled with intoxicating starburst lilies for the occasion. He also decided that he wanted his old flame Joe Fanelli to do the cooking, and flew him out from London. When Joe arrived, the pair kissed and made up, if not as lovers, and prepared together a menu of Freddie's favourite dishes, Coronation Chicken and Prawn Creole among them.

The lesbian waitresses in white shirts and black slacks were provided by a female Elektra Records executive whose gay lover was the cleaner at the Stone Canyon house.

'It was a magnificent scene in the lush outdoor gardens of the estate,' recalls Eddie, who attended the party alongside Elton John, Rod Stewart, Jeff Beck and John Reid. There were relatively few famous faces among the hundred guests, most of whom were Freddie's cherished anonymous friends. Freddie's partner for the night was Vince the barman.

'There were servers, bartenders, magicians and classical musicians,' remembered Eddie. 'A grand time. The night flew by quickly until it became apparent that the after-party crowd was one that I didn't particularly fit in with' – Eddie being as straight as Freddie and his acolytes were gay.

The first single release from the album was Roger's 'Radio Ga Ga' in January 1984. Originally entitled 'Radio Caca', reportedly after a lavatorial remark by Roger's young son Felix (whose mother Dominique is French), it reached Number Two in the UK, Number One in nineteen other countries, and was one of Queen's smartest compositions yet. Within its bland, pop-chant lyrics lurked a thinly disguised snipe at pop radio, for having sold out. Its image and function were now deemed to be hugely at odds with what it had once represented. The epic record required equally epic visuals to promote it. Produced by Scott Millaney and directed by David Mallet – whom Freddie referred to as 'Mallet B. DeMille' – it featured scenes from Fritz Lang's 1927 sci-fi film *Metropolis*, as well as a photo album depicting frames from earlier videos such as 'Bohemian Rhapsody' and 'Flash'. With the help of the Queen fan club, 500 disciples descended on London's Shepperton Studios, donned silver boiler suits and stood in straight lines, where they clapped and raised their hands to the beat of the chorus line. The sequence would soon be mirrored by Queen fans at gigs the world over, and was to become an indelible image of their Live Aid performance the following year. Their most expensive promo to date, it was one of the most impressive videos Queen had ever attempted.

'David (Mallet) and Freddie would spend hours thrashing things out,' recalls producer Scott Millaney.

'"Darling, just make it better than Elton's," Freddie would say. "I want the best."

'I'd do the budget, send it to Jim Beach, he'd say, "No, that's too much", and I'd say, "No, you don't get it, that's *Freddie's* budget."'

Millaney and Mallet were also responsible for the video for the more controversial track, 'I Want to Break Free', in which all four band members appeared in drag. The video also incorporated a forty-five-second ballet sequence, inspired by Claude Debussy's *Prélude à l'Après-Midi d'un Faune*, in which Freddie danced with the Royal Ballet corps.

'Freddie was beside himself with excitement about that video,' remembers Millaney. 'He was all "Well, darling, we've simply *got* to dress up in drag, and I have to shave off my moustache." David said, "NO! You have to keep it on, because that's the *point!*" Freddie was never happier than when he booked the Royal Ballet and could dance with them all day . . . he even got to writhe all over them!'

Make-up artist and body painter Carolyn Cowan, responsible

for the human paintwork on the video, developed such a close relationship with Freddie on the shoot for 'Break Free' that she was booked for several videos in succession.

'I wasn't a normal make-up artist and Freddie wasn't a normal rock star, if there is such a thing, so we met in the middle,' Carolyn tells me.

'We were both very strong, and I could defuse his mood in an instant. In return, Freddie always looked after me. It was a very symbiotic relationship. We liked each other, to put it simply.

'The make-up room is a sacred place. People are naked, and allowing you to see them as they are. This requires a huge degree of trust, and Freddie got that. I paint a body quickly. I'm fast. You have to be. People get cold; they get bored; they fidget. They remember to be self-conscious. You have to capture the moment, and simply get on with it.

'I remember arriving at Limehouse Studios to do "Break Free", and clicking immediately with all of them.

'I was doing massive amounts of booze, cocaine and marijuana at the time, which may have helped [she was rescued by David Bowie in 1991].

'Like Freddie, I have a highly addictive personality. I think he recognised that in me. I had long dark hair in those days, and looked like Charles II. Short skirt, long boots, an anything-goes kind of attitude. I suppose I just fitted in with the band's general eccentricity.

'I made them all up in drag, in that *Coronation Street* style, and the results were incredible. Freddie had such a great face anyway. Everything came together that day. It all worked. I had to do pointy wax ears on the ballet dancers. They were all so badly-behaved that the make-up kept getting fucked and I had to keep doing it all again. Meanwhile, Freddie was all, "Give me another line of coke, darling, please!" It was all outrageous. I remember we got through these incredible amounts of drugs.

'You have to remember,' Carolyn says, 'that we were inventing an art form. We were under pressure because of that. Even so, I got on well with all the band, collectively and individually. They hadn't yet got tired and bored and pissed off. They were still loving the madness and freedom and hedonism of it all. And it *was* fun. Freddie's energy was extraordinarily creative, and he had a better sense of humour than anyone I've ever known.'

But that video proved another nail in the coffin of Queen's reputation in the States. The cross-dressing was deemed too excessive for MTV.

The channel exerted such control over the music industry and popular culture during the 1980s that decisions not to play certain artists' videos had devastating effect. The tongue-in-cheek element and *Coronation Street* send-up was lost on Queen's American fans, who found it offensive and unfathomable. The video was even banned in several States. The band were speechless.

'We had done some really serious, epic videos in the past,' said Roger, 'and we just thought it was time we had some fun. We wanted people to know that we didn't take ourselves too seriously. That we could still laugh at ourselves. I think we proved that.'

'Middle America felt that Freddie might be gay, and Middle America was very important,' said former journalist and EMI PR executive Brian Southall.

'You could be terribly arty in New York or Los Angeles, but don't try it in Kansas.'

The band were unrepentant, and refused point-blank to make an alternative promo for the American market. Hubris had kicked in yet again. It killed them in America.

'When Queen did "Break Free", that was a problem here,' agrees Peter Paterno, the US entertainment lawyer turned record company president who would later sign Queen to Disney's Hollywood Records.

'All the miniskirts and the make-up. It offended a lot of people. And "Ga Ga": radio stations in the US took big offence. "We won't play those guys' music if they're making fun of us, why should we?" was the consensus. Queen went off the boil here overnight.'

The Works would struggle to Number Twenty-Three in the States, and 'Ga Ga' to Number Sixteen.

'Also,' adds Paterno, 'they had reached a point at which they were at odds with the image. The typical hard-rock fan here back then was a macho guy, he didn't look like them. For me, they were still making really great music. I was a fan. "Hammer to Fall", Brian May's anti-nuke number, went on to feature on the soundtrack of the *Highlander* movie. It is an amazing song which got no traction in the US at all. It didn't exist here. It was the beginning of the end for Queen in America at that time.'

Capitol Records' dispute with independent radio promoters didn't help. Neither did the strange attitude of Freddie's personal manager, Paul Prenter, who appeared to be single-handedly responsible for Freddie's ever-increasing taste for sordid behaviour, namely rent-boy sex and drugs. It seemed to some as though egging Freddie on to ever deeper depths of danger and depravity satisfied Prenter's own lust for extreme decadence.

'He was a very bad influence on Freddie,' commented Roger, 'and hence on the band.'

Little did Freddie or his friends suspect how ruinous his relationship with Prenter would eventually prove.

In February, as EMI were preparing to launch *The Works*, which would become their biggest album to date, despite leaving the States lukewarm, Queen joined Boy George and Culture Club, Paul Young and Bonnie Tyler for the San Remo song festival. It was a gauche fiasco for veteran performers, but a fun few days off in Italy's Bournemouth . . . and good for promo, despite Brian and Roger being at loggerheads throughout, arguing about everything from the set list to the stage set.

Interviewed during the festival, Freddie opened up about his friendship with Michael Jackson.

'Michael and I have grown apart a bit since his massive success with *Thriller*, he confessed. 'He's simply retreated into a world of his own. Two years ago, we used to have great fun going to clubs together, but now he won't come out of his fortress. It's very sad. He's so worried that someone will do him in that he's paranoid about absolutely everything.'

John and Roger embarked on a whistle-stop promotional tour of Australia and the Far East before vanishing on holiday. Brian went off to guest on a track for American rocker Billy Squier's new album, while Freddie returned to Munich to live it up, venturing from time to time into the studio to continue his solo work.

May 1984 took them back to Montreux to mime for 400 million TV viewers at the Rose d'Or festival. From there, Queen announced their next European tour, commencing in August. Roger then turned to some solo recording, releasing a widely-ridiculed single and album the following month. Freddie raced back to Munich. In June, the band regrouped in London to receive a special Silver Clef Outstanding Contribution to British Music award from the Nordoff Robbins Music Therapy charity.

July saw the release of the single 'It's a Hard Life', which hit Number Six in the UK and gave the band their third Top Ten single from *The Works*.

'It's a Hard Life' was Freddie at his huge, heart-rending best, resuming the half-exuberant, half-tragic theme of 'Killer Queen' and 'Play the Game'. The track's opening lyric and melody both echo '*Vesti la giubba*', the most famous aria from Ruggero Lenoncavallo's opera *Pagliacci*: '*Ridi, Pagliaccio, sul tuo amore infranto!*' ('Laugh Pagliaccio, at your broken love'). Freddie may also have had Smokey Robinson in mind when he wrote 'Hard Life'. In 'Tears of a Clown' from The Miracles' 1967 album *Make It Happen*, Smokey compares himself to characters like Pagliacci, the clowns who hide hurt and anger behind vacant smiles. Robinson had deployed the sad-clown comparison before in his composition for Motown's Carolyn Crawford, 'My Smile Is Just a Frown (Turned Upside

Down)'. Similarly harking back to 'Play the Game' and the frequently futile quest for true love, Freddie's 'Hard Life' was an impassioned take on his real-life dilemma. He was blessed with greater material wealth than most mere mortals could ever dream of. But it wasn't enough. This was 'money can't buy me love' territory, famously visited by The Beatles twenty years earlier. As Paul McCartney put it, 'the idea behind (that song) was that all these material possessions are all very well, but they won't buy me what I really want'. Freddie had to learn the hard way how true this was.

That Freddie felt cursed by a lack of true emotional and romantic fulfilment was an open secret among his closest friends, who had watched over Freddie and mopped his tears throughout an epic march of disastrous relationships down the years. It was also obvious to his fans, thanks to the many heart-rending songs he wrote on the subject.

'His lyrics reflected his life,' says Frank Allen of The Searchers. '"I Want It All". "Somebody to Love". "Don't Stop Me Now". "Who Wants to Live Forever" all illustrate some aspect of his hopes and desires. Naturally a songwriter expresses his ethos and personality in his lyrics, and as Freddie became more comfortable with his sexuality, it gave him the freedom to open up to the world. I would venture that his involvement with women boosted his confidence. Within most people there is an element of bisexuality. Very few come to terms with it. The guilt and the consequences, even in these so-called liberated times, are too great.'

Millions loved Freddie, but from afar. Few got close. I believe that those who did, and who were admitted to his inner circle, needed *him* too much. Their adoration of Freddie spoke more loudly of their own desires and dreams than of his. Freddie's exuberance and 'gay abandon' was a foil to throw the outside world off the scent, concealing a growing spiritual despondency. In his heart, he feared, he would never find that truly special 'somebody to love' – another reason why he clung so tenaciously to Mary.

Referring to 'It's a Hard Life', on which he worked tirelessly with

Freddie, Brian said, 'This is one of the most beautiful songs Freddie ever wrote. It's straight from the heart.'

The lavish video for the single was filmed by director Tim Pope in Munich. It featured many of Freddie's clubland cohorts, including Barbara Valentin, and left the band both ruffed and ruffled. All of them looked distinctly uncomfortable in their medieval troubadour get-ups. Freddie's own skin-tight, eye-studded scorcher, in homage to risqué French *fin de siècle* singer Mistinguett, raised further eyebrows across the pond. So did a mostly unexplained leg injury, serious enough to require plastering, which he claimed to have sustained during a contretemps in a Bermuda Triangle bar.

Queen were still on a mission to play virgin territory. The Vatican was denied them, the Russians described them as 'decadent', and the Chinese and Koreans were not playing ball. On agreeing to perform twelve shows at the Super Bowl in South Africa's controversial Sun City in October 1984, the band found themselves embroiled in the most politically compromising phase of their career. The multimillion-dollar Bophuthatswana desert complex was a Las Vegas-style enclave financed partly by the government while apartheid was still in place. To the outside world, it represented a V-sign by the privileged white South African minority to the many poverty-stricken black inhabitants of the country's squalid townships. The British Musicians' Union had imposed a strict ban on performances there by its members. Artists Against Apartheid, founded by Steven Van Zandt, formerly of Bruce Springsteen's E Street Band, would capture the anti-apartheid mood on their single 'I Ain't Gonna Play Sun City'. Its line-up included Miles Davis, Bob Dylan, Ringo Starr and his drummer son Zak Starkey, Lou Reed, Jackson Browne, Pat Benatar, Peter Gabriel, and Stones Keith Richards and Ronnie Wood. The political single was not a massive hit in America on its release in December 1985, but was a huge success in Australia, Canada and the UK.

Queen were unrepentant.

'"I Want to Break Free" is an unofficial anthem among the African Congress Movement, and "Another One Bites the Dust" is one of the biggest-selling songs in South African black history,' explained Roger.

But controversy raged as the band prepared to depart on *The Works* tour – on which they welcomed a fifth member, keyboard player Spike Edney, to perform on stage as part of the band.

They had not played together live for almost two years. Although rehearsing was not their favourite pastime, it was a necessity. Into a Munich hangar they went, equipped with state-of-the-art production, sound and lighting.

'The very first thing I played with them in rehearsals was "Tie Your Mother Down",' recalls Spike. 'Which was fine, because they'd been playing that for a hundred years. Then "Under Pressure". Then they wanted to try out one of the new ones: "I Want to Break Free". Not really a very difficult song, you might think. We got going into the first verse of it, crumbled and stopped. It occurred to me that they had never played it live together. I had everything written down, so I said, "Actually, it goes like this . . . " then John came over to the piano, then Brian, and they sort of stood there. Then Freddie pitched up. "You wouldn't happen to have the *words*, old chap, would you?" he asked. So there we all were round the piano, and I thought to myself, "This is gonna be OK. I can do this."'

The band's UK shows included three nights at the Birmingham National Exhibition Centre, where Spandau Ballet front man Tony Hadley met his idol Freddie for the first time. Hadley's own voice was so powerful and versatile that he was already being compared to the young Frank Sinatra. Unbeknown to him, Freddie was one of *his* biggest fans.

'Mutual admiration society,' laughed Tony.

'I'd grown up listening to Queen records, and Freddie was the world's greatest front man. I'd been dying to meet the band. At the time, I was famous enough that I could get a backstage pass to more or less anything. We went back to meet the lads, who were really friendly and polite. They invited us to their after-show party at the hotel next door. I walked in with Leonie [his first wife], there was a spare seat next to Freddie, and he said to me, "Come on, darling, come and sit next to me, dear." Leonie ended up down the table. We were chatting away when all of a sudden a couple of strippers came on to entertain the troops.

'It seemed to me that Queen always had more fun than anybody else. The parties were big, the records were big, the personalities in the band were bigger than any other group's. Even John Deacon, who was the quiet one.

'I sat there talking to him that night about the on-stage persona, and he gave me free advice. "Never make excuses for being on stage," he said. "Never apologise. The audience have come to see *you*, so it doesn't matter if you're a bit off one night. You've just got to front the whole thing out." I was twenty-three, twenty-four years old, singing in a band that was doing OK. He was rock royalty. He didn't have to bother with someone like me. But he was so enthusiastic, so keen to impart his knowledge and experience. He was the only one who ever did that, and I really respected him for it.

'"Every artist is wracked with self-doubt," he said to me.

'"Even you?" I asked. "*Especially* me," he replied.'

Queen's 5 September Wembley show culminated in a party for five hundred friends at Xenon nightclub to celebrate Freddie's thirty-eighth birthday. The cake was perhaps his most spectacular yet: a five-foot vintage Rolls-Royce. That week, their twenty-sixth single 'Hammer to Fall' was released on the same day as Freddie's debut solo single, 'Love Kills', recorded for the movie *Metropolis*. As the band flew into Dortmund, it was noted that nine Queen albums currently featured in the UK Top 200. In October, Queen and entourage, including Mary Austin and her new live-in lover Joe Bert, the bass player in Tom Robinson's band, departed for South Africa for their Sun City run. At the debut show, Freddie's voice gave out just a couple of numbers in, his old throat problem aggravated by the desert heat and dust. That show and the next five were abandoned, the band regrouping for the final six.

On their return to London, Brian and Roger went to the Musicians' Union to plead their case.

'It was not as if the trip had been a complete jamboree,' reasons Spike. 'Queen had done quite a bit of charity stuff out there, including fundraising for the Kutlawamong school for deaf and blind children. They later released a special live album there, and donated all royalties to the school. The reaction to the band was so fantastic that I still don't believe it was the wrong thing to do. Within a couple of years, of course, the whole political thing had changed, and the world started going there.'

Dismissed with a heavy fine, the band were also blacklisted. At least they held out for their money to be donated to charity instead of swelling the union bank balance. They remained puzzled for years by the fiasco.

'We're totally against apartheid and all it stands for,' said Brian. 'But I feel we did a lot of bridge-building. We actually met musicians of both colours. They all welcomed us with open arms. The only criticism we got was from outside South Africa.'

Spike concedes that Queen had a reputation for incredible arrogance.

'That's true. They *were* arrogant. But it was because, most of the time, they were right. I got the impression that they believed they had been unfairly treated when they started out, which had taught them to be self-sufficient and to rely on their own judgement. The only downside to their arrogance was that it filtered down through the ranks of their organisation. People who worked for them started being arrogant on Queen's behalf, when they didn't have a right to be. It could all get pretty unbearable at times.'

Freddie returned to Munich, and in December the band produced their first Yuletide single, 'Thank God It's Christmas'. Intended as a send-up of the hackneyed genre, their twenty-seventh single was produced in London, with Freddie's vocal added in Germany. It failed to make the UK Top Twenty, and never appeared on any Queen album. But it has haunted them annually ever since, on every Christmas compilation going. The season's soaraway Number One, meanwhile, was Band Aid's 'Do They Know It's Christmas?'. History was about to be made.

20

Live

Let's face it, all us rock stars still want to be in the limelight, and this is going to showcase us. Let's be open about it. OK, we're helping out, but from the other point of view it's going to be a worldwide audience, an all-over simultaneous broadcast. That's what we're all about as well, and we shouldn't forget that. I doubt there is one artist that's going to appear who hasn't realised that fact.

Freddie Mercury

Music isn't always about what you play. It is also about what you don't play.
Freddie Mercury was at least three different people. On stage, off stage, and in that twilight zone somewhere between. He embodied his music. The performance perfectly reflected every song.

Louis Souyave, guitarist, Daytona Lights

To Rock in Rio, 'the biggest rock festival the world had ever seen'. 1985's eight-day New Year extravaganza, also featuring Rod Stewart, Yes, Iron Maiden, Def Leppard, Ozzy Osbourne, George Benson, James Taylor, and some of Brazil's best-selling artists, was planned on a scale that promised to live up to even Queen's expectations. The fact that their own faithful tour manager Gerry 'Uncle Grumpy' Stickells was in charge of the event, and that Queen were invited to headline, clinched the deal. They set off for South America yet again on Sunday 6 January.

Freddie's personal entourage comprised Mary Austin, Barbara Valentin, Peter Freestone, Paul Prenter and a minder. Between 250,000 and 300,000 fans travelled for two days or more through blistering heat to become part of the largest rock audience of all time.

Spike Edney had been involved in some major events in his time, but nothing like Rio.

'I knew that Queen's earlier South American tours had been pioneering adventures, but this was the biggest show ever.'

But his abiding memory is of how sorry he felt for Freddie.

'He was a massive star in South America by then. He was a god. Queen's "Love of My Life" had been Number One in Argentina forever. It was their "Stairway to Heaven". Consequently, Fred was a total prisoner once he got down there. He couldn't go anywhere – not even with armed guards. It was distressing for him. He did manage to slip out once or twice, but it wasn't worth the aggro.'

Part of the reason for Freddie's mind-blowing popularity, Spike believes, were his looks.

'I heard it said that when Fred shaved his head and grew the moustache, he became the epitome of the good-looking South American male – a sort of Latin Clark Gable. Perhaps there was a bit of that in what they adored about him.'

The Barra da Tijuca Rockodromo site had taken months to construct, and featured a gigantic semi-circular stage with a huge fountain on either side. In the event, the fountains proved useful for fans to wash in, torrential rain having rendered the site a mud bath. Giant press stands had been installed, with international telephone lines and picture-wiring facilities for the thousands of journalists and photographers attending. At night, huge searchlights sliced the sky, as if heralding a Hollywood premiere. The purpose-built heliport proved a logistical necessity rather than a luxury. Forget

Freddie's deep fear of the chopper: there was no other way in to the stage. All roads to the Barra had been jammed for days.

On the first night, Queen were due on after Leyton metal-heads Iron Maiden, but they were two hours late going on stage.

'I can't remember any specific reason why,' says Spike Edney, 'maybe it was just running late.'

Queen eventually made it on at gone two a.m., by which time the crowd was practically in riot mode.

'Jim Beach had fixed it for me to be in the wings when Queen went on,' remembers Peter Hillmore, covering the event for the *Observer* newspaper.

'I peered out and saw this colossal audience. "What's it like being out there on stage?" I asked Brian. "Go and have a look," he said.

'I went on. Thousands upon thousands of faces staring up at me, all screaming for Queen. I felt the raw power of Freddie Mercury, and tasted what it was like to have a quarter of a million people wanting nothing more than for you to open your mouth and sing. I felt scared, because I couldn't actually *do* anything. Queen ambled on and it all started to happen. Roadies rushing about, nobody even noticing me. I floated away to one side.

'I knew, there and then, that more than anything in the world I wanted to be in Queen. I wanted to be Freddie Mercury. He'd lift his hand and they would sing along. He'd drop his hand and they would fall silent, because *he* said so. The effect was unbelievable. Like seeing a nuclear reactor split the atom.'

Freddie was supernatural, thought Hillmore.

'He'd have people jumping out of cars at traffic lights, salivating over his limo, going "Freddie, we love you, you're God!" He and Queen had an entire organisation pumping away and costing a fortune, just to make sure they were comfortable wherever they went – before they even did a day's work. They'd never unpack. They'd never have to worry about excess baggage, or queuing at airports, or lining up for their duty frees. It was VIP lounges and first-class transatlantic flights all the way, with someone to cater for every whim. Which all adds up to why I think it's impossible for a star like Freddie to have a private life. In the end, all that is going to have an effect on even the most normal person's sanity.'

Freddie's widely reported 'Brazilian boob' was in fact exaggeration on the part of the press. Strutting onto the stage in the girlie get-up that he'd worn in the video for 'Break Free', Freddie was astonished by the reaction of the audience. When they started pelting the stage with cans, stones and other rubbish, Freddie took this to be in protest. When a huge piece of cardboard hit Freddie, Brian retreated, taking several paces back until he was level with Roger's drum riser. Freddie, however, stayed defiantly at the front of the stage, and made the mistake of losing his temper. Misinterpreting what was happening, he taunted the crowds back. Although a number of journalists reported that the locals had adopted 'Break Free' as an anti-dictatorship anthem, and did not approve of it being sent up by a rocker in drag, this was not what the crowd were angry about.

Dave Hogan, snapping the event for the *Mail on Sunday*'s *You* magazine, described the occurrence as a 'complete misunderstanding'.

'Usually, at gigs of that size, fans would all rush to be closest to the front,' Hogie said. 'But on that occasion, the organisers had built such a high stage that those at the very front weren't getting a look-in. They couldn't see anything at all, it was happening above them. Some were trying to hoist themselves up to watch the band, but the security guys kept coming along and stamping on their fingers. Then Freddie came out as the transvestite in his wig and boobs, just as there was a surge of fans sitting on other fans' shoulders to try and see. There was a flurry of stamping security guards, and an onslaught of angry fans picking up gravel from the ground in the stadium to chuck at the security guards in protest. No one was throwing stones at Freddie. On the contrary, they loved him. But it was written up as fans booing and stoning Freddie because of the way he was dressed. Imaginative reporting, let's call it, by journalists who were only trying to get a headline. Fair enough. But Freddie, I have to say, did his usual and went down a storm. He wasn't stoned; I can vouch for that personally. I was right there in front of him. But why let the truth get in the way of a good story!'

Installed in great style in the presidential suite of Rio's Copacabana Palace hotel, Freddie held court.

'His room was where all the American presidents had stayed,' remembers David Wigg. 'He asked me up there for drinks. It rained heavily, and there was mud everywhere, but Freddie's attitude was always "the show must go on". That night, I went to dinner at his invitation. Mary Austin was there – she always sat on his left, while his current boyfriend always sat on his right. Afterwards we all went off to a disco (Alaska, the most popular gay disco in Rio at the time). The night went on until about four a.m. I had to write my article for the *Express*, and thought I'd better get some sleep. I went over to Freddie to congratulate and thank him before I left. "Where are you going?" he said. "I'm going to walk home to my hotel," I told him. "You jolly well aren't!" he replied. He snapped his fingers. "Steve! You take David home in *my* car, and don't drop him outside, see him *in* to the hotel." Freddie was so well-mannered, sensitive and caring. All his family were like that – the parents, the sister, all of them. He was so old-school British, which was very unusual for a rock star.'

To Paul Prenter fell the dubious task of picking out men that Freddie might fancy. Few resisted the invitation 'to join Freddie Mercury at his personal private party in his hotel suite'. Most onlookers agreed that Prenter's duties had taken on a sordid dimension. Not only was he responsible for rounding up talent – usually young male prostitutes known as 'taxi boys' – but for procuring copious quantities of alcohol and cocaine.

One former taxi boy, a blond, blue-eyed Jew named Patricio, joined Freddie at his private parties on several occasions. Having travelled from Buenos Aires to Rio to try his hand at acting, Patricio had fallen into prostitution through destitution and despair. He would make one more significant journey in his lifetime: to Israel, to die of AIDS. Patricio, by his own admission, had a number of sexual encounters with Freddie.

'The boys who were chosen joined Freddie back in the privacy of his hotel suite, which was very luxurious and overlooked the hotel pool,' he remembered.

'First we drank, and then snorted some cocaine – there was a little low, wooden table with the lines of cocaine already chopped out, all prepared. Next, we'd shed our clothes and enter Freddie's room, where he would greet us, wearing just his dressing gown. Throughout proceedings, Paul (Prenter) remained fully clothed. Freddie engaged in sexual activity with each in turn, in front of the others. When he was tired, Prenter paid the boys and asked us to leave. Freddie was always passive. When you start being gay, you tend to be active. But if you are popular, and everyone wants to go with you, you turn passive, as it's the easiest way to have fun. To act like "the man" is very tiring. Most gay men come to prefer the "female" role.'

Freddie had grown addicted to casual sex. According to Patricio, the star was not even turned on by it most of the time. The wilder the evening got, he said, the more impassive Freddie appeared.

'He did not even seem to be enjoying himself. Just going through the motions.'

Many such parties were held down in Rio, all concluding the same way. Freddie's quests for kicks had exceeded what he could handle. He continued to crave the outrageous, if only for its own sake. His relentless indulgence in all manner of excess proved one thing: that he was tired. He could have anything money could buy, but he had to work harder and harder for pleasure. Loveless sex was all very well, but the excitement had faded. It is hard to imagine that he wouldn't have despised himself at times for such self-indulgence, but he seemed driven to it. He could not stop himself. Something, soon, would have to give.

'When Paul and Barbara were both around,' admits Peter Freestone, 'it became a competition as to who could provide the more outrageous spectacle, until it all reached burn-out point. Freddie had long since lost interest, but he was too polite to say anything. He'd always had such enormous fun doing those things before, and of course people didn't expect him to have changed.'

A huge performers' party was held on 12 January at the Copacabana Beach Hotel. It was a rowdy affair, televised to millions across South America, during which even normally dignified Brian ended up in the pool. Queen took to the stage again on 19 January, to close the festival. Queen had made history yet again, and not for the last time.

The band arrived in Auckland on 5 April for the start of their New Zealand tour. They were met by anti-apartheid protesters still inflamed by the Sun City fiasco, who demonstrated at the airport and outside their hotel. Freddie barely noticed, preoccupied as he was by the UK release of his second solo single, taken from the debut solo album which many believed would never see the light of day. Although the record made Number Eleven at home, it made zero impact in America. All four band members began to confront their worst fear, that their reign in the States might actually be over.

There was further disruption on the New Zealand tour in the shape of Freddie's old mucker Tony Hadley. Spandau Ballet had recently completed a two-month tour of Europe, and were in for a round Down Under. Promoter problems had resulted in the New Zealand leg being cancelled, with loss of earnings for many involved. In Auckland, Tony was under strict instructions from his manager Steve Dagger to lay low. This stance did not come naturally to Tony – especially not with his drinking pal Freddie in town.

'It was rare indeed for Freddie to go on stage drunk,' said Spike Edney. 'Queen's first gig at Auckland's Mount Smart stadium, after a ridiculous afternoon spent with Hadley, was one of the few times.'

Tony turned up to surprise the band. 'I checked into their hotel, rocked up at the sound check, had a chat, then Freddie and I went back to the hotel together, and wound up in the bar for a drink. The next thing, Freddie's saying "Let's get some Stoli." We sat putting the world to rights, exchanging rock 'n' roll war stories, while we did the whole bottle of vodka. Neat. Then he was saying, "Come on, darling, up to my room, I've got a bottle of vintage port."

'By then, we were both off our heads,' winces Tony.

'Freddie then says, "You've *got* to come on stage tonight." "I don't want to intrude," I said, although I was up for it. "No no no," he insisted, "it'll be great." He got on the phone to Roger and John. "Tony's coming on stage with us tonight, OK, darling? Wonderful." It seemed fine by them. "The only problem we might have is Brian," Freddie confided. "He tends to get a bit funny about these things." So he called Brian and came on all diplomatic: "Brian, darling, Tony's coming on stage with us tonight and we're going to do 'Jailhouse Rock' – OK? Tony, love, Brian's on, and he's absolutely fine about it." Then I remembered. "I don't know the bloody words, mate," I told him. "Never mind," said Fred, all jolly, "I don't fucking know them either!"'

The drunken pair sat down to try and learn the song. Half the words they made up, and the rest they guessed. Then Tony staggered off to get some sleep.

'I got down the gig that night, and everybody was going to me, "What the hell have you done to Freddie! He's off his head!" "Well," I said, "we've been boozing big-time." They all frowned at each other. "But Freddie *never* boozes before he goes on stage!" someone said.'

Never before had a harder time been had of it, getting Freddie ready to go on stage.

'At the time, everyone was wearing those Adidas boxing boots with lots of laces, which tie up quite high – because they feel good and are great for running and jumping about on stage,' Spike says.

'That night, Freddie was laid out on the sofa backstage. Tony Williams, one of the wardrobe assistants, and Joe Fanelli were dressing Fred together, because Fred was too out of it to do it himself. They'd got his gear on, and then his boots. But when he stood up and went to walk forward, he couldn't. The announcement came: "Tape's starting now!" – by which time we were all supposed to be at the side of the stage. And Freddie went, "You stupid c***s, you've put my tights on back to front!" The next moment he was lying on his back like a beetle with his legs in the air, Tony and Joe going like maniacs trying to undo these laces, so that they could get his boots and his tights off. They eventually got everything back on the right way, and we went hurtling down the stairs, the intro tape having finished and all this smoke filling the stage. We made it by the skin of our teeth.

'Fred, bless him, was so out of it that he was going to fly,' adds Spike. 'He was ad-libbing, making things up, singing crap, for about the first half-hour of the show. Roger had his head down, couldn't look at anyone. Brian's staring wildly, like, "What the fuck's going on here?" By the time we'd made it halfway through the show, Freddie had sobered up a bit. It went great after that, amazingly. Until Hadley came on.'

Smarting from a telephone conversation with his manager, who was angry to hear that Tony was keeping anything but a low profile, Tony was dying to get in front of an audience.

'I was standing at the side of the stage while Queen were playing, still trying to remember the bloody words to "Jailhouse Rock", he laughs.

'Freddie came across and draped himself over Spike's piano, hissing, "Hadley you bastard, I am so pissed," in front of 45,000 people. There I was, mumbling away to myself like an idiot, with a few key words scrawled on my hand: "wardens ... county jail ... party ... jailhouse ... rock". I couldn't get the lyrics into my head. Eventually, Freddie went "Ladies and Gentlemen, Mr Tony Hadley!" The crowd went crazy, I rushed on, and launched into the bop-bop bit of "Tutti Frutti". Wrong song! And Freddie's going, "Yeah! All right!" and Brian's going, "What the fuck is *this*?" The rest of them were just pissing themselves. Freddie and I didn't care, we were just giving it loads. Simulating sex with Brian's guitar while he was playing it, the lot.'

The Melbourne gigs were sedate by comparison. Four nights at Sydney Entertainment Centre towards the end of April, to be followed by six shows in Japan, were rendered the more enjoyable by news that Elton John was in town. Freddie, Elton and Roger wasted no time in painting the tiles pink, in advance celebration of Freddie's solo album.

'Freddie Mercury could out-party me, which is saying something,' commented Elton. 'We'd be up for nights, sitting there at eleven in the morning, still flying high. Queen were supposed to be catching a plane, and Freddie would be like, "Oh fuck, another line, dear?" His appetites were unquenchable.'

The band's final show in Sydney happened also to be Columbia Records' release date of *Mr Bad Guy*. Again, Freddie was wearing his heart on his sleeve in his songwriting. A flash and funky departure from the original Queen sound, the most telling tracks were 'Living On My Own', 'There Must Be More To Life Than This', and the plaintive ballad 'Love Me Like There's No Tomorrow', which he had written for Barbara Valentin.

Although the album went in at Number Six in the UK, it was an unmitigated disaster in America. While 'I Was Born to Love You' scored reasonably, 'Made in Heaven' went nowhere – despite the compellingly pompous promo video directed by David Mallet. Presented as a ballet performance on a formal curtained stage, it featured Freddie in red and black bondage gear and a flimsy red cape atop a huge rock. Negligibly-clad ballet dancers climbed up the rock and all over each other to get to him, until it fractured to reveal a beautiful blue revolving Planet Earth.

The Works tour nailed, Brian remained in Australia with his family for a holiday, John and Roger repaired to Roger's new home on Ibiza, and Freddie made a beeline for Munich, for more mirth and misdemeanours with his lovers.

Thank God for Live Aid.

'We were shite,' shrugs Francis Rossi, recalling Quo's valiant opening of the London leg on 13 July.

'Really bad. Under-rehearsed. Not rehearsed at all, truth be told. If we'd taken it on board a bit better, what it was all about and the fact that we'd have a global audience, we'd have rehearsed. Queen, of course, had just been out on tour, and were as slick as can be. *And* they rehearsed.

'Maybe Bowie was good, but no one else stands out much in the memory. Bono jumps off the stage, so fucking what. It was Queen's day, no question. What you have to remember is that, at that point, no one realised it was as big as it turned out to be. Bob was this loud upstart Irish bloke mouthing off about what he was going to do. And he pulled it off. It's tricky to keep your ego out of it completely, of course. Because we're stars, darling. But there wasn't too much of that going on, on the day.'

'When we got to Wembley that day for the show, Freddie put me straight about a lot of things, if I can use that expression,' Francis goes on.

'I remember we were moved to this holding area for artists, and we were all messing about. But then something happened. I don't have any problem with gay guys: how could I, I have two gay cousins and a gay son. But I had always been one of those straight guys who believed that gays aren't as manly as the rest of us. How wrong could I be? Freddie and I were engaged in a little bit of a tussle, having a laugh, when suddenly he had me in a half-Nelson and I just couldn't fucking move. He was so strong. So much information went flooding through my brain at that point. It was the steepest learning curve. I can see the expression on my face even now – *and* on his. I froze. I stared up at him. He was the strongest person I'd ever met in my life. "Don't worry darling," he said with this wicked laugh, "if I wanted you, I could have you," just like that.

'I know a lot of people think that homosexuals – I prefer the word "faggots", actually, none of this pussyfooting about – can't fight. These schmucks who get on telly and pontificate about why we shouldn't have gays in the army: what do they *think* we've always had? Our industry's full of gays. I find camp people marvellously entertaining, and a lot of the time easier to deal with than the rest. Rick (Parfitt) used to camp it up loads, in the good old days. Lots of us did. I've often thought that gays are better adjusted than the rest of us. They have to be, coping with what they have to deal with in the first place. No one was better than Freddie at that. He knew who he was; at least he did by then. Live Aid was definitely his day, no one else's. I fucking loved him for it.'

'Credit must go to all of them for that phenomenal performance,' says Paul Gambaccini. 'When Queen went on I was backstage, interviewing artists for the TV broadcast. You could feel the frisson. All the artists stopped talking among themselves, stopped doing whatever they were doing, and turned towards the stage. Everyone knew, as it was happening, that Queen were stealing the show. Freddie was doing his dance with the cameraman, in what was a blatant sexually-charged performance. They were rehearsed, they were ready, they were utter professionals. We thought, oh my God, this is as good as a live rock performance gets. Queen were the best. When you think back to who else was on that bill, that's just incredible. Queen were over. They'd had their day. Yet here Queen were, reinventing themselves and going again before our very eyes. It still takes my breath away when I think about it. Freddie Mercury delivered the greatest front-man performance anyone had ever seen.'

Uplifted by the Live Aid experience, Queen had soul-searching to do. Perhaps they had been bracing themselves for a natural conclusion to their mostly phenomenal career. They couldn't go on indefinitely, could they? Bands that do run the risk of diminution into caricature. Legendary status is achieved by quitting ahead. Each member of Queen had sidetracked into solo projects, with mixed results, and only Freddie with a modicum of success. Now forced to accept that they were better off sticking together than stalking separate paths, particularly at their time of life, they resolved to defer oblivion and to go again. Live Aid had gifted them a second chance. No rock act worth its stash would pass that up. Queen couldn't wait to get back on the road. 1986, Europe, would be the most ambitious tour of their career.

But first, Freddie's thirty-ninth birthday party, an excessive £50,000 black-and-white ball at Henderson's, one of his favourite Munich clubs. The party would be combined with a shoot to create a video for 'Living On My Own'. It featured 300 friends, including Barbara Valentin and Ingrid Mack, wife of Reinhold. Many of the extras were flown in from London and most were in drag – except Freddie, who wore Harlequin tights, epauletted military jacket and white gloves, and Mary Austin, who came as a St Trinian's schoolgirl. Brian was a witch, Peter Freestone a gypsy. The resultant video was an acid-trip – hedonistic, hallucinatory, bare-buttocked, throbbing – and was never screened in the US. In Britain, the single only managed a chart position of Number Fifty.

Barbara Valentin organised the party's black-and-white cuisine.

'Caviar and mashed potato – Freddie's favourite – a cake in the shape of a grand piano, and magnums of Cristal champagne, which people carried away under their arms. Everybody stole from Freddie, she sighed. 'Even two containers of his birthday presents went missing.'

Next came a commitment to Russell Mulcahy, partner of David Mallet and Scott Millaney in MGMM, to create music for his forthcoming film, *Highlander*, starring Christopher Lambert. Again, Queen managed to incur the wrath of the press, with the release of the single 'One Vision'. Denounced for having 'cashed in on their Live Aid success' with this 'blatantly themed' Top Ten hit, Queen were incensed. The song was in fact inspired by civil rights leader Martin Luther King's famous 1963 speech on the steps of the Lincoln Memorial, and not by Live Aid, retorted Roger, the song's composer. The track stands out for its reversed vocals at the beginning, which convey comprehensible lyrics when played forwards: 'God works in mysterious ways . . . mysterious ways . . .'

In defiance, they agreed to make a mini Queen documentary to use as a promo video for the record. This was the first time they worked with Torpedo Twins Rudi Dolezal and Hannes Rossacher, but by no means the last. In 1987 the Twins completed a visual anthology of the band's career entitled *Magic Years*.

At Fashion Aid for Ethiopia at the Royal Albert Hall on 5 November 1985, featuring eighteen of the world's top fashion designers, including Yves St Laurent, Giorgio Armani, Calvin Klein and Zandra Rhodes, Freddie played gracious groom to actress Jane Seymour's blushing bride. Each wore an outfit designed by David and Elizabeth Emmanuel, who had created the wedding dress of Lady Diana Spencer for her marriage to the Prince of Wales. Freddie then put himself at the disposal of his friend Dave Clark, the former singing drummer with Sixties group The Dave Clark Five. Dave was writing and producing an inventive new stage musical destined for the Dominion Theatre on Tottenham Court Road. Entitled *Time*, it would star Cliff Richard as well as Sir Laurence Olivier, the latter appearing as a hologram. Freddie collaborated on a couple of tracks for an album which also featured Stevie Wonder, Dionne Warwick and Julian Lennon, and made a one-off stage performance. EMI, meanwhile, were reaping rewards with a luxury boxed set of Queen albums (with a few glaring omissions). Still Freddie was not enjoying the solo success he had longed for. 'Love Me Like There's No Tomorrow', the fifth single from *Mr Bad Guy* and the ballad he had written for Barbara, didn't even chart.

Queen's soundtrack for *Highlander* would now be combined to form their new album. After appearing at the Montreux Rock

Festival, rehearsals began for the European tour. Kicking off in Stockholm, it would peak at Wembley Stadium and at Knebworth Park, earning more than £11 million over twenty-six shows. The tour saw Queen break the UK's all-time attendance record, performing to more than 400,000 fans. Did they somehow have an inkling this would be their last chance to experience the Freddie magic live?

21

Budapest

I want to go to places I've never been. To me, it's all about people. Music should go all around the world. I want to go to Russia and China and places I haven't seen, before it's too late – before I end up in a wheelchair and can't do anything. I'll still be wearing my same tights, too. I can imagine them wheeling me on stage in a wheelchair, up to a piano, and still singing 'Bohemian Rhapsody'.

Freddie Mercury

I rather liked the surrealism of going to the Hungarian Embassy for a rock 'n' roll party, knowing that they were more accustomed to welcoming a completely different kind of Queen.

Peter Hillmore

A Kind of Magic, Queen's fourteenth album and the *Highlander* soundtrack, was released at the end of May 1986 to mark the start of their European tour. As expected, it soared to Number One. At dawn on Wednesday 4 June, 13 huge trucks of equipment rumbled out of London to begin an odyssey across 11 countries. Queen would perform 26 concerts for a million fans in 20 cities, including Stockholm, Paris, Munich, Barcelona and Budapest. Each city was chosen, for personal reasons, by the band.

Denis O'Regan, now in big demand, was hired by Jim Beach through Queen's latest publicist, Phil Symes, to act as the tour's official photographer. He says he was nervous, but not about taking pictures.

'I'd heard about what they got up to. Tony Brainsby, their first PR, told me he'd once found Freddie in a dustbin behind the Embassy Club.

'Roger, John and Brian were the lads. Pretty easy-going. Freddie was the most enigmatic. There were often times when he couldn't keep up with what he was thinking. His brain would be doing nineteen to the dozen, and his mind raced ahead of his mouth. He'd say things like "What I want to get is the flow of the, um . . . oh, fuck it!" He'd have whole conversations in which it was just "fuck it, fuck it!", because he couldn't get his lips round what he wanted to say.'

No rock tour virgin, even Denis was taken aback by how hard this band enjoyed themselves – as if on a mission to parody what a rock 'n' roll supergroup was meant to be like.

'There were parties in brothels, Roman baths, Turkish baths. More lesbian strippers backstage at Wembley, and all those naked women painted to look like they were wearing uniforms at the Roof Gardens party, after the Wembley show. Not to mention the outrageous goings-on in the toilets.'

It wasn't all fun. Indeed, the crew seemed to live the dream better than the band most of the time. From what he witnessed at close range, Denis could not help but sympathise with Freddie for his loathing of life on tour. But contractual obligations dictated the pace. Make an album, tour to promote it: the pattern back then was set in stone.

'Freddie was not happiest on the road,' Denis admits. 'He once told me that he enjoyed performing, but *hated* touring. He seemed so vulnerable. Not at all what I'd expected. He could be dainty and sweet, like a little child. He'd sit at the end of the table clapping his hands and getting all excited about some dinner or other. Everything had to be just so. It was so cute. He was quiet, reserved and quite introverted a lot of the time. But he'd go from one extreme to the other in a flash. Considering what a big strong guy he looked on stage, he seemed petite and sometimes effeminate behind the scenes.'

Although Denis did not find him difficult to photograph, he was surprised to note how shy Freddie was.

'He would never really pose, as such. He would clown around, or ignore me and just be "himself". He might appear at the door wearing a crown, and throw a few shapes, knowing I was there – but not specifically inviting me to take photographs. He always knew what he was doing, of course.'

Denis hadn't expected Freddie's temper.

'He would frequently get angry, and could be very dismissive. He was always saying, "Tell them all to fuck off!" But he was pretty apologetic too. Freddie's magic was all down to the live performance. I think you have to be born with that kind of star quality. Not being "straight", if you like, he almost didn't have as much to prove up there as the rest of them. He'd go on stage and take the piss out of an audience, where the others might have felt they couldn't risk it. He had clearly been a really wild party animal in his day. Most of that was well out of his system by 1986.'

Spike Edney, master of keyboards on the 'Magic' tour, agreed.

'The mad partying scene had quietened down tremendously. Making a point of two camps staying in separate hotels wasn't relevant any more,' he said, referring to the band's sometime habit when on the road of dividing their accommodation into 'homo' and 'hetero' territory. In Munich, for example, when the band first arrived, and bunked down at the Munich Hilton, there had been the 'PPP' ('Presidential Poofter Parlour') and the 'HH' ('Hetero Hangout').

'By the time of the "Magic" tour, we were all staying together in one place,' said Spike. 'Fred was much more settled. He didn't have the taste for going out clubbing and staying up all night, the way he used to. Also, he was really looking after his voice. We'd often end up back in his suite, drinking champagne and playing Scrabble or Trivial Pursuit. I can remember several occasions still being up at nine a.m., just me and Fred, finishing off a game. Or playing Reverse Scrabble, where you have to take the letters off but still leave complete words. Previous Queen tours had been about sex, drugs and rock 'n' roll. By the mid-1980s, it was Scrabble.'

This new measured, middle-aged pace notwithstanding, there was one final party-to-end-all-parties left in Queen. The invitation of the season was to their post-Wembley celebration at the Roof Gardens club that July. London's oldest and finest roof garden is there to this day, a hundred feet above Kensington High Street, on top of what was once Derry & Toms department store. During its brief tenure there, Barbara Hulanicki's Biba emporium attracted a million customers a week to its themed retail floors and Rainbow Restaurant, where the public mingled freely with rock stars and celebrities. It was special to Freddie for a very personal reason, being the place where he had first set eyes on Mary Austin.

Oh what a night. Excess all areas. Dwarfs, drag queens, bottomless, topless – talking of which, Page 3 girl Samantha Fox, who in the 1980s was as famous as Jordan/Katie Price, took to the stage with Freddie in an impromptu set, and belted out Free's 1970 hit 'All Right Now'. She wasn't bad.

'Absolutely OTT,' agrees lensman Hogie, 'the party to end all parties. If you went in innocent, you came out wide-eyed. Naked, body-painted people. A vast fish tank with nothing in it except nudes sprayed to look like stones and reptiles, all lying on top of each other. Even coming up in that tiny lift, where were you supposed to look? Naked nipples and belly buttons everywhere. Queen did rock 'n' roll parties the way they should be done.

'Freddie adored Sam Fox. She had an amazing, er, personality. Whatever she did was in the papers, and she was just breaking into pop singing. That night, Freddie was enchanted by her boobs. All he wanted to do was pick her up and shake her, to see if he could get those puppies out. He was so excited. "Ooh look, fresh meat! A plaything!" Sam was game, she went along with it. He did get hold of her, and threw her around like a rag doll. Those great pictures made all the papers next day, which didn't do either of them any harm.'

'There will never be another band quite like Queen,' commented James 'Trip' Khalaf, the American sound engineer who had bigged up Queen's volume on Live Aid day.

'They were always ready for wretched excess. The parties were always bigger, the women always had larger breasts, the entire thing was on such a stupendous level that I could hardly keep up with it most of the time.'

As long as Trip had known Freddie, he never ceased to find him 'a strange person'.

'He was lovely, but he wasn't one of us . . . Fred was just a star. What else could he have been but this huge, bombastic rock star? The sonofabitch did a great job.'

On 9 August, Queen performed an open-air gig to more than 120,000 fans in the grounds of Knebworth Park, Stevenage. The stately home gave Queen their biggest-ever UK audience, and they celebrated into the night. The only person missing was Freddie: he had retreated discreetly at the end of the show, arm in arm with Jim Hutton and Peter Freestone. As Peter explained, Freddie had never enjoyed 'that kind' of party: 'He especially hated record company dos. No offence, but he didn't want to hang about making small-talk with employees.'

Perhaps Freddie sensed that Knebworth would be his final curtain. We all wish we'd known.

In the chopper conveying him back to the Battersea heliport that night, Freddie was informed of the fatal stabbing of a fan during the show. The crowd had proved impossible to penetrate. Officials had tried but failed to get an ambulance through to the scene.

'Freddie was very upset,' said Jim. 'He was still subdued the next morning, as friends arrived for Sunday lunch. There was great coverage about the concert in the newspapers, which did seem to cheer him up a bit. But that fan's death preyed on his mind. He only ever wanted his music to bring happiness.'

If the good times had to stop rolling, at least the memories are preserved. Of all the shows on the last tour Queen would ever play with Freddie, one remains etched on the minds of all who were fortunate enough to be there.

Queen's appearance at the Népstadion (People's Stadium), Budapest, on Sunday 27 July 1986 was more than just a gig. While Elton John, Jethro Tull and Dire Straits had performed modest concerts in Hungary, this was to be the first open-air stadium concert by a Western rock group staged anywhere behind the Iron Curtain, then still in place. It attracted 80,000 fans, both Hungarian and from neighbouring states. Tickets cost the equivalent of about £2 each, which for many was more than a month's wages. Even so, promoters were fielding overwhelming demand, to the tune of more than a quarter of a million applications.

The Hungarian press went berserk as the big day approached. Newspapers even hinted at 'lenient restrictions on audience behaviour', from which we assumed that they were going to be allowed to clap. They would certainly not be drunk, drugged, disorderly nor aggressive, the venue being patrolled by submachine-gun-toting police. The only booze available was orange squash. Even smoking was banned from the field. A sedate, well-regulated occasion was anticipated. Thank God for the backstage pass.

Queen's primary press officers – Roxy Meade and Phil Symes – bombarded we journalists with facts and figures. Seventeen cameras would film at the Népstadion, one of them operated by Gyorgy Illes, seventy-one, a veteran cameraman and revered tutor at Hungary's Film Academy. Illes was famous because his pupil Vilmos Zsigmond had earned an Oscar for his work on Spielberg's 1977 movie *Close Encounters of the Third Kind*. Queen and crew would cruise down the blue Danube from Vienna to Budapest on Soviet President Mikhail Gorbachev's official hydrofoil. Other

'Magic' tour fact sheets informed us that the stage measured up to 6,000 square feet, depending on indoor or outdoor venue; that the entire performance area would be carpeted in grey Axminster; that 8.6 miles of cable would be used on each date to connect instrumental, sound, lighting and other stage equipment to five full-power generators providing 5,000 amps; and that the sound system would be powered by more than half a million watts, with revolutionary delay towers. You didn't get that kind of press release from Michael Jackson or Elton John.

Queen's appearance was now being hailed as a giant step for East–West relations. Chargé d'Affaires David Colvin, acting British Ambassador to Hungary, rose to the occasion, hosting a pre-gig reception at a different kind of Embassy club from the one we were used to, for the band and cautiously selected special guests.

Our evening at the Hungarian Embassy assembled an incongruous mix of English expats, Eastern Bloc musicians, Western rock stars, Her Britannic Majesty's press corps, and the usual smattering of liggers. Freddie, while appearing bemused by it all, confessed that he would 'rather have gone shopping' than be standing there listening to people 'boring the pants off' each other with the ins and outs of Eastern European history. He had long maintained a dignified apolitical stance. While his private views bordered at times on imperialist, he knew better than to be drawn into socio-political discussions in public. An international celebrity, he said, was better off 'leaving politics to the chaps who are paid to do the job, dear.'

'That was Freddie to a T,' said Peter Freestone. 'He even considered U2 too political. He knew he was where he was because he was an entertainer. He wasn't there to lead people in their political beliefs.'

A few days later, Freddie gave the British press an elegant party in his presidential suite at the Duna Intercontinental hotel. 'Presidential' was an understatement, despite his blasé dismissal that 'all suites are equal'.

'Well, this one's a fucking sight more equal than mine,' retorted Roger, when he stopped by to check it out.

The gracious host, Freddie shook hands and exchanged platitudes as he welcomed us. Smaller than his stage persona, more muscular and fitter-looking than plenty half his age – he was less than two months off his fortieth birthday – he was scrubbed, fragrant, and sporting a bright floral shirt and tight pale denim jeans. His impeccably groomed hair revealed a small, threadbare patch just beginning to shine at the crown.

'Thank you for coming,' he said. 'Have you people been having a good time?' His voice was quiet, his half-smile polite, as he beckoned crystal goblets of champagne.

Freddie nodded and chuckled quietly as we related our Budapest adventures: taking the waters at the Gellert baths, submitting to carbolic massage by gelatinous 'Sumo-women' – although we later agreed that Freddie must be an old hand at all that. He wanted to know if we had 'bought' anything. We described our quirky purchases with gush.

'Very good, very good,' he smiled, waving us through a further reception room towards a sumptuous buffet heaving with lobsters, prawns, caviar, sugared fruits and exotic ice creams. At a gleaming grand piano, a tuxedoed musician sat fingering lobby tunes.

The sliding glass windows of the suite were drawn back, giving access to a balcony as wide as the room. In the indigo distance loomed silhouettes of famous tourist attractions: Fishermen's Bastion, the citadel on Gellert Hill, the soaring, floodlit spire of Matthias church. Mary Austin stood chatting quietly with Jim Beach, perhaps discussing, offered some wag, the wisdom of more fibre in the diet. Jim Hutton kept a limbo-dancer's profile in the corner, as did Brian, Roger, John, and a few of the crew.

Come Sunday, plastered with Access All Areas passes, we coached it through concrete suburbs to the Népstadion. Hungarian folk dancers in red, white and black costumes twirled handkerchiefs to music to psych us for the main event. It was a tidal wave when it came. Pomp, circumstance, billowing smoke and blinding lights, the deafening, all-encompassing experience of Queen.

What lingers in the memory? Brian, keener than an audition novice, frantic fingers tearing a sixpence plectrum through the strings of his fireplace guitar. His rendition, with Freddie, of popular Hungarian song 'Tavasi Szél Vizet Áraszt' – 'The Spring Wind Makes Waters Flood'. The crowd roaring their appreciation that the rockers had gone to so much trouble to learn their ditsy folk ballad, hardly noticing Freddie checking the lyrics every few seconds, which he had scrawled phonetically in pen on his left palm. The audience belting out 'Ga Ga' word-perfect, their synchronised hand-clapping a vision for sore eyes. The grand semi-finale: Freddie, stripped to the waist, leaking sweat into the seams of a vast Union Jack; and his flamboyant about-turn, moments later, revealing the broad horizontal red, white and green stripes of the Hungarian national flag.

It was not all. For his dramatic final appearance, Freddie sailed onto the stage draped in designer Diana Moseley's regal *pièce de résistance*, an ermine-edged velvet cape and train, and sporting a Coronation-style crown. Brian's inimitable take on 'God Save the Queen' ripped through the stadium in accompaniment, to tumultuous applause. That sequence, first recorded for the band's fourth album *A Night at the Opera* in 1974, and which had been performed as an outro at virtually every Queen gig since, was hardly unexpected. But it sounded somehow more majestic than ever in that corner of a foreign field.

'That was our most challenging and exhilarating gig ever,' Brian told us backstage afterwards.

We the hacks? We'd seen it all before. We were too blasé, God knows. We hadn't even paid for our tickets. What we'd seen, we knew the next morning, once the champagne had worn off, was just another knock-out Queen concert. We had been taking their brilliance for granted for years. Why stop now? The wonderment, the ambience, that Christmas-morning-like magic, had emanated entirely from the Hungarian audience. To those fans, some of whom had handed over four weeks' wages for the privilege, it will still be the most phenomenal spectacle of their lives.

Rock's greatest front man had triumphed again. It was, if only we'd known, a hollow victory. The irony of the tour's title was just beginning to dawn. For Freddie, the writing was on the wall. The magic that night thrilled everyone but him.

22

Garden Lodge

Whenever I watched Hollywood movies set in plush homes with lavish decor, I wanted that for myself, and now I've got it. But to me it was much more important to get the damn thing than to actually go and live in it. I'm very much like that – once I get something I'm not that keen on it any more. I still love the house, but the real enjoyment is that I've achieved it. Sometimes, when I'm alone at night, I imagine that when I'm fifty I'll creep into Garden Lodge, as my refuge, and then start making it a home. When I'm old and grey and when everything is finished and I can't wear the same costumes and jig around on stage any more – not quite yet – I have something to fall back on, and that's this wonderful house.

Freddie Mercury

From chart positions and awards to re-releases and video releases, the Queen machine was in perpetual motion. The wonder would never cease. Unspendable income was guaranteed for life. Freddie would never need more money than he had already. He could buy anything he wanted, could have gone anywhere he fancied. Instead, he retreated into his private world and the relatively modest comforts of home. He had his cook, valet, chauffeur, cleaner, and a handful of trusted friends. Mary Austin was responsible for the household and accounts, including staff wages and cash, and came to see him every day. Jim Hutton was there for him too. To anyone who asked – including Freddie's parents Bomi and Jer if they came for Sunday lunch – Jim was simply the gardener, and they pretended that another bedroom was his room. Was Jim offended by this pretence?

'Not a bit,' he insisted. 'They were lovely people. I understood the reason for the secrecy. They were religious. Zoroastrianism did not allow homosexuality. He had not come out to his family.'

Did his parents realise during his lifetime that Freddie was gay?

'No,' his mother Jer told *The Times* in 2006, fifteen years after his death.

'That area's too sensitive,' added her son-in-law, Roger Cooke, confirming that Freddie never came out to his family.

Was it that he was afraid of declaring the truth to the world?

'At the time,' said Jer. 'Society was different then. Nowadays it's all so open, isn't it?'

She indicated her belief that, had he lived on, Freddie would in time have felt able to be open.

'He didn't want to upset us,' she added. 'When he came home, he was just "Freddie".'

Jer revealed that her all-time favourite song by her son is 'Somebody to Love', the song which Freddie also loved best.

Peter Freestone remembered one particular celebration, which Freddie gave for his parents' wedding anniversary, just before he officially took up residence at his new house. None of the future Garden Lodge entourage was invited.

'Just his family and Mary, of course, who looked very good in a scarlet Bruce Oldfield which I had helped her pick out from a vast selection, and which Freddie had bought for her.'

Jim Hutton met Freddie's parents 'many times', and got on well with them.

'They came to Garden Lodge very rarely – usually for Sunday lunch, or for one of Kash's children's birthdays,' Jim said. 'But when he was in London, Freddie saw them every week. I'd drive him over to visit them every Thursday afternoon at their small terraced house in Feltham, the same one they'd always lived in, and we'd all sit in the kitchen together, having tea. Mrs Bulsara got the tea at her own pace; she didn't rush around. She was very independent. She still drove herself all over the place in her little car. Their place was very homely. One thing I found odd was that they didn't have any pictures of Freddie in frames anywhere, which you'd think they would have. It was also strange to me that they were still living in that tiny house when Freddie could easily afford to buy them something grander. He'd offered, but they'd said they didn't want to move. They were happy with the home they had. It was very endearing actually, since a lot of rock stars' parents jump at the chance of all the material things, once their offspring has made it.'

Jim had little in common with Freddie's mother, but shared with his father Bomi a love of nature and gardening.

'He was proud of his garden,' said Jim. 'I'd go out there with him. He loved his old rose trees, and a wonderful eucalyptus.'

As for Jer, Jim was touched by the fact that she always made Freddie his favourite cheese biscuits, which she'd pack into a little lunchbox for him to take home.

'I met Freddie's sister Kashmira for the first time when she and her family came to stay at the Mews. You could see at once that she and Freddie were sister and brother – they had the same big, dark brown eyes. Her daughter Natalie was a sweet, boisterous kid, and she also had a baby son, Sam.'

Freddie's family was always very important to him, affirmed Jim.

'Whenever he was away, no matter where, he always made a point of sending cards to his parents and his sister.'

Freddie's father Bomi died in 2003. His mother Jer now lives in Nottingham, having moved there to be close to her daughter Kashmira, her son-in-law and grandchildren. Jer's house was 'christened' 'Fredmira' – a blend of the names of her own two children.

★　　★　　★

'I can't carry on rocking the way I have done in the past,' Freddie declared after what turned out to be Queen's final gig in August 1986.

'It is all too much. It's no way for a grown man to behave. I have stopped my nights of wild partying. That's not because I'm ill, but down to age. I'm no spring chicken. I prefer to spend my time at home. It's part of growing up.'

He continued to entertain, but mostly under his own roof. His fortieth birthday party on Sunday 7 September 1986 was modest by his standards: a 'Mad Hat' garden party for 200 guests.

Designer Diana Moseley prepared a range of eccentric headwear for Freddie to choose from. He opted for a white fur construction with Martian-style antennae.

'It was a sedate party for him, but really lovely all the same,' remembers Tony Hadley, who was there, along with Tim Rice, Elaine Paige, Dave Clark, comedian Mel Smith, *EastEnders* actress Anita Dobson, Brian, Roger and John.

'Freddie insisted on taking me upstairs to show me the carpet he'd had made for his bedroom,' remembers Tony. 'It had no join in it; the loom must have been enormous. It also had a big star on it, like a star of David. He was so proud of that carpet it wasn't true.'

'Freddie was very proper and very "British" about household things,' revealed Jim.

'I remember his parents were coming to Sunday lunch once, and Freddie was practically having a nervous breakdown. Talk about a mother hen. He was in and out of the kitchen all morning, fussing over the food. He was into everything. The dining table he had to lay himself. It was important to him. The knives and forks had to point perfectly towards the ones opposite, and the place mats had to line up just so. He was the absolute perfectionist.'

Despite the fact that they were essentially there to serve the master, there were neither politics nor pecking order at Garden Lodge. All who lived there were treated equally, and were expected to keep just one rule: 'You didn't bring anyone back,' said Jim. 'No pals, no overnight partners. It was Freddie's domain. Security was paramount. Otherwise we were a family bunch, not just Freddie's staff. It mostly ran on an even keel. Joe the chef got away with blue murder. He could be a sweetie, but he had his tantrums. Freddie would throw a paddy quite often, but he wasn't bossy, he didn't lord it. He never flung his weight around or gave us orders. It was much more relaxed than that. We often all ate together, *en famille*, but mostly it was just Freddie and myself. I don't think I gave the others reason to feel resentful towards me. Everyone had their own room, including Barbara. Her room had been my bedroom, in fact. Later, when Freddie and I no longer slept together, I moved back into it. There was never any favouritism. Whenever Freddie's friends came back for a few drinks, everyone in the house was included in the party. Garden Lodge was everybody's home.'

For all the fun, frolics and wild times that Freddie and Jim shared – a million-pound holiday in Japan, the madness of Live Aid, the tranquillity of Switzerland – and the tender relationship which sustained Freddie until the end, Jim claimed to have derived the most satisfaction from his lover's creativity.

'He never stopped,' Jim said. 'Always into something. Always planning. His brain was perpetually doing overtime. First, it was Garden Lodge to get finished. Then he bought the mews house directly behind Garden Lodge, in Logan Mews. Then he was off to buy a place in Switzerland. He could never rest, nothing was ever completed. He had to be *doing* all the time.'

Freddie was not in the habit of talking to Jim about his music.

'But when it came to lyrics, he'd talk to anyone who was there. He'd say, "I've got this idea", or "I've got these words", or "Help me out with this line here." He was always scribbling things, on anything at all. He never sang around the house – only occasionally in the bath. But not Queen songs. I've got a video of him in the Jacuzzi (which surfaced on the internet, after Jim's own death), and he's warbling away at the top of his voice.'

Freddie had promised his lover the holiday of a lifetime in Japan at the end of September 1986, and Freddie kept his promises. He relished the fact that for the first time ever he could enjoy as a tourist the country he had always adored. Freddie and Jim saw the sights, wined and dined, shopped outrageously – their purchases even included a huge kimono stand, an item Freddie had always wanted. The experience for both was unforgettable. On their return to London, they settled into an orderly domestic routine with their cats, their koi carp, and their closest friends.

Their cosy world was detonated on Sunday 13 October 1986, by the *News of the World*, after which a cloud descended over Garden Lodge. It was never to lift.

The sensational revelations were nauseating: Freddie, the paper alleged, had taken a secret AIDS test the year before, the same year that the band stole the show at Live Aid. The deaths of two of his former lovers were also revealed: airline steward John Murphy, one of the beloved 'New York Daughters', and young Tony Bastin, the smiling blond courier Freddie had picked up all those years ago in Brighton. Jim Hutton was identified as Freddie's live-in lover. Wild nights spent taking cocaine with David Bowie and Rod Stewart were exposed in detail, as was the reason why Michael Jackson and Freddie had fallen out. The paper's informant claimed that Michael had been upset by Freddie's prodigious use of cocaine, and that Jacko had caught him snorting the drug in his lounge. There was even a spread of personal photographs, featuring Winnie Kirchberger and other lovers, under the headline 'All the Queen's Men'.

The sordid exposé also destroyed the perception of Freddie's friendship with Kenny Everett, revealing their terminal falling-out after a row over cocaine.

'Everett thought Freddie was taking advantage of his generosity, whereas in reality it was more likely the other way round – not that Freddie would ever have given him a hard time for it,' Jim explained.

'They never made up, and Kenny never again came to Garden Lodge, not after I moved in. If we'd see him out and about around the gay clubs, they never spoke. All those newspaper stories about Kenny being at Freddie's bedside were fabricated.'

Freddie was speechless when he discovered that this explosive 'exclusive' was the work of Paul Prenter, his trusted former personal manager and supposed close friend. Prenter had held Freddie's hand on the road all those years. He had sold what was left of his charge's dignity and privacy for a mere £32,000.

'Freddie couldn't bear the betrayal,' said Jim. 'He couldn't believe that someone who had been so close to him could behave in so mean-spirited a way. There were days and days of it, followed up in the *News of the World*'s sister paper, *The Sun*: Freddie and drugs, Freddie and men; it got worse and worse. Freddie got angrier with each new revelation. He never spoke to Prenter again.'

Prenter was also frozen out by Elton John, John Reid and others in their circle, who closed ranks to protect Freddie.

Why did he do it?

Some observers say that Prenter resented Freddie's relationship with Jim. That, in taking a permanent live-in lover, Freddie was effectively dispensing with Prenter. Realising that his power over Freddie had been destroyed, he sought revenge. Although Prenter phoned Freddie and tried to explain himself, Freddie refused to take his calls.

'Paul tried to excuse himself by claiming that he'd been hounded and tormented by the press for so long that he eventually cracked,' said Jim.

'He tried to say that he said all that stuff by mistake. He said he was misquoted. As if. Only Paul could have known some of the stuff that was written.

'It crushed Freddie's ability to trust others, except for a select few,' lamented Jim. 'He made no new friends after that.'

'Freddie had taken Paul on after the band got rid of him,' said Peter Freestone. 'Even though Freddie knew that Paul was taking advantage of him, financially and so on. That made it all the harder to bear.'

'Prenter was the one who had always taken advantage of Fred's forgiving nature,' added Spike Edney.

'People were constantly saying, "How does he get away with this shit?" Yet Fred maintained their friendship. He got shafted by more people over the years than anyone I've ever known . . . considering that he was a pretty shrewd judge of character, it's amazing how many leeches got through. Fred never actually had any true privacy, ever. People like Prenter saw to that.'

In the United States, the falsification of death certificates was sensationally on the rise. Many prominent figures on the way out thanks to AIDS-related illnesses had talked their doctors into preserving their image by registering information that wasn't true. Even as cabaret supremo Liberace lay dying, his spokesman was still insisting that the star was 'suffering the ill-effects of a water-melon diet'. Macho heart-throb Rock Hudson, last of the square-jawed romantic leads and co-star of screen sweetheart Doris Day, had been the first major movie star to die openly of AIDS, in 1985. By then, 264 cases had been reported in the UK. The disease was declared the most serious health threat to the nation since the Second World War. New laws were passed, empowering magistrates to order hospitalisation of AIDS sufferers, to prevent them from engaging further in careless sex. Attacks on homosexuals became commonplace, and misinformation was rife. *Burke's Peerage*, ironi-cally the former employer of Jeremy Norman, the Embassy Club and Heaven founder, made the shock announcement that, in order to preserve the 'purity of the human race', it would not list families of which any member was known to be infected with AIDS.

There were sound reasons for keeping a low profile, as far as Freddie was concerned – not least the shame of having to admit to his parents that he was gay. The pain and embarrassment that this could cause them in their Parsee community was unthinkable. There was also, for Queen and Jim Beach, the not inconsiderable question of their recording contract. With albums still owing, the last thing they needed was the suggestion that Freddie might not live long enough to fulfil their obligations to EMI.

Christmas 1986 saw the release of Queen's *Live Magic* album, featuring live recordings of many favourite hits. The band would now take the next year off, to rest, take stock, and focus on solo work.

For all his inner torment, Freddie appeared serene. At long last, he had struck the perfect work/life balance. Although he knew that he was marking time, he would do it in style. He'd get up late; invite a few friends over for brunch, or eat out locally; sit chatting for hours, rest a while, then give a supper party at home or take his entourage out to a restaurant for the evening. On his return, he would work in his studio into the small hours. Now and then he would make the short journey to Queen's production offices on Pembridge Road, Notting Hill; attend a couple of business meetings; pop in to Christie's or Sotheby's to see what antiques or oriental art might be coming up for sale. He was 'always busy, seldom rushed. It was a pleasant, convivial lifestyle'. But there was a sell-by date, and it was looming.

23

Barcelona

With the Barcelona *album I had a little bit more freedom and a bit of scope to actually try out some of my crazy ideas. Montserrat kept telling me that she found a new lease of life and a new-found freedom. Those were her own words, and I was very taken by it. She told me on the phone that she loves the way our voices sound together . . . and I was smiling from my ass to my elbow, my dears. I sat at home like I'd just swallowed the canary, thinking 'Ooh! There's a lot of people who'd like to be in my shoes right now.'*

Freddie Mercury

People say that Barcelona is in some respects a rather trivial pop song, that it's cod opera. It isn't at all. In other circumstances, with that melody, it could have been part of a grand opera. It wouldn't have been laughed out of court.

Sir Tim Rice

His first attempt at a solo album having failed to stun, Freddie was hell-bent on proving himself.

He chose Townhouse Studios on the Goldhawk Road, West London, for his follow-up, primarily because it was easily accessible from Garden Lodge. One of Britain's most famous recording studios, Townhouse, now closed, was built by Richard Branson in

1978 and later taken over by the EMI/Virgin group. Frank Zappa, Bryan Ferry and Tina Turner to name a few, had toiled there. Studio Two can be seen in Bob Dylan's strange feature *Hearts of Fire*. Elton John would record his tribute to Diana, Princess of Wales there, on the afternoon of her funeral in 1997.

At Townhouse, Freddie experimented with Buck Ram's classic 'The Great Pretender'. A huge hit for Ram's protégés the Platters in 1956, the song, recorded over the years by Pat Boone, Roy Orbison, Sam Cooke, Dolly Parton, and The Band, and having inspired the name of Chrissie Hynde's group The Pretenders, was notably covered by Gene Pitney in 1969. Pitney's was clearly the version on which Freddie based his, although early demos lean more towards the Platters' take.

So delighted was Freddie with his efforts that he couldn't wait to film the promo video. The dramatic £100,000 effort was filmed in three days by MGMM, and produced by Scott Millaney with David Mallet directing. Freddie even shaved off his moustache for the shoot, in keeping with the slick image he and Mallet created.

With its sweet, sentimental overview of Queen history – the film incorporated iconic scenes from earlier videos such as 'Bohemian Rhapsody', 'Crazy Little Thing Called Love', 'It's a Hard Life' and 'I Want to Break Free' – it was to become one of the best-loved promos ever. Although this would not be the last video he would make, it was widely regarded after his death as 'Freddie's Farewell'. He dragged up again with Roger Taylor and Peter Straker as 'backing singers' – although Taylor and Straker were seen but not heard. Despite the fact that they are credited as backing vocalists on the single, they only mimed for the video. Freddie recorded all the vocals for the track himself. In a number of sequences, Freddie sported the same costumes he had worn for the original shoots, which Diana Moseley had in storage. They still fitted him perfectly. An even more outrageous video was released a month later, showing the making of 'The Great Pretender' in graphic detail.

'The Great Pretender' single was released in February 1987, and reached Number Four in the UK. It has since appeared on countless compilations. It stands today alongside 'Bohemian Rhapsody' as a testament to the tormented soul behind the rock star, a rare glimpse into the mind of the Freddie within. In his final filmed interview, in spring 1987, Freddie admitted that this song more than any other summed up his career. The 'tears of a clown' motif creeps in again – 'Just laughing and gay like a clown' – and the song's most telling lines tear at the heart strings: 'Oh yes, I'm the Great Pretender/ Pretending that I'm doing well/My need is such/I pretend too much/I'm lonely but no one can tell'.

He said it reflected perfectly how performing on stage for thousands of fans at a time really made him feel. Was it worth it, I wonder? We'll never know. But we can see, given Freddie's genius for the craft of songwriting, that his rendition of 'The Great Pretender' is a tragic irony. The song he chose as being the one that best described him was a song that Freddie had not written for himself.

During the 'Magic' tour, in August 1986, Freddie had given a radio interview during which he was asked, 'Who has the best voice in the world?' 'I'm not just saying this because I'm in Spain,' he replied, 'but as far as I'm concerned, Montserrat Caballé has the best voice of anybody in existence.'

'Montserrat heard about what Freddie had said,' Peter Freestone told me. 'She had already been approached regarding the 1992 Olympics, Barcelona being Montserrat's home town.'

While no one remembers whose idea it was, a plan began to evolve featuring Freddie and Montserrat duetting on an Olympic anthem.

'Jim Beach had some discussions with Carlos, Montserrat's brother and business manager,' said Peter. 'It was then put to Freddie, who readily agreed – it would give him his longed-for opportunity to work with her. He was completely seduced by the idea of another worldwide television audience, having got the taste for it at Live Aid. A meeting was duly arranged in Barcelona in March 1987. Montserrat sent Freddie some videos of her performing. In return, she asked for the complete works of Queen.'

Freddie was unusually nervous as he flew to Spain with Peter, Jim Beach, and the producer Mike Moran, whom Freddie had met and befriended on Dave Clark's musical *Time*. When they arrived at the Ritz Hotel that Tuesday, they were kept waiting for what seemed like hours. 'Montsy' was in the habit of turning up late.

'Lunch took place in a private garden dining room with a piano placed specially in one corner,' Peter said. 'Freddie had a rough tape with a song and a few little ideas on it, which I had to guard with my life. There was 'Exercises in Free Love', plus what would become 'Ensueño', and some ideas for other tracks. I noticed that Freddie and Montserrat were both very much in awe of each other, but so excited at the prospect of working together. They hit it off, and the lunch was a great success.'

Montserrat had an engagement at the Royal Opera House in London a few days later, after which she visited Freddie at home for the first time.

'Opera stars love to go to bed early, because of The Voice,' said David Wigg.

'But Montserrat came to Garden Lodge one night for dinner, and she stayed up with Freddie until five in the morning, he and Mike on the piano, her singing Queen songs, mostly. How she knew them, I'll never know. Freddie had the most incredible range of any rock star, but he was blown away by hers. Montserrat and Freddie met their match in each other.'

'Mike Moran was there, and it didn't take them long to hit the piano,' recalls Peter. 'It was an unforgettable night. Freddie and Montserrat were completely natural with each other. They drank champagne and fooled around, just jamming – if that term can be applied to an opera singer. Their formal studio work together was never as relaxed as that night at Garden Lodge.'

The following month, Queen were honoured with another Ivor Novello award, for Outstanding Contribution to British Music, after which Freddie turned his attention to what would be his final solo album. *Barcelona* would be produced by Mountain Studios' David Richards, whose work was cut out: 'La Stupenda' was in huge demand by opera houses and concert halls all over the world, and her diary was booked up five years in advance. She did not have much time to hang out or dabble in the studio, the way Freddie liked to work. The bulk of the production was done long-distance over the next nine months, with Freddie despatching tapes of near-completed tracks featuring his own falsetto vocals, for her to add her soprano in their place. If not an ideal way to work, the result was stunning, and one of the greatest achievements of Freddie's life.

Tim Rice's companion at that time was *Evita*, *Cats* and *Chess* star Elaine Paige, who was working on an album of Queen covers approved by Freddie. Freddie and Tim had met through Elaine, and had become good friends. Tim contributed lyrics to 'The Golden Boy' and 'The Fallen Priest' on the *Barcelona* album. The first featured a celebrity gospel choir line-up including Blue Mink's Madeline Bell, Peter Straker (again) and South African session singer Miriam Stockley. The second was something of a Moran masterpiece, on which he conducted the orchestra, wrote all the arrangements, and played piano and keyboards.

'Montserrat and Freddie sang these two songs as duets,' Tim told me. 'They were both interesting. Neither of them great songs, but great musical chunks. Freddie was a man of great culture, taste and musical gifts, who was really obsessed by opera. That was his big love in the last few years of his life. When we went round to his house, he would play videos of all these divas, and he'd get so excited by them. Maria Callas, Montserrat Caballé, Joan Sutherland, all singing these great arias. To a certain extent he educated me, as I really didn't know anything much about opera.

'I believe it was one way of Freddie having love for women which he could really express and indulge in. Because Freddie adored women. He revelled in their femininity, the way they looked and dressed, and smelled, even. In their differences from men. He quite obviously loved Mary. When I used to go out to dinner with him and Elaine, he really enjoyed her company. There was no question of him cutting women out. He very much wanted them in his life. I never went to any of his wild parties, but I did go to some dinner parties of Freddie's. There might be twenty, thirty people there, and at least half of them were always ladies.'

Towards the end of May, Freddie left Garden Lodge for Ibiza, accompanied by Jim, Peter, Joe and Terry, his chauffeur. AIDS now having been officially diagnosed, he was desperate to get away. On the advice of Freddie's GP, Dr Gordon Atkinson, a small medical trunk was now a vital part of his luggage, which contained Freddie's preparations for AIDS.

Their holiday was spent at Pike's, a charming 500-year-old farm-house converted into an exquisite hotel. Freddie felt very much at home there. He played some tennis, lounged by the pool, and ventured out to the odd gay club or bar at night.

'He had developed a bad wound on the bottom of his right foot,' said Jim. 'He found it increasingly difficult to walk, and it would dog him for the rest of his life.'

During their trip, Freddie was taken to the famous Ku Club outside San Antonio, where he had an engagement with his new bosom pal. The Ibiza '92 festival, being staged to fanfare Spain's forthcoming hosting of the Olympics, and featuring Marillion, Duran Duran, Chris Rea and Spandau Ballet, was to be closed by Freddie and Montserrat performing 'Barcelona'. The cham-pagne flowed at the Ku Club, and well into the night back at Pike's. Freddie partied into the early hours. He expected few tomorrows.

He spent the summer working on his house, converting the cottages he'd acquired in Logan Mews in Kensington, and planning a conservatory. It was as if, Jim remarked, he wanted to leave behind his own little bit of paradise. In September he returned to Pike's on Ibiza for his forty-first birthday, accompanied by Peter, Joe, Terry, Peter Straker and David Wigg. The other members of Queen were already on the island, where Roger owned a secluded holiday home. The party at Pike's was to have been a joint affair, shared with Queen's former manager John Reid. But Reid withdrew at the last minute. An embarrassed Freddie was left to cope with the arrangements, including a dual-name firework display and a Gaudi-inspired chocolate birthday cake for two. 'Fuck Reid', was Freddie's only comment. A chartered plane carrying dozens of his friends was due at any moment, and Freddie was not going to let Reid's absence spoil his fun.

Roger, working on an album with his new solo band The Cross, invited Freddie to contribute to a track to be recorded at Maison Rouge studios in London. The track, 'Heaven for Everyone', eventually made it onto Queen's *Made in Heaven* album.

'Of course, Freddie's version is fantastic,' said Spike Edney, who also worked on the project. 'But he wasn't actually allowed to be singing on a Roger Taylor solo album, because of his own solo recording contract. So Fred couldn't be credited in the notes. Consequently, on that first Cross album, *Shove It*, you hear this track called 'Heaven for Everyone', and it's Freddie's vocal . . . but when they put it out as a single, they had to release the Roger version!'

'Barcelona' the single emerged in Spain on 21 September. Ten thousand copies were purchased in under three hours. Released in the UK the following month, the first collaboration by a rock superstar and an internationally-acclaimed operatic soprano, it stunned the critics and soared to Number Eight. It would later be performed at the '92 Olympics, a year after Freddie's death, when it would reach Number Two in the charts in the UK, the Netherlands and New Zealand.

Flowers left outside Freddie's former home in Logan Place, following the news of his death.

Tributes at Freddie's home on the 3rd anniversary of his death.

Freddie Mercury tribute concert, Wembley Stadium, London, 1992.

Opera diva Montserrat Caballé with Freddie's parents, Bomi and Jer Bulsara, at the unveiling of their late son's commemorative statue, 25 November 1996, Montreux, Switzerland.

Brian May and Roger Taylor with Freddie's mother Jer at the 16th Annual Rock and Roll Hall Of Fame Ceremony, 2001, New York.

The author, Barbara Valentin and friend, Munich, 1996.

Queen's official photographer Denis O'Regan with the author, London 1996.

The Teddy Bar, a favourite Munich nightspot.

HansSachs Strasse, Munich: the apartment building in the infamous Bermuda Triangle district where Freddie purchased a flat with Barbara Valentin.

The Munich building which housed Henderson's, one of the nightclubs Freddie frequented. Here, in 1985, he combined his 39th birthday party, a £50,000 black and white ball, with a video shoot to promote 'Living On My Own'.

Jim Hutton in his garden in County Carlow, Ireland, July 1996, 5 years after Freddie's death.

Jim Hutton, Peter Freestone, Barbara Valentin and the author, the Groucho Club London, August 1997.

Back, from left; the author, Barbara Valentin, Jim Hutton, Peter Freestone. Front, from left: the son of Freddie's school friend Gita Choksi, and Indian friend, at the Groucho Club London, August 1997.

Peter Freestone and Jim Hutton at a private party given by the author at the Groucho Club, London, August 1997.

Queen's rarest and most sought-after record: *The Works* LP, pressed on red vinyl in Colombia.

Limited Edition: Two hundred hand-pressed copies of 'Bohemian Rhapsody' pressed on 7-inch blue vinyl to commemorate Queen's label EMI Records receiving the Queen's Award to Industry, 1978.

A replica of the Freddie Mercury statue sculpted by Czech artist Irena Sedlecka, which stands above the entrance to London's Dominion Theatre, home to 'We Will Rock You' since 2002.

Graffiti tributes to Freddie and Queen on the walls of the entrance to the former Mountain Studios, Queen's own facility in Montreux, Switzerland. The studios are long-gone, but the entrance and doorway are preserved as an informal shrine. March 2011.

Fans gather at sunset to honour their idol at Freddie's statue on Lake Geneva, March 2011.

Freddie Mercury's statue by Irena Sedlecka,
overlooking his beloved Lake Geneva beneath
the Swiss Alps, March 2011.

Christmas 1987 brought new housemates to Garden Lodge: a pair of kittens named Goliath and Delilah. For the latter, a beautiful tortoiseshell that would become his favourite cat, Freddie wrote an eponymous song. She soon took to sleeping at the foot of his bed. As Freddie's illness took hold, his pets, which he adored as though they were children, brought him comfort.

He now worked only when he felt strong enough. In January 1988, Queen reunited at Townhouse to commence their next album, *The Miracle*. All were now aware that Freddie was gravely ill. The signs were obvious. The extent of his illness was discreetly ignored at first, until to do so became impossible. Freddie sat Brian, Roger and John down one day, and gave them the lowdown.

'First of all, he said: "You probably realise what my problem is – my illness",' Brian remembered. 'And by that time, we kind of did. It was unspoken. And then he said, "Well, that's it. I don't want it to make any difference . . . I don't want it to be known, I don't want to talk about it, I just want to get on and work until I can't work any more." I don't think any of us will ever forget that day. We all just went off and got quietly sick somewhere.'

'Freddie knew his time was limited, and he really wanted to work, and keep going,' Roger said.

'He felt that was the best way for him to keep his spirits up, and he wanted to leave as much behind as possible. We certainly agreed, and backed him right up to the hilt . . . but *The Miracle* was an effort – a long album to make.'

'I think [work] was the one thing that gave him much happiness,' Mary Austin would explain, after his death. 'It made him feel alive inside . . . instead of things becoming dull, and life becoming painful . . . there was something else that he was working for. Life wasn't just taking him to the grave.'

'Freddie felt safe in the environment of the group,' added Brian. 'Things were just as they always had been. Probably we all tried too hard. But we tried to make things just very normal. It seemed to work.'

On 8 October, Freddie arrived in Barcelona for the huge open-air La Nit festival, before King Juan Carlos, Queen Sofia and Princess Cristina of Spain, during which the city received the Olympic torch from Seoul. Freddie and Montserrat mimed to a recording of 'Barcelona', with the opera house orchestra and choir. It was an odd climax to a bizarre evening which had featured an eclectic line-up: José Carreras, Spandau Ballet, Eddy Grant, Jerry Lee Lewis and Rudolf Nureyev.

The rest of 1988 was spent quietly on separate pursuits. The band reconvened in January 1989 to finish *The Miracle* album. Bitter creative altercation and fall-outs when someone failed to get their own way having hallmarked Queen's studio style, their working time together was at last harmonious. 'I Want It All', their thirty-second UK single, was released in May, followed by their sixteenth album. *The Miracle* went platinum within a week. Freddie and Jim left for Montreux and 'The Cygnets', the beautiful lakeside house he rented there, so named for its view of 'Freddie's swans', which he would rush down to see as soon as he arrived. Freddie had renamed the place 'The Duck House'. Roger went one better, with 'Duckingham Palace'. Freddie would spend hours wandering along the water's edge. The mountain air refreshed him. He felt more at peace in Montreux than anywhere else. Speculation about his health dominated the headlines back home. The band took a swipe in return with their single 'Scandal'.

Voted 'Best Band of the Decade' by the readership of *TV Times* magazine, Queen appeared on a television special, 'Goodbye to the Eighties', to receive their award from Liverpool's much-loved pop singer turned personality Cilla Black, and her sidekick, a young Jonathan Ross.

Still restlessly creative, and ever anxious to augment his legacy, Freddie turned his thoughts to the promotion of Queen's next single from the album, also called 'The Miracle'. They should use child lookalikes of the band members, he suggested. The kids they wound up choosing were astonishingly good, and the video was mesmerising. Over the New Year, 1990, with heavy hearts, Queen gathered at Mountain Studios to begin recording *Innuendo*. The album, they thought, would probably be Freddie's swansong. It wasn't quite.

24

For the Road

I've had upheavals and I've had immense problems, but I've had a
wonderful time and I have no regrets. Oh dear, I sound like Edith Piaf!

Freddie Mercury

Certain people in this industry are not meant to grow old. Freddie was
one of them. I could never see Freddie at seventy. Nor Michael Jackson. In
any case, Freddie wouldn't have liked the way albums are recorded today.
He lived his life to the full. He died young, but he crammed in an amazing
amount. More than most people could in five lifetimes.

Rick Wakeman

New Year 1990. As Queen regrouped at Mountain Studios to
begin work on the album *Innuendo*, Jim Beach entered challenging
negotiations with Capitol to terminate Queen's recording contract.
Unbeknown to the band, a new American label was waiting in the
wings. The entertainment lawyer who had negotiated Queen's exit
deal from the Elektra label was now president of the Walt Disney
Company's Hollywood Records, and poised to sign one of his all-
time favourite bands.

'A lot of people thought it was a stupid move, destined for failure,' says Peter Paterno. 'In fact, signing Queen was successful
beyond all possible hope.'

'Despite all the negative commentary at the time, the deal was *not* risky. We'd get our money back in eight years. Did I know that Freddie had AIDS? I knew he was ill. He kept the details secret. But frankly, I knew I couldn't lose. If he passed, we projected that we'd be even in three years. As it happened, the movie *Wayne's World* came out, featuring that insanely brilliant 'Bohemian Rhapsody' head-banging sequence in the car, and we were even in three *weeks*.

'Up until then, they were a dead issue in the United States, but huge throughout the rest of the world. I thought the *Magic* album was an amazing album, but it did nothing in the US. Even so, I had a hunch. I sent Jim Beach a message saying, "I hear Queen are free." "Not only are they free," came the response, "but the entire catalogue is available." That's how we got started.'

The complete output of Queen's long career would now be digitally remastered and re-released on CD, which was suddenly overtaking vinyl in popularity. It was a massive gamble on Paterno's part, the band not having had a Top Twenty album in the States since 1982.

All was progressing well for the Hollywood Records president until someone tipped off Disney chief executive Michael Eisner that Freddie was dying of AIDS.

'Michael got hold of me and demanded, "What's going on?" remembers Paterno. 'This was news that made him extremely nervous. He sensed that somehow we were being taken for a ride, that the deal would make Disney look ridiculous. He thought we should put a clause in the contract regarding what would happen if Freddie died. But I said, "If he does, as morbid as it sounds, that sells records too. I've heard music from the new album, and I'm not worried."

'It was a *very* expensive deal: ten million dollars. The Disney board at first turned me down, I had to argue my corner. Then I got my way, we did the deal, and it was one of my proudest moments.'

'I said to Jim Beach, "For ten million dollars, do I at least get to meet the guy?" I flew from Los Angeles to Montreux to spend just one memorable afternoon with Freddie Mercury. He was pleasant and gracious. Played me some of the album in the studio. We walked around the town, had dinner together. It was all a lovely experience, but you could tell that he was facing his mortality.

'Suddenly, Queen were *huge* here again!' Paterno exclaims. 'My hunch didn't fail me! Thing was, they'd never stopped putting out great albums. Had they started to sound like jaded has-beens, I wouldn't have bothered. But they were still making terrific music, and I always thought they had a comeback in the States in them. How gratifying to have been proven right, even though the loss of Freddie Mercury is tragic.'

Having at last achieved an elusive BPI (British Phonographic Industry) Award for Outstanding Contribution to British Music, and mindful that time was running out for Freddie, Queen cooked the calendar to make 1990 their twentieth anniversary. They hosted a celebration for 400 friends at London's Groucho Club. The venue was chosen for its name, in homage to early Queen albums named after Marx Brothers movies. Liza Minnelli, George Michael, Patsy Kensit, Michael Winner and Rod Stewart turned up. The celebration cake was in the style of a Monopoly board, with Queen hits pasted into the squares.

As bloodthirsty picture editors foamed at the mouth over gaunt, give-away snaps of Freddie as he arrived at and left the party, the death-rumours were denied by fellow band members, management, publicists, friends and personal entourage.

'That was what Freddie wanted,' said Peter Freestone. 'Those of us closest to him were even lying to members of our own families. We did it for Freddie. He never wanted a fuss, or to shock his parents. Other than that, he didn't see that his illness was anybody's business but his own.'

'There were a lot of people at that party, but curiously, not many people were talking to the band,' remembers Phil Swern.

'It was almost as if they were afraid to approach them. I found myself standing near the bar with Freddie, chatting for about twenty minutes. I couldn't quite believe that I was talking with this icon like we were old pals. He was very pale and quiet. I suddenly realised that I was shaking and nervous. Why? The aura. He had it. Who else? Frank Sinatra: I was once invited backstage at the Royal Albert Hall to meet him. Before I even set eyes on Sinatra, and even though my back was to the door, I knew the second he walked into the room. You felt it like a nuclear wave. Very few people have it. Not Paul McCartney. Not Mick Jagger. They're too accessible. Barbra Streisand does: she's ethereal, of another world. Not even movie stars have it. That wave brings you out in a sweat.

'Whatever it is, I believe that you are born with it. You never lose it. You can't work on it. You can't buy it. It is magical. You can't cut through it – so an ordinary mortal cannot have a successful relationship with someone like that. It's the primary reason why they have such disastrous love lives. You win the adoration of millions, but you cannot get or retain the love of just one person.

'Freddie and I chatted a bit about Queen's long career,' said Phil. 'We even discussed the structure of his songs. He grew quite animated when he started talking about his music. It's what defined him, there's no question. I'd written a few songs in my time, which had achieved chart success. Songwriters are always fascinated by how other songwriters do it. So I had to ask the inevitable: where did he get his inspiration from?

'"The lines just come to me," he smiled.

'It was very hard talking to him,' Phil added, 'because I knew that he was dying. It hadn't been announced at that point, but I knew. Jim Beach told me. And I remember thinking that, if you have this aura, it crushes you in the end. It suffocates you. It is a huge cross to bear, and it's probably the price you pay for genius. Within that aura, you're only human like everyone else.

'A lot of very talented people die young. Maybe it's because they reach their creative peak, and they "commit suicide" in some way. Because they can't handle fame any more. Although some take their own lives directly, such as Marilyn Monroe with an overdose, most don't do that. Instead, they sabotage their existence in some way. James Dean drove a sports car so fast that it was inevitable that he would one day crash it and kill himself. Elvis was only forty-two when he died, but he was wrung out, he had nothing left, and he knew it. Maybe Freddie's death-wish was excessive sex, which, in the climate we were in, was always going to lead to AIDS. It's a way of relinquishing responsibility for a life that has become too much.'

Their final party over, the band returned to Mountain Studios.

'*Innuendo* was very much made on borrowed time, as Freddie really wasn't very well,' Roger would reveal after Freddie's death.

During the last year of his life, hounded by the press, he would return to Montreux as often as his health would permit, at last allowing that peaceful place to become his refuge.

By chance, Freddie's old college friend Jerry Hibbert found himself commissioned to work on animation for a video to promote *Innuendo*.

'I'd heard all the rumours that Freddie wasn't well, and of course I was very concerned. So I said to Jim Beach at the meeting, "Are we animating these because Freddie's ill and can't appear in the video?" "Freddie's *not* ill," Jim said. "Where on earth have you heard *that*?"'

Freddie's forty-fourth birthday was by Freddie's standards a low-key dinner party for twenty at Garden Lodge. Mary came with her then partner Piers Cameron. Jim Beach with his wife Claudia. Mike Moran was there with his wife, alongside Dave Clark, Barbara Valentin, Peter Straker, Freddie's GP Dr Gordon Atkinson, and the usual suspects who made up Freddie's household. It was to be his last formal birthday celebration, and he knew it. He didn't let the knowledge get the better of him. Generous to the last, he presented each guest with 'something to remember me by' from Tiffany, and was delighted, in turn, by his magnificent birthday cake. It was a replica of one of his favourite monuments on earth, the Taj Mahal.

Innuendo's title track was released as a single in January 1991. It gave the band their first UK Number One for a decade. The February album, their fourteenth and final studio effort to be released during Freddie's lifetime, hit Number One in the UK, Switzerland, Italy, Germany and the Netherlands, and became the first Queen album since *The Works* in 1984 to go gold on release in America. In the video for the single 'I'm Going Slightly Mad', a painfully gaunt, heavily made-up Freddie aped a crazed Lord Byron. 'Headlong', their thirty-ninth single, emerged in May. On a relentless mission now, against all clocks, Queen returned to Mountain Studios to begin work on *Made in Heaven*. The album would not be released until four years after Freddie's death. Despite his dwindling strength, Freddie drove himself harder than ever, and vodka'd his way through long and arduous studio sessions.

'I think maybe there was a part of him that thought the miracle would come,' said Brian. 'I think we all did.'

'Those were very sad days, but Freddie didn't get depressed,' said Peter Freestone. 'He was resigned to the fact that he was going to die. He accepted it . . . Anyway, can you imagine an *old* Freddie Mercury?'

Back at Garden Lodge, Freddie was struck by the urge to pick up drawing and painting again. He had given barely a thought to these skills since graduating from Ealing Art College.

'Jim went out and bought him a watercolour set and some brushes,' recalled Peter Freestone.

'He would sit for hours trying to do a portrait of Delilah, his favourite cat. It proved too much for him. But he did manage a couple of abstracts. That was down to Matisse. We were looking through an auction catalogue one day, and there was a Matisse going for £10,000. "*Ten grand?*" cried Freddie. "*I* could do that!"

'He went swish, swish with the brush, and said to Joe and me, "There you go, one each! See how much *those* are worth!" I suppose they could be worth all of that now.'

Life went up a gear. It was going too fast. In August came the news that Paul Prenter had died of AIDS. In the same month, Freddie told his sister Kashmira and her husband Roger the truth.

'We were sitting in his bedroom having coffee when he said suddenly, "What you have to understand, my dear Kash, is that what I have is terminal,"' recalled Roger Cooke.

'"I'm going to die," he said. We saw these marks on his ankles, and knew he was ill. After that, we talked no more about it.'

'We continued to live our life as normally as we could,' said Jim.

'We were in Switzerland just three weeks before he died. While he obviously wasn't in full health, he was well enough to be there. He was in a recording studio, for God's sake. We never talked about how long he had left. But I think, if you have a terminal illness, there comes a point when you have a pretty good idea.

'A few of us went out to the Duck House for a break. There was Mary and her baby Richard, and Terry and his family. One day we had to all go and look at this lovely 1950s chalet lake-house with a garden and its own moorings. It was gorgeous, but it wasn't going to work for Freddie. What he really needed was a flat. It was Jim Beach who found the penthouse in a building called la Tourelle. It had three bedrooms, for Freddie, Joe and me, a huge sitting room with vast windows and a balcony looking out over the lake.'

Freddie had longed to spend that Christmas at his new Montreux apartment. Everyone at Garden Lodge now knew that it was not going to happen, but kept up the pretence for Freddie's sake.

'Perhaps it does seem a little pointless now, that he got his own flat in Montreux so near the end,' admits Peter Freestone.

'But Freddie loved doing up houses. The Montreux place was just something else to keep him going. Freddie had all these plans about what he'd do to each room, and he bought a lot of furniture from Sotheby's for it.

'Freddie knew exactly how he wanted the flat to look, and he chose all the décor and furnishings himself', said Jim.

'Joe and I were allowed to decide the colour schemes for our own rooms – he had pale green while I had pale blue. I was put in charge of creating mini gardens for Freddie on the balconies. He wanted as much greenery as we could cram in. It was a tragedy that he never got to spend his last Christmas there, or live there in the end'.

On Freddie's forty-fifth birthday, Jim gave Freddie his final gift to him, a set of Irish crystal champagne glasses intended for the flat in Montreux. Both of them knew that they would never make it out there.

'That birthday was his quietest ever', remembered Jim. 'It was very sad. He was coming to terms with the fact that his life was running out fast, and of course he wasn't happy about it. By then, he had lost the will to face most people. He didn't want them seeing how he looked at that stage. How distressed he was. He didn't want to upset them, and sort of wanted them to remember the old Freddie.'

Freddie's final birthday cake, created by Jane Asher from photographs taken by Jim and Joe Fanelli, was a replica of his cherished Montreux apartment building, la Tourelle. Also on that last birthday, in the United States, the single 'These Are the Days of Our Lives' was released, its video featuring Freddie's final haunting film appearance. The same single, backed by 'Bohemian Rhapsody,' would be released in the UK in December, after his death.

Freddie informed his housemates of his decision to stop taking his medication.

'He stopped everything except painkillers,' remembers Peter.

'He never really talked about being afraid of dying. There was no point in being frightened. He never let the disease take control of his life. As soon as it looked as though that might happen, he took control again.

'*He* was going to decide when to die', explained Peter.

'For weeks, twenty-four hours a day, the press had camped on his doorstep. He was a prisoner in his own home. Nothing could be done about it, except, perhaps, what he did do – which was to let go.'

He'd had enough. Not only was Freddie losing his sight, but the will to live was ebbing away.

'I think his only regret at the end was that there was so much more music inside him,' said Peter.

'The Show Must Go On', Queen's brave, heart-rending single, backed by 'Keep Yourself Alive', was released in October. The band, their management, their publicists and entourage, all sworn to secrecy, continued to contradict rumours. Meanwhile, EMI continued to pump out product – *Greatest Hits II*, *Greatest Flix II*. With Freddie's life hanging by a thread, the band appeared more prolific than ever.

'Freddie hated the idea of his family being upset', said David Wigg, 'and of his home being besieged by the media if his illness were made public. That is why everyone close to him carried on denying everything. The show went on, all right.'

Peter Freestone and Joe Fanelli nursed Freddie through the final days.

'I learned to do it. I had to. There was nobody else who could have done it,' shrugs Peter.

'Freddie had now begun to cut people off. He just didn't want to see certain people. His parents, for example. They had been to the house in those last two or three weeks, and they wanted to come again on the Saturday before he died. But he said, "No. I've seen them." Part of it was, he didn't want them seeing him as he now was. He'd prefer to be remembered as he had been. That was the reason he turned his back on so many people during the final year. Sometimes it would be a silly argument or something. But he knew the real reason, and so did I.'

A few really close friends were wonderful to Freddie during those final days: 'Dave Clark, Elton, Tony King. And Joe and I, who were nursing, had help from the Westminster Hospital where Freddie had been treated: an oncologist who tried to relieve his Kaposi's sarcoma, and a skin specialist.

'It's amazing how quickly you learn things you never expected to have to do. Freddie had a Hickman line inserted into his chest, for example, through which we were able to give him his drugs. One comfort is that one of us was with him all the time – Jim, Joe, myself – even through the night, during those last weeks. Freddie was never once left alone.'

Gordon Atkinson, Freddie's doctor and friend, made his regular visits throughout the week. Terry Giddings, his driver, still came every day, despite the fact that Freddie wasn't going anywhere.

'Even though she was seven months pregnant, Mary still tried to get to the house daily for a short visit, in order to continue her work. Freddie had determined that business was still to be as usual.'

Later, Peter wrote that Bomi and Jer did visit Freddie during that final week before he died, along with Kash, Roger and their two children. All had tea together in Freddie's bedroom.

'With superhuman effort he was able to entertain them for some two or three hours,' said Peter in his memoir. 'This was still Freddie protecting them, making them believe that there was nothing for them to worry about. We brought up the tea, which included home-made sandwiches and shop-bought cakes. Little did any of us know that this would be the last time they would see Freddie alive.'

Brian and Anita came, as did Roger and Debbie Leng, his model partner. Neither couple knew that Freddie was so close to death, and that they would not see him again.

'Both visits were fairly short,' said Peter. 'Without them knowing it, Freddie was saying goodbye.'

On 23 November, with Jim Beach at his bedside for a long meeting, they agreed Freddie's last-ever statement, admitting to his fans and to the world that he had AIDS. This would be released immediately by publicist Roxy Meade. It came as a terrible shock to his friends.

'After all the years of keeping this huge secret to ourselves,' said Peter, 'it was now going to be broadcast to the world. After discussion, we accepted the reasons behind it. A lot of good could come out of Freddie admitting to having the disease while still alive.'

Twenty-four hours later, Peter Freestone made the call to Jer and Bomi Bulsara with the news they were dreading to hear. Their beloved son, the Great Pretender, was dead.

25

Legend

We'd spent so many years making sure that Freddie was presentable before he left the house. The last thing I could do for him, in preparation for his final departure, was to make everything as perfect as I possibly could.

Peter Freestone

Every generation discovers Queen and makes them relevant in some way. Brian and Roger understand their legacy, and have been really clever with it. Queen is now a massive business venture. They are bigger today than they were during Freddie's lifetime. They are laughing all the way to the bank, and good on them. Plenty of people think they've sold out, that they've compromised their art – but why should they care? They are rolling in it. As Roger Taylor says, 'fuck 'em if they don't get it!'

Richard Hughes, producer, Transparent Television

Zoroastrians take an optimistic view of death, which they regard not as the end, but as a beginning. Earthly existence is thought to be merely a prelude to the after-life, where many blessings await. Holding fire, earth and water sacred, Parsees are neither cremated, interred, nor buried at sea.

With the body perceived as an empty vessel, it is not preserved but is committed for 'celestial burial' and laid within 'Towers of

Silence' beyond city walls. There, at the mercy of the elements, it may also be consumed by birds of prey. Not even for a superstar could this process happen in England.

'It had to be cremation, and it had to take place as soon as possible after death,' confirmed Peter, who signed Freddie's death certificate himself, giving cause of death as 'a. Bronchopneumonia. b. AIDS,' as confirmed by Dr Atkinson.

Having been attended round the clock by doctors, a postmortem to determine cause was not required. Peter Freestone consequently made rapid funeral arrangements, consulting with Freddie's parents.

'They had to be considered. We were burying a rock superstar, but they were burying their son. Naturally they wanted things done according to their Parsee tradition. Their requests were all taken into account.'

'When he died, Freddie said to me, he wanted to be taken straight out,' said Jim.

'He wanted it all to be over as quickly as possible, with as little fuss as possible. Had we been able to arrange it, he would have liked to be cremated the same day. Get it over and done with, so that everyone could get back to normal ... Freddie never wanted people to go around tearing hair out or gnashing teeth. Get on with life. That's what it's for.'

Freddie was cremated at West London Crematorium, Kensal Green, at ten a.m. on Wednesday 27 November.

'It was all perfect, just the way Freddie would have wanted it,' Peter smiles. 'There were five Daimler hearses for the flowers alone. Freddie was in a Rolls-Royce hearse, with four cars following that. His simple, pale oak coffin with a single red rose on top was carried in by pall-bearers to "You've Got a Friend", sung by Aretha Franklin. We all followed. There were some fourteen on the "friends" side, and about thirty relatives on the "family" side.'

Elton John arrived in his green Bentley. Brian came with his on-off girlfriend Anita Dobson (now his wife). Mary Austin, pregnant with her second son, Jamie, arrived with Dave Clark. Jim Callaghan, Queen's faithful security guard, stood silently at the door of the chapel, waiting to greet Freddie's parents and escort them in.

'When the coffin disappeared, we played a recording of Verdi's '*D'Amor sull'ali rosee*', an aria from *Il Trovatore* – sung, of course, by Montserrat Caballé. That had been Freddie's favourite musical piece of all. He'd often go into the studio, put it on and turn it up to such a volume that you could hear the musicians turning the pages of their music, and even moving their chairs. It was incredibly moving,' said Peter, 'and I was rather upset. I needed to be on my own. My mother is buried at that crematorium. I remember running down to where her ashes are buried, and asking her to look after him.'

Freddie's floral tributes covered more than a quarter of an acre outside the crematorium. From his parents, white dahlias and lilies bearing the message, 'To our very beloved son Freddie. We love you always, Mum and Dad'. From David Bowie, yellow roses. From Elton John, a heart of pink rosebuds with the words 'Thank you for being my friend. I will love you always'. Boy George's tribute read simply 'Dear Freddie, I love you'. Mary Austin's wreath was a pillow of roses in yellow and white, with the note 'For my dearest, with my deepest love, from your Old Faithful'. A wreath from her little son said 'To Uncle Freddie with love from your Ricky'. Roger Taylor's carried the moving farewell: 'Goodbye old friend, peace at last!' All flowers were later donated to London hospitals.

Back at the house, and finding that he could not handle the crowd inside, Jim wandered alone into the garden.

'I had lost my father years earlier,' he told me, 'but I wasn't in Ireland when it happened. So you could say that Freddie was the closest person to me who died. It hit me very hard.'

Jim would become incensed over the weeks to come by the words and deed of others. The press reported that Dave Clark had said he was the only person in the bedroom when Freddie died.

'He was *not* the only person in the room,' stated Jim. 'But it was quoted all over the place.'

The error must have perturbed the sensitive and caring Clark, for on his birthday, Jim received a beautiful card from him.

'The inscription he wrote inside read "You *were* there." I don't know why people would say otherwise. Dave was brilliant when Freddie was ill. He would come round to the house all the time and muck in. Yes he *did* sit by Freddie's bed for hours on end, to give us a break. Dave *was* in the house the night Freddie died. But it wasn't how he said.

'Freddie's favourite cat Delilah hadn't been on his bed all day long, I noticed, which was strange. That was where she slept. It was where she lived, practically. That evening she was at the foot of his bed, on the floor. I picked her up. Dave was holding one of Freddie's hands at the time. He stroked Delilah with it. There was a glimmer of recognition from Freddie as Dave did so. Then Freddie expressed a wish to go to the toilet. I flew downstairs to get Peter to come up and give me a hand, Freddie wet the bed, and we had to change the sheets. For the sake of dignity, Dave left the room. It was then that Freddie passed away.'

Jim would never truly recover from the loss.

'There are still times when I can be pottering around in the garden, and Freddie's facial expression when he died will come into my mind,' he told me in Ireland. 'I can blank out what happened consciously, but not subconsciously. It is impossible to forget. I learned so much from him, not least a positive outlook. Freddie's attitude was always, "But you can, don't you see? You *can* do it. Put your mind to it, you'll see what you can do." That was one of the loveliest things about him.'

Jim died from lung cancer in Ireland in 2010.

★   ★   ★

In Munich, poor Barbara Valentin was forced to deal with her grief alone. She'd gone out and bought 'the black outfit', and had booked and paid for her plane ticket. She was about to leave for the airport when the phone call came, commanding her to stay away. She would not say who had made the call, and Peter Freestone told me that he did not remember. The likelihood was that it was one of Jim Beach's team. Mary Austin was to be 'the widow' that day, and Barbara would not be welcome.

'I couldn't even be there to bury him,' she wept. 'After all we'd been through. The pain was terrible. I have never got over it. The love I shared with Freddie I had never had before, and I've never had it since. Not that I've gone looking. Once was enough. He was the greatest love of my life. He still is. Twenty women would each have to live a hundred years to have what I had. It's better to stop at the right time. I guess that's what he did too.'

At least Freddie got to do what he always said a star should do, she went on: 'He quit while he was ahead. He used to tell me that you can never afford to fall from the top, be not as great as you once were. Fame had made him the loneliest person in the world. To compensate for this, his life became wilder and wilder, until it controlled him. He was over-compensating for his loneliness: Freddie did everything to extremes. The price he paid was the most terrible. I know he wouldn't have planned it like that. But he got his way. Immortality was what he wanted, and immortality was what he got.'

Barbara died of a stroke in Munich in 2002.

Garden Lodge never did 'get back to normal'. As Mary prepared to move in, she gave the impression that she wanted the others out. Jim thought that he would be allowed to stay as long as he wanted. In the event, he was asked to leave immediately.

'And me. And Joe,' remembered Peter Freestone sadly. 'We didn't have anywhere else to go, and needed a while to sort things out. We would have left soon enough ... Mary's behaviour was certainly baffling.'

'How on earth could the three of us be treated the way we were, after all we had been through with Freddie?' said Jim. 'It didn't make sense. I left that house with nothing, not even my own things.'

The legal and financial wrangling that ensued left Freddie's former carers in limbo, and Barbara Valentin almost homeless. With the help of her friends at Garden Lodge, she successfully contested the opposition. Freddie's will raised countless questions, some of which would never be resolved.

Jim Hutton later explained that it was anger, not money, that prompted him to write his memoir. He wanted the world to know the truth, and could see no other way.

'I think Jim Beach was angry that my book ruined "the myth of Freddie",' reckoned Jim. 'All it did was return him to his original status of human being. It told the truth. Beach wanted fans to believe that sweet Mary Austin was the love of Freddie's life, and what a great, tragic, romantic tale it all was. I believe that the fans don't give a monkey's whether or not Freddie was gay. I also believe that fans prefer to know the truth – good and bad.'

Peter Freestone also thought that. Freddie would have been horrified to see the people he loved and cared about falling out after he had gone.

'Those concerned have to live with themselves. Mary once said of Jim [Hutton] that he had "a very vivid imagination". I knew Jim a very long time, and never knew him to be anything other than totally honest. Jim's conscience, like mine, was always clear.'

As for his ashes: were they scattered on Freddie's 'Swan Lake', in Montreux? Preserved in an urn on his parents' mantelpiece? Had they been returned to a beach in Zanzibar to be offered to the ocean, sent for safe-keeping to his Aunt Sheroo in India, or buried beneath a cherry tree in the grounds of Garden Lodge – as Jim Hutton maintained? Could they even be concealed within the grave of some anonymous deceased, in Surrey's Brookwood Civil and Military Cemetery, which has a dedicated Parsee plot? Freddie's old schoolfriend Gita Choksi from St Peter's, Panchgani, believes so. On her first-ever visit to her own father's grave at that cemetery, Gita ran into a caretaker in the grounds, and the pair got chatting. 'The rock singer Freddie Mercury's ashes are buried over there,' he told her.

'I was completely shocked and overcome,' Gita said.

'The caretaker obviously had no way of knowing anything about my connection with Freddie, and had no apparent reason to lie. I had not seen my old schoolfriend all those years, and here he was, his ashes buried just a few feet from my own father's. I am absolutely sure that it is the truth. I don't think the caretaker would tell me, a Parsee like Freddie, such a thing if it were not true. It was the most extraordinary thing to happen to me in my life. But I was grateful for it.'

Could the man not have been mistaken? It is possible. Bizarrely, though, when I visited the Brookwood Parsee plot myself, a caretaker told me the same thing. It crossed my mind that this could be a deliberate ploy, to throw fans off the scent. Surely not . . .

While not surprised to hear Gita's story, Peter Freestone was unable to confirm it. 'I simply don't know. I suspect that his ashes were divided, and that perhaps the parents got some, and Mary got some . . . but who's to say? Only they know for sure.'

'Bohemian Rhapsody' was re-released as a Christmas 1991 single, soon after Freddie's death. It raced to Number One, raising more than a million pounds for the Terence Higgins Trust AIDS charity. Queen's signature single was also re-released in America, with profits shared among AIDS charities across the States through the Magic Johnson Foundation.

On 20 April 1992, the band were ready to give Freddie his rock 'n' roll send-off – with a concert that would subsequently be voted the greatest live rock event of the 1990s. Brian, who described Freddie's death as 'like losing a brother', stressed that the Freddie Mercury Tribute Concert at Wembley Stadium on Easter Monday that year 'is not Queen', although most of those who took part would perform Queen songs. On the day of the concert's announcement,

72,000 tickets sold out within two hours, even though no line-up had yet been agreed. The event would be broadcast on radio and TV to seventy-six countries, and filmed for a documentary by David Mallet.

The dazzling show kicked off with recorded footage of Freddie doing vocal scales. Annie Lennox and David Bowie sang 'Under Pressure', Roger Daltrey 'I Want It All'. Extreme did 'Hammer to Fall', George Michael and Lisa Stansfield duetted on 'These Are the Days of Our Lives', and Elton John tackled 'Bohemian Rhapsody' with Axl Rose. Seal chose 'Who Wants to Live Forever'. Mick Ronson and Ian Hunter, of Mott the Hoople, veered from the basic format, to offer a moving tribute with Bowie's 'All the Young Dudes'. So did Robert Plant, with the Led Zeppelin number 'Thank You' – although he also sang 'Innuendo' and 'Crazy Little Thing Called Love'. But it was Liza Minnelli who blew them all off the stage, brilliantly, with 'We Are the Champions'.

Yet where were Dave Clark, Peter Straker, Tony Hadley, Elaine Paige? Aretha Franklin, Prince, and Michael Jackson? Plenty of us were surprised by the unexplained absence of singers who had meant so much to Freddie, as well as by the fact that the 'metal' element of the line-up was perhaps not quite what Freddie would have wanted. The music of Guns N' Roses, Metallica and Def Leppard was much more to Brian's and Roger's taste. It has been claimed that many of the artists who did perform were chosen because their own sound had been influenced by Queen. Others agree with the theory that the Tribute concert was actually about Brian, Roger and John welcoming their beloved front man back into the Queen fold, where in their hearts he belonged, and about a retrospective of the band's original flavours, ethos and ideals.

Tim Rice says that Elaine Paige was 'wounded' that Liza Minnelli was invited to sing at the tribute instead of her. Many, too, were surprised by the absence of the 'out' gay element – Boy George, Holly Johnson, Jimmy Somerville, Leee Johns – to celebrate that aspect of Freddie's lifestyle. Against the line-up who did perform, Pavarotti, Carreras and Domingo delivering the classical arias Freddie adored would have looked and sounded wildly out of place. As for Montserrat Caballé, she herself has explained that she had full commitments to EXPO in Seville, performing live every night during its inaugural week, which kicked off on the same date as the tribute concert. She had expressed a wish to contribute to Freddie's concert, by satellite. But in the event, a satellite link into London could not be established, because the concert itself was being transmitted live worldwide. Not even the late Hollywood legend and AIDS campaigner Dame Elizabeth Taylor, in her tearful address to the audience, could compensate for the absence of La Stupenda.

George Michael, who stole the show with 'Somebody to Love', echoing the band's Live Aid triumph seven years earlier, revealed that he was 'living out a childhood fantasy'.

'When I think of Freddie, I think of everything he gave me in terms of craft,' George said. 'Just to sing those songs, especially "Somebody to Love", was really an outrageous feeling. It was probably the proudest moment of my career.'

'George Michael at the tribute concert was *amazing*,' enthused Peter Paterno. 'It did cross my mind, and I'm sure a lot of other people's minds, that they really should consider having him take Freddie's place. In the end though, I guess, no one ever could.'

Spike Edney, who contributed keyboards with Mike Moran, was saddened by the post-concert fall-out, when many critics blasted contributors for falling short of Freddie's standards. Those who expressed disappointment failed to remember or understand that very few artists in rock history have been blessed with Freddie's extraordinary vocal range.

'It may not be fair to say that none of those great artists could sing any of the songs as well as Freddie,' he reasons. 'But I know a lot of them felt as if they were there in his shadow. Of course, he would have loved that. It would have tickled him to see them all suffer. As well as appreciating it for what it was – a great tribute – he would have relished the agonies they all had to go through, not managing to match his keys!'

The experience was summed up, relates Spike, by the scene at the after-show party at Brown's nightclub.

'Upstairs, I saw Roger propped up against the wall, just staring into space. Then I spotted Brian a couple of feet away, doing the same thing. I went over to them. "How do you feel?" I said. "Can't feel anything," one of them replied. Nobody could remember anything about it. You just couldn't take it all in. Once it was over, it was, "God – what have we done for the past month? And what do we do now?"'

The fundraising wheels were in motion. The Mercury Phoenix Trust, established in 1992 to handle revenue from the concert and other sources, took as its emblem the phoenix from Queen's crest, which Freddie had designed at the very beginning of the band's career. To this day, the trust continues to raise money for AIDS causes throughout the world.

George Michael, Lisa Stansfield and Queen donated royalties from the *Five Live* mini album to the Mercury Phoenix Trust. In April 2002, the Trust received a further major boost when the concert was released on DVD to mark the tenth anniversary of the charity. It entered the UK chart at Number One. Today, twenty years on, money continues to flow into the fund.

There is no doubt that Jim, the bereft lover, embarked upon his selective 1994 biography with the intention of creating a tender tribute to an adored partner. This was blurred by a co-writer who dwelled on more sensational aspects of the relationship, as well as on intimate details of Freddie's final days.

Jim was consequently banished from the Queen camp. This reaction, which left him bewildered and confused, surely occurred because Freddie's band mates, management, family and friends were grieving too. They found it unbearable to see the stark details of Freddie's death out there for all to consume.

During the time I spent with Jim in picturesque County Carlow, in the southeast of Ireland, where he lived out his days in a comfortable bungalow built with Freddie's £500,000 legacy, I was in no doubt that the love Jim claimed to have felt for Freddie was genuine. He was a warm and decent man who was content with his lot. He was eternally grateful, he told me, for having experienced the superstar lifestyle through Freddie. In his garden, he proudly showed me his lilac 'Blue Moon' roses, which Freddie adored.

Given Jim's Catholic background, and the fact that his mother was still alive when he published, it must have taken immense courage to write the book.

'I did discuss it with my family,' he said. 'In a way, I asked their permission. I shouldn't have worried. They simply said that they were there for me, and that was that.'

Freddie, Jim knew, had faced a greater dilemma because of his family's religion.

'But Freddie didn't practise Zoroastrianism,' reasoned Jim, with which Peter Freestone agreed. 'Because Freddie's parents had him cremated according to the faith, it was assumed that he had practised,' added Jim.

'But in all the years I knew him, he never worshipped. I know nothing about his family's religion. We never discussed it. But I do remember lying in bed beside him at night, and hearing him praying. In which language? In English. To whom? I don't know. I'd sometimes ask who he was talking to, and he'd just shrug and whisper, "I'm saying my prayers."'

Queen Productions' offices in Pembridge Road closed down after Freddie's death. So did Mountain Studios, when David Richards dismantled his production facility and moved into the Alps above Montreux. The heavily-graffitied doorway (and the studio's ghosts) are all that remain. But the many who presumed that the Queen story would end, bleakly, with Freddie's demise, were mistaken.

Made in Heaven, Queen's fifteenth studio album, debuted at Number One in 1995, four years after Freddie's death. Estimated to have sold twenty million copies worldwide, it is an immaculate compilation made with diligence and devotion. Brimming with vitality and mortality, it is also a Requiem to and a showcase for the diva in Freddie. One stand-out track, for me, is 'Mother Love'. To music composed by Brian, Freddie's haunting vocal draws us back on a channel-surfing rewind into a blast of incandescent live Queen, an echoed riff from 'It's a Kind of Magic', and a shred of Gerry Goffin/Carole King's 'Goin' Back', by Freddie, released as Larry Lurex in Queen's earliest Trident days . . . 'I think I'm going back/ to the things I learnt so well/in my youth . . .' A heart-tugging baby cry plays the song to a ghostly conclusion, which surely symbolises his death as the singer's rebirth.

The other favourite on this album is 'A Winter's Tale', Freddie's swan song, which he wrote and composed at his Montreux apartment overlooking the lake he loved. The lyrics, describing what he saw from his window, celebrate the peace and contentment he found there towards the end. The song's title, whether intended or not as a homage to the romance 'The Winter's Tale' by William Shakespeare, reveals perhaps more about Freddie's early songwriting inspiration. One protagonist of Shakespeare's play is Polixenes, the King of Bohemia – an ancient kingdom which corresponds loosely to the modern-day Czech Republic. As such, it may have germinated 'Bohemian Rhapsody'. If, as presumed by many Bard scholars, this play was an allegory on the demise of Anne Boleyn, its character Perdita was based on the daughter of Anne and King Henry VIII, who would become Elizabeth I, England's *Queen* . . . The band's original greatest hit laced through Freddie's final offering? It's not impossible.

There are many memorials, not least the statue of Freddie crafted by Irena Sedlecka which stands on the edge of Lake Geneva in Montreux. It was unveiled by Montserrat Caballé on 25 November 1996, marking the fifth anniversary of Freddie's death.

The ceremony was opened by the Mayor of Montreux, in the presence of Freddie's parents, his sister Kashmira, Montreux Jazz Festival founder Claude Nobs, and Brian and Roger. The statue remains one of the most-visited tourist sites in Switzerland. It has also become the focal point of Queen fans' annual pilgrimages, to celebrate their idol's September birthday.

'One of my hardest moments was unveiling the statue', Brian told *Q* magazine in 2011. 'Obviously it's a very nice tribute, and the ceremony was very moving, but I just suddenly became overcome by anger. I thought "This is all that's left of my friend, and everybody's thinking it's normal and fabulous, but it's actually awful that I'm looking at a piece of bronze which is the image of my friend, and my friend's not here any more".'

A special Ballet for Life, '*Le Presbytère n'a rien perdu de son charme ni le jardin de son éclat*' ('The presbytery has lost none of its charm, nor the garden its sparkle') was choreographed five years after Freddie's death by Maurice Bejart of the Bejart Ballet of Lausanne, to celebrate the lives of Freddie and the Bejart's principal, Jorge Donn. Featuring Queen songs and Mozart compositions, the moving piece opens with 'It's a Beautiful Day' – the first track of *Made in Heaven*, and closes with 'The Show Must Go On' – the final track on *Innuendo*, Queen's last album during Freddie's lifetime. It was first performed in the Theatre de Chaillot, Paris, in January 1997, in the presence of Madame Chirac (wife of the then President of France) with Elton John, Brian, Roger and John Deacon. This was the bassist's last live performance with his band mates.

John suffered serious depression after Freddie's death. Having lost his own father when he was only eleven, Freddie's demise brought back memories of emotions John had not dealt with at the time. At one point he started frequenting a lapdancing club and took up with a twenty-five-year-old dancer, lavishing her with an apartment, a car and luxurious gifts. The ill-advised relationship foundered, after which John was understandably keen to retire with his wife and family. He left the band officially in 1997.

'He's very private now', commented Brian. 'He communicates by emails when there's a business discussion, but that's it.'

Brian and Roger were anything but ready to let go. The right project would come along in good time.

In June 2002, Brian performed 'God Save the Queen' on the roof of London's royal residence (in memory, he said, of Jimi Hendrix), to open Party at the Palace, a concert held to commemorate Her Majesty Queen Elizabeth II's Golden Jubilee. In 2004, he collaborated for the first time with former Free and Bad Company front man Paul Rodgers, at the Fender Strat Pack concert. Excited by the obvious chemistry between them, Brian persuaded Paul to play with Queen for their induction into the UK Music Hall of Fame. Brian, Roger and Paul then announced a world tour as 'Q + PR' in 2005, making clear that Paul was not replacing Freddie, but that the project was a variation on a theme. They played at a concert in South Africa for Nelson Mandela's 46664 AIDS awareness campaign in 2005, following which they toured together for the rest of that year, with Spike Edney happily back on keyboards.

Q + PR went on to play a twenty-three-date tour of North America. Two years later, they performed in Hyde Park for Nelson Mandela's ninetieth birthday celebration, bringing their troubled South African episode to a sublime conclusion. They then departed on a full-scale tour of Europe. Although the collaboration is concluded for now, both parties insist that the arrangement remains open. All, meanwhile, push on with solo interests, notably Brian in 2011 with West End and Broadway star Kerry Ellis, on a sell-out musical-theatre-meets-rock presentation entitled 'Anthems'.

On the eighteenth anniversary of Freddie's death, 24 November 2009, some 2,000 Queen fans from around the world convened in Feltham town centre to watch Brian and Freddie's mother unveil a granite Hollywood Star-style plaque dedicated to her son's memory. It was the first UK monument to commemorate the Queen front man (not counting the mock-up statue welcoming fans to *We Will Rock You* above the Dominion Theatre on Tottenham Court Road).

'Feltham was his first home in England after we arrived from Zanzibar, and it was a place where he began to explore his musical future,' said eighty-seven-year-old Jer Bulsara.

'Freddie, we pursued your dream, our dream, and we love you, and we always will,' said Brian. 'We are very happy to honour you in this way.'

'Stormtroopers in Stilettos' (the title taken from the track 'She Makes Me' on Queen's third album, *Sheer Heart Attack*, 1974) is a nostalgic international touring exhibition of Queen's early days. It opened to commemorate the band's fortieth anniversary in 2011 – a year of celebrations which would also see them sign a new record deal, with Island Records, through Universal.

In late 2010, a major Hollywood film based on Freddie's life was announced by GK Films. Graham King's Freddie Mercury movie is co-produced by Robert de Niro's TriBeca Films and Queen Films. Freddie is played by *Borat* and *Bruno* star Sacha Baron Cohen, to a script by Peter Morgan, author of many acclaimed screenplays including *The Queen*, *Frost/Nixon* and *The Last King of Scotland*.

'Freddie Mercury was an awe-inspiring performer,' commented King, 'so with Sacha starring in the role coupled with Peter's screen-play and the support of Queen, we have the perfect combination to tell the real story behind their success.'

Morgan's script returns the band to the early 1980s, when Queen had damaged their profile in America, and were well in decline. Their best years apparently over, each member was pursuing solo projects. Then Geldof announced Live Aid, Queen embraced his vision, and went out at Wembley Stadium to stun the world. Re-awakening to their collective power, they plan and embark on a massive world-wide 'comeback' tour, and look forward to a healthy second innings. But Freddie falls to AIDS, and the dream is dashed ... The film is slated for release in summer 2012, in time for the twenty-first anniversary of Freddie's death.

Since Freddie's passing, Queen's global reputation and impact have soared, in no small way thanks to the phenomenal success of their stage musical *We Will Rock You*. Set in a futuristic parallel universe in which rock music has been banned and where the Bohemians, a gang of music-loving rebels, hold out for a hero, it was written by comic Ben Elton to classic Queen tracks. Since it opened at London's Dominion Theatre, Tottenham Court Road in 2002, the 'jukebox theatre' production has played to consistently full houses, and shows no signs of losing pace. Twenty-seven international versions have been staged; it won the BBC Radio 2 Olivier Audience Award in March 2011, and will extend to a long-awaited movie version in 2013.

We Will Rock You may not be to everyone's taste. Indeed, Brian and Roger stand accused in some quarters of having 'sold out'. Who cares? Queen don't. The show's enduring popularity speaks for itself. As Roger says, 'Fuck 'em if they don't get it'.

Says Paul Gambaccini, '*We Will Rock You*'s vital role has been in bringing Queen's sensational music to millions of young people who weren't born when Freddie was alive, and when the original band were still touring.'

How would Freddie himself feel about the fact that Queen are even bigger today than they were during his lifetime?

'He would love it,' insists Paul Gambaccini. 'He would *just love* it. He's bigger than Liza Minnelli: what a kick he would have got out of that. He loved the divas. Adored them. Liza, Montserrat: he worshipped these women. He would be thrilled that the outsized projection of himself is so greatly esteemed. I mean, I get Facebook requests from young European men on the grounds that they know I knew Freddie. Peter Freestone is an idol of this group. It's a career. They do the dress-ups, the tributes, the Freddie-for-a-Day (when fans all over the world dress as their idol on Freddie's birthday to raise money for the Mercury Phoenix Trust), the works. It's fascinating. None of them was alive, or they were not aware, when Freddie was active. They are reacting to the historically-preserved Freddie Mercury, not to a man they would have known for themselves.'

Those still living get on with what will never be ordinary lives. John Deacon is today a quiet family man, the years of Queen madness consigned to the top shelf of his troubled mind. Brian, who has been made a Commander of the Order of the British Empire for Services to the Music Industry, is into second wife Anita, his three adult children, astronomy and preserving foxes. Roger, post-Debbie, married his young girlfriend Sarina after six years together, and had five children at last count. Music remains a priority for both Roger and Brian.

Incredibly, Queen have overtaken The Beatles to become the official UK album chart leaders. In 2006 their *Greatest Hits* album was Britain's all-time best-selling album, with sales of more than 5,407,587 copies. Their *Greatest Hits II* album ranked seventh, with sales of more than 3,631,321 copies. The band have released a total of eighteen Number One albums, eighteen Number One singles, and ten Number One DVDs worldwide, making them one of the world's best-selling rock acts. Their total album sales have been estimated at over 300 million worldwide – including 32.5 million in the United States alone. Queen is also the only group in which every member has composed more than one chart-topping single. 'We Will Rock You' was adopted as the anthem of both the New York Yankees and Manchester United football club. 'We Are the Champions' remains the most played Queen song of all time, chanted by sports fans everywhere. Freddie himself described it as 'the most egotistical and arrogant song I ever wrote'.

'I feel that Freddie is still here, in some ways, because his music is still here,' says his sister Kashmira. 'He was my brother, but a megastar too. Simply speaking, I don't know what it was like to have an ordinary brother. That's because my own brother was so extraordinary.'

★   ★   ★

'Freddie was my best friend,' Roger Taylor told me in a candid moment. 'I have never got over his death. None of us has. I think we all thought that we would come to terms with it quite quickly, but we underestimated the impact his death had on our lives. I still find it painful to talk about. Our present and our future without Freddie are impossible to contemplate. I deal with it day by day.'

The Freddie he misses is the soul behind the superstar: a deeply human man who fell for a fantasy. To the disapproval of some, it was to the delight of millions. It was on his terms. Offering no apology, he expected no sympathy. If he felt trapped, at times, by the contradictions that shaped him, his songs set him free.

To the tearful clown who had the last laugh . . . and to Brian and Roger, venturing onwards, in his memory. Can anyone fault them as keepers of the flame? Not I.

Acknowledgements

WITH THANKS AND LOVE:

To Hannah Black, my awesome editor, for spirited effort and guidance.

Also to Camilla Dowse, Kate Miles, Alice Howe, Kerry Hood, Bea Long, Jason Bartholomew and everyone else at Hodder & Stoughton who worked with such commitment to the cause. Their exuberance and 'extra-mile' attitude has been a joy.

To Ivan Mulcahy, my brilliant agent, for constant encouragement, friendship and support. Also to Laetitia Rutherford, Stephanie Cohen and Jonathan Conway at Mulcahy Conway Associates. It's a privilege to know and work with such upbeat people.

To Freddie Mercury, Brian May, Roger Taylor and John Deacon, for the music that thrills my children as much as it has always thrilled me.

To the many generous friends, colleagues and associates, as well as key figures in Freddie Mercury's life, who opened their hearts and memories or helped to make this book happen in some way – most of whom (I hope) are remembered here:

Tim Rice, Steve Harley, Phil Swern, Andy Hill, Jim Diamond, Steve Levine, Mick Rock, Dan Arthure, Jonathan Morrish, Leee John, Frank Allen, David Wigg, Clare Bramley, Francis Rossi, Dave Hogan, Nigel Angel, Bob Lefsetz, Peter Paterno, James Saez, Eddie Delena, Reinhold Mack, Rick Wakeman, Ben Wakeman, John Waite, Elton John, Jamesie, Kim Wilde, Nick Boyles, Chris Hewlett, Henry

Semmence, Alan Edwards, James Nisbet, Scott Millaney, Simon Napier-Bell, Richard Hughes, Robert Lee, Gray Jolliffe, David Hamilton, David 'Kid' Jensen, Paul Gambaccini, Spike Edney, David Stark, John Fleming, Jeff Griffin, James Khalaf, Nick Fitzherbert, Paula Fitzherbert, Louis Souyave, Tony Hadley, Carolyn Cowan, Bernard Doherty, Tony Bramwell, Harvey Goldsmith, Pete Smith, Peter Freestone, Mike Read, Michael Appleton, Bob Geldof, Fiz Shapur, Andrew MacGillivray, Lindsay Martins, Jude Martins, Alicia Martins, Daniel Martins, Jeremy Norman, David Thorpe, Rolf Harris, Denis O'Regan, Peter Hillmore, Edmund Preston, David Quantick, Phil Symes, Jerry Hibbert, Chris Poole, Shernaz Screwaller, Michael Anastasios, Dominic Denny, Jim Jenkins, Gerd Kochlin, Nick Elgar, Stuart White, David Syner, Toby Rose, Sandy Evans, Bonzo Fernandez, Perviz Darunkhanawala, Diana Darunkhanawala, Nancy Galloway, Nasser K. Awadh, Professor Abdul Sheriff, Hamari Omar, Kevin Patience, Sheroo Khory, Morris W. Innis, Cyrus Ghandy, Janet Smith, Gita Choksi, Mr and Mrs Davis, Marcela Delorenzi, Hollow Skai, Tomas Petterson, Paul Davies, Saskia Campbell, Annabel Lord, Frank Warren, Laura Morris, John McFaul, Stephen Kahn, Mike Stone, Michael Charidemou, Anthony Lee, Linda Plant, Rita Rowe, Robert Kirby, Chris Griffin, Wendy Reid, Phil Mackney, Jessica Mackney, Rachel Tarnoy, Dominic Collier, Alison Miller, Claire Weeks, Lia Policane, Sharron Nasir, Pauline Thomson, Julie Ives-Routleff, Karen French, Bill and Rachel Leigh, Maureen and Ghee Ong, Jan Moore, Jane Stone.

Professor Edward G. Hughes MD MB ChB, McMaster University, Hamilton, Ontario.

Dr Cosmo Hallstrom MD FRCP FRCPsych MB ChB DPM, London.

Bernie Katz, June Cluskey, Kent Olesen, Matthew Hobbs, Vincent McGrath and friends, the Groucho Club.

Bob, Jim, Nick and Dave, Right Turn Left RIP.

Kelvin Mackenzie, Rod Gilchrist, Lynda Lee-Potter, Nigel Dempster, Bob Hill, Nick Gordon, John Koski, John Chenery,

Herbert Kretzmer, Jack Tinker, Baz Bambigoye, Sean Usher, Pat Hill, Anne Barraclough, Steve Absolom, Geoff Sutton, Roger Tavener, Richard Young, Alan Davidson, Alan Grisbrook, Dave Benett, Geoff Baker, Annette Witheridge, Gill Pringle, Rick Sky, Martin Dunn, Nick Ferrari, David Wigg, John Blake, Piers Morgan, Hugh Whittow, Adam Helliker, Martin Townsend, Lisa Clark, Rachel Jane, Stephen Rigley, Clair Woodward, Amy Packer: the Fleet Street Years.

Special thanks to Dave Hogan, and to David Stark.

I am indebted to Roger Tavener for his notes and recollections of our night with Freddie Mercury, Moutreux, 1986.

Grateful thanks to Jim Beach, Phil Symes, to Freddie's mother, Jer Bulsara, and to his sister, Kashmira Cooke.

Christopher Millard and Elizabeth Bell, the Royal Opera House
Imperial College, London
Ealing Art College, London
University of Westminster, London
Trident Studios, London
De Lane Lea Studios, London
I Like Music, London
Associated Newspapers, London
News International, London
Trinity Mirror PLC, London
British Library Newspapers, Colindale, London
The Groucho Club, London
Soho House, High Road House & Shoreditch House, London
Babington House, Somerset
Zanzibar Museums, Zanzibar
University of Dar es Salaam, Tanzania
St Peter's School, Panchgani, India
Norbert Muller & Montreux Music, Switzerland www.montreux-music.com
Billboard USA www.billboard.com

Record Plant Studios, Los Angeles
Hollywood Records/The Walt Disney Company, Los Angeles
Soho House, West Hollywood
New York Daily News
Soho House New York

The Mercury Phoenix Trust
  www.mercuryphoenixtrust.com

46664 Nelson Mandela HIV/AIDS Awareness Campaign
  www.46664.com

Child Hope
  www.childhope.org.uk

UK National AIDS Trust
  www.nat.org.uk

Bone Cancer Research Trust
  www.bcrt.org.uk

Official Queen website
  www.queenonline.com

Official Freddie Mercury website
  www.loveroflifesingerofsongs.com

Freddie For a Day Global Charity Network
  www.freddieforaday.com

Official website of The Who
  www.thewho.com

www.lesleyannjones.com
email: laj@lesleyannjones.com

IN MEMORIAM

Rose Allocca, Poly Styrene, Peter Batt, Gerry Sanderson, John Entwistle, Roger Scott, Kenny Everett, Ginny Comely, Barbara Valentin, Pat Stead, Giles Gordon, Tony Brainsby, Tommy Vance, Jim Hutton, Liam McCoy, John Sutton, Lester Middlehurst, Sir Henry Cooper.

Any omissions are unintentional. I am sincerely grateful to all concerned for invaluable assistance. None of the above mentioned is in any way responsible for the author's views as expressed in this book.

Picture Acknowledgements

Author collection: 1 (top left & middle left), 1 (bottom)/photo by kind permission of Gita Choksi, 8 (bottom), 10 (bottom left), 16 (middle), 17, 18 (top), 19 (top left & right), 21 (bottom), 23, 24, 27, 28, 29, 30, 31, 32. By kind permission of Mrs Jer Bulsara & The Mercury Phoenix Trust: 1 (middle right). © Corbis: 14 (middle & bottom), 15 (top)/photos Denis O'Regan.© Getty Images: 2 (top)/photo Mark & Colleen Haylard, 2 (bottom)/ photo Michael Putland, 4 (top & middle), 9 (bottom), 12 (top)/ photo Denis O'Regan, 12 (middle)/photo Phil Dent, 16 (bottom), 20 (top left & middle)/photos Dave Hogan, 26 (top)/photo Fabrice Coffrini, 26 (bottom)/photo KMazur. © Gray Jolliffe: 10 (middle right). © Mick Rock: 5, 6, 7 & 8 (top & middle). © Denis O'Regan: 15 (bottom), 16 (top). © Photoshot: 10 (bottom right). © Press Association Images: 11 (middle) & 20 (bottom)/ photos Paul Smith, 25 (top)/photo Edward Hirst. © Rex Features: 3 (bottom)/photo Andre Csillag, 3 (top)/photo Ian Dickson, 4 (bottom), 9 (middle), 12 (bottom), 13 (top left & right), 14 (top), 18 (bottom left & right), 21 (top), 22, 25 (bottom)/photos Richard Young, 9 (top)/ photo David Thorpe, 10 (top left)/photo Mark Mawson, 25 (middle)/ photo Nils Jorgensen. © The Picture Library Ltd: 11 (bottom), 13 (bottom), 15 (middle), 19 (bottom)/photos Alan Davidson.

Every reasonable effort has been made to contact the copyright holders of material reproduced in this book. But if there are any errors or omissions, Hodder & Stoughton will be pleased to insert the appropriate acknowledgement in any subsequent printing of this publication.

Chronology

5 September 1946	Farrokh Bulsara born in Zanzibar.
1951	Farrokh enrols at Zanzibar Missionary School.
1955–1963	Farrokh becomes a boarder at St Peter's School, Panchgani, India. Changes his name to Freddie. Launches his first band, The Hectics.
1963	Freddie returns to Zanzibar and completes his education at St Joseph's Convent School.
1964	Zanzibar revolution, January. Freddie and his family flee to the UK.
1964–1966	Freddie studies Art at A Level at Isleworth Polytechnic School.
1966	Freddie arrives at Ealing College of Art to begin his course in graphic design and illustration. He leaves home, and meets Tim Staffell, who plays in a band with Brian May.
1969	Freddie graduates from Ealing College of Art with a diploma; runs a Kensington market stall with Roger Taylor; meets the bands Smile and Ibex; launches his second band, Wreckage; meets Mary Austin.
April 1970	Brian May, Roger Taylor and Freddie join forces as Queen. Freddie changes his surname to Mercury.

1970	Freddie's rock idol Jimi Hendrix dies, 18 September.
1971	Bassist John Deacon joins Queen, February.
1972	Queen sign deal with Trident Studios.
1973	Queen sign recording contract with EMI. Queen's debut single 'Keep Yourself Alive' and debut album *Queen* released July. Queen tour UK supporting Mott the Hoople. First official Queen fan club launched.
1974	'Seven Seas of Rhye' single and *Queen II* album released, March. The band embark on their first headlining UK tour. Queen support Mott the Hoople on US tour, April. 'Killer Queen' single and *Sheer Heart Attack* album released, October/November. Both single and album break the US Top Ten.
1975	Queen's first headlining US tour. First tour of Japan. Freddie wins Ivor Novello songwriting award for 'Killer Queen'. Queen conclude their deal with Trident. Elton John's manager John Reid becomes Queen's manager. 'Bohemian Rhapsody' single released, 31 October. *A Night At the Opera* album released, November. 'Bohemian Rhapsody' earns Queen their first UK Number One, November, and wins Freddie another Ivor Novello award.
1976	Queen's second US tour. All four Queen albums in the UK Top 20, February. The band tour Japan and Australia. Queen give massive free concert in Hyde Park, London, 18 September. *A Day at the Races* album released, December.
1977	Queen tour the world. 'We Are the Champions' single released, October.

'Bohemian Rhapsody' wins Britannia Award. *News of the World* album released. Lawyer Jim Beach negotiates Queen's exit from contract with John Reid. Beach assumes control of Queen's legal affairs. Queen create their own personal management team, including Paul Prenter.

1978   Queen tour Europe. The band celebrates launch of the album *Jazz*, October, with an outrageous Hallowe'en party in New Orleans.

1979   Queen begin recording at Musicland Studios, Munich. *Live Killers* album released June. Freddie performs in charity dance gala with the Royal Ballet at London Coliseum. He meets Peter Freestone, his future personal assistant.

1980   'Crazy Little Thing Called Love' hits Number One in countless countries, earns Queen their debut US chart-topper. Freddie purchases Garden Lodge, his lavish home in London. Queen embark on an epic US tour. *The Game* album, released June, becomes their first US Number One album. 'Another One Bites the Dust' single Number One in US and numerous countries. Two Grammy nominations. Queen enter *Guinness Book of Records*. *Flash Gordon* album released.

1981   Queen tour South America. Freddie throws five-day birthday party in New York City. *Greatest Hits* album released, November.

1982   Queen sign new contract with EMI for a further six albums. *Hot Space* album released May. 'Under Pressure' single with David Bowie reaches Number One. American tour.

The band receive keys to the city of Boston, 23 July.

1983   Freddie meets Winnie Kirchberger and Barbara Valentin in Munich, and Jim Hutton in London. Begins first solo album in Munich.

1984   *The Works* album released February, UK and US. Queen awarded Outstanding Contribution to British Music at the Brit Awards, June. Spike Edney joins Queen as touring keyboard player. Queen's controversial excursion to Sun City, South Africa, result in them being blacklisted by the Musicians' Union.

1985   Queen headline at Brazil's Rock in Rio festival, January, then tour New Zealand, Australia and Japan from April. They steal the show at Live Aid, Wembley, July. Freddie quits Munich for good and returns to London.

1986   Queen's 'farewell' 'Magic' tour of Europe. *A Kind of Magic* album, the soundtrack to the film *Highlander*, released June. Freddie retires from touring to set up home at Garden Lodge, London, with Jim Hutton, Peter Freestone and Joe Fanelli.

1987   Freddie releases cover version of 'The Great Pretender', February. Meets with Montserrat Caballé in Barcelona to discuss possible collaboration, March. Former personal manager Paul Prenter betrays Freddie in print. Freddie performs at La Nit Festival, Barcelona, in the presence of the king and queen of Spain, October. Freddie's album with La Stupenda, *Barcelona*, released October.

1989	*The Miracle* album released, May. Queen voted 'Band of the Eighties'.
1990	Queen presented with BPI's Outstanding Contribution to British Music award.
1991	'Innuendo' gives Queen first Number One single for ten years. *Innuendo* album released, February. The band begin recording their final album *Made In Heaven*, eventually released in 1995.
24 November 1991	Freddie Mercury dies. 'Bohemian Rhapsody' released as Christmas single, raising more than £1 million for Terrence Higgins Trust AIDS charity. Also released in US, with profits shared among AIDS charities across the States through Magic Johnson Foundation.
1992	Mercury Tribute concert, Wembley Stadium, Easter Monday. Mercury Phoenix Trust AIDS charity launched.
1994	Jim Hutton publishes memoir of life with Freddie.
1995	*Made in Heaven* album debuts at Number One, four years after Freddie's death.
1996	Statue of Freddie by Irena Sedlecka unveiled in Montreux on fifth anniversary of Freddie's death.
1997	*Le Presbytère: Ballet for Life*, in honour of Freddie, debuts in Paris, January, with live music by remaining Queen members. Bassist John Deacon leaves the band.
2002	Brian performs 'God Save the Queen' on roof of Buckingham Palace for Queen Elizabeth II's golden jubilee. Queen stage musical *We Will Rock You* opens at London's

Dominion Theatre, and goes on to play in twenty-seven countries.

2004   Brian performs at Fender Strat Pack concert, where he is reacquainted with Free/Bad Company frontman Paul Rodgers.

2005   Brian, Roger and Paul Rodgers announce world tour as 'Q + PR'. The band also perform at concert in South Africa for Nelson Mandela's AIDS awareness campaign. Brian awarded CBE for services to the music industry.

2006   Q + PR play 23-date tour of North America. Queen's *Greatest Hits* album becomes UK's all-time bestselling album, outselling The Beatles' *Sgt Pepper's Lonely Hearts Club Band*. Total album sales are estimated at 300 million worldwide.

2008   Q + PR perform in Hyde Park for Nelson Mandela's ninetieth birthday.

2009   Freddie memorial plaque unveiled by his mother in his English home town, Feltham, attended by 2,000 fans.

2011   Queen's fortieth anniversary year. *Stormtroopers in Stilettos* touring exhibition opens in London. New record deal signed with Island through Universal. The band's first five albums, remastered and expanded, are released in March, followed in June by their second five albums. The final five of their fifteen studio albums are re-issued on 5th September, on what would have been Freddie's 65th birthday. Major Hollywood feature film starring Sacha Baron Cohen is set for release in 2012, to mark the twenty-first anniversary of Freddie's death.

Discography

In 2011, as part of their fortieth-anniversary celebrations, Queen released remastered, expanded and repackaged versions of all fifteen of their studio albums. Visit www.queenonline.com

QUEEN ALBUMS

Dates given in brackets are US releases.

Queen	13 July 1973 (4 September 1973)
Queen II	8 March 1974 (9 April 1974)
Sheer Heart Attack	8 November 1974 (12 November 1974)
A Night At The Opera	21 November 1975 (2 December 1975)
A Day At The Races	10 December 1976 (18 December 1976)
News Of The World	28 October 1977 (1 November 1977)
Jazz	10 November 1978 (14 November 1978)
Live Killers	22 June 1979 (26 June 1979)
The Game	30 June 1980 (30 June 1980)
Flash Gordon	8 December 1980 (27 January 1981)
Greatest Hits	2 November 1981 (3 November 1981)
Hot Space	21 May 1982 (25 May 1982)
The Works	27 February 1984 (28 February 1984)
The Complete Works	2 December 1985: limited-edition boxed set containing all of Queen's albums to date except *Greatest Hits*, and including a special album, *Complete Vision*, featuring singles and B-sides otherwise unavailable at that time (no simultaneous release in US).

A Kind Of Magic	2 June 1986 (3 June 1986)
Live Magic	1 December 1986 (not released in US)
The Miracle	22 May 1989 (6 June 1989)
Queen At The Beeb	4 December 1989: re-released May 1997 as a double album, remastered, featuring every song Queen ever recorded for the BBC (no simultaneous release in US)
Innuendo	4 February 1991 (5 February 1991)
Greatest Hits II	28 October 1991 (not released in US)
Classic Queen	3 March 1992 (US only)
Live At Wembley '86	26 May 1992 (2 June 1992)
Box Of Tricks	26 May 1992 (not released in US at the time). Includes *The 12" Collection*
Greatest Hits	(different tracklisting,15 September 1992: US only)
Made In Heaven	6 November 1995 (7 November 1995)

RECOMMENDED

The Platinum Collection:	
Greatest Hits I, II & III	November 2000
Absolute Greatest	November 2009
Deep Cuts, Volume I (73–76)	March 2011
The Singles Collection Volume I	December 2008
The Singles Collection Volume II	June 2009
The Singles Collection Volume III	October 2010

FREDDIE MERCURY SOLO RELEASES

ALBUMS

Mr Bad Guy	29 April 1985 (7 May 1985)

With Montserrat Caballé:

Barcelona	10 October 1988 (released posthumously in US, 14 July 1992), and re-released UK 10 August 1992

The Freddie Mercury
  Album   16 November 1992 (released in the US as
                          The Great Pretender, 24 November 1992)
Freddie Mercury
  Remixes   various territories (not US) 1993

RECOMMENDED:

The Solo Collection Box Set   23 October 2000
A complete overview of Freddie's career. One of the most extensive
boxed sets Queen Productions have ever produced, this collection
also includes exclusive bonus tracks and remixes; instrumentals; the
'Rareties', or Mr Bad Guy sessions, Barcelona sessions and other
sessions; and the unique recorded interviews with Freddie by David
Wigg. There are also many rarely-seen photographs, drawings and
writings by Freddie, and a comprehensive text.

Lover of Life, Singer of Songs: The
  Very Best of Freddie Mercury   5 September 2006
A two-disc compilation released to mark what would have been his
sixtieth birthday, this is a genuine celebration of the man and his
music. It's all here.

SINGLES

As Larry Lurex:
'I Can Hear Music'   29 June 1973

Freddie Mercury:
'Love Kills'   10 September 1984 (11
                               September 1984)
'I Was Born to Love You'   9 April 1985 (23 April 1985)
'Made In Heaven'   1 July 1985 (not released in US)
'Living On My Own'   2 September 1985 (2 July 1985)
'Love Me Like There's   18 November 1985
  No Tomorrow'   (not released in US)

From Dave Clark's musical *Time*:
'Time', the title theme 6 May 1986 (not released in US)
'The Great Pretender' 23 February 1987 (3 March 1987)

FROM *BARCELONA*, WITH MONTSERRAT CABALLÉ

'Barcelona'   26 October 1987
'The Golden Boy'   24 October 1988
'How Can I Go On?'   23 January 1989

POSTHUMOUS SOLO SINGLE RELEASES

'Barcelona'   re-released 27 July 1992
'How Can I Go On?'   re-released October 1992
'In My Defence'   30 November 1992
'The Great Pretender'   re-released 25 January 1993 (12
                         November 1992)
'Living On My Own'   re-released 19 July 1993

This re-release of 'Living On My Own' was Freddie's biggest-selling hit single ever. It topped the chart on 8 August 1993 – the first time any solo single by any member of Queen had reached number one.

For much more information than there could be room for here regarding singles, boxed sets, bootlegs, unofficial releases, tribute albums, Queen + Paul Rodgers releases and more, visit: http://www.queenpedia.com/index.php?title=Discography.

Select Bibliography

Blake, Mark, *Is This the Real Life? The Untold Story of Queen*, Aurum Press Ltd: London, 2010

Brooks, Greg & Lupton, Simon (compilers/editors), *Freddie Mercury: His Life In His Own Words*, Omnibus Press: London, 2008

Cann, Kevin, *David Bowie: Any Day Now: The London Years*, Adelita Ltd: London, 2010

Courauld, Pari, *A Persian Childhood*, Rubicon Press: London, 1990

Dean, Ken, *Queen: A Visual Documentary*, Omnibus Press: London, 1986

Evans, David & Minns, David, *Freddie Mercury: More of the Real Life*, Britannia Press Publishing: Culver City, 1995

Freestone, Peter with Evans, David, *Freddie Mercury: An Intimate Memoir by the Man Who Knew Him Best*, Omnibus Press: London, 2001

Geldof, Bob, *Is That It?*, Sidgwick & Jackson: London, 1986

Gunn, Jacky & Jenkins, Jim, *Queen: As It Began*, Sidgwick & Jackson: London, 1992

Hodkinson, Mark, *Queen: the Early Years*, Omnibus Press: London, 1995

Hogan, Peter K., *The Complete Guide to the Music of Queen*, Omnibus Press: London, 1994

Hutton, Jim with Wapshott, Tim, *Mercury and Me*, Bloomsbury: London, 1994

Kent, Nick, *Apathy for the Devil*, Faber: London, 2010

Norman, Jeremy, *No Make-up: Straight Tales From A Queer Life*, Elliot & Thompson Ltd, 2006

Norman, Philip, *Sir Elton: The Definitive Biography of Elton John*, Pan Books: London, 2002

O'Regan, Denis, *Queen: the Full Picture*, Bloomsbury: London, 1995

Palmer, Robert, *Dancing In the Street: A Rock and Roll History*, BBC Books: London, 1996

Rider, Stephen, *These Are The Days Of Our Lives*, Castle Communications: London, 1991

Rock, Mick, *Mick Rock, A Photographic Record 1969-1980*, Pinewood Studios: Century 22nd Ltd, 1995

St Michael, Mick, *Queen In Their Own Words*, Omnibus Press: London, 1992

Sheriff, Abdul & Ferguson, Ed, *Zanzibar Under Colonial Rule*, James Currey Ltd: Oxford, 1991

Shilts, Randy, *And the Band Played On: Politics, People, and the AIDS Epidemic*, Penguin Books: London, 1987

Sky, Rick, *The Show Must Go On*, Fontana Press: London, 1992

Smith, Pete, *Live Aid*, Penn & Ink Ltd: Vancouver, WA, 2012

Southall, Brian, *The Rise and Fall of EMI Records*, Omnibus Press, London 2009

Index